Deeds
of
Pitt County
North Carolina
- 1761-1785 -

(Volume #1)

Compiled by:
Judith DuPree Ellison

Southern Historical Press, Inc.
Greenville, South Carolina

Please direct all correspondence and book orders to:
SOUTHERN HISTORICAL PRESS, Inc.
PO Box 1267
Greenville, SC   29602-1267

Originally printed: Miami, FL. 1968
Copyright 1968 by:
    Old SouthHistorical research &
    Atlantic Printers and Lithographers
ISBN #978-1-63914-133-3
Printed in the United States of America

DEDICATION

This Index is dedicated to my father,

Thomas O'Hagan DuPree

(b. Greenville, North Carolina, May 3, 1890
d. Miami, Florida, March 10, 1961)

always an intensely loyal and proud Tarheel
who, although he became a successful business man
and a community leader in Dade County, Florida,
never for one moment forgot his North Carolina heritage.

ACKNOWLEDGEMENTS

My special thanks to *Mrs. LaDean Childres*, without whose persistence this book would never have been planned; and

to *Mr. Jas. I. Stinson* of Eastman Kodak Co., without whose encouragement this book would never have been started; and

to *Mr. Edward E. Deegan* of Atlantic Printers and Lithographers, without whose enthusiasm and confidence this book would have been much less ambitious; and

to *Dr. H. G. Jones* and his staff of the N.C. Department of Archives and History, without whose advice and assistance this book would never have been possible; and

to my husband and daughter, *Martin* and *Melissa*, without whose patience and understanding this book simply could not have been done at all.

FOREWORD

Until now, a person interested in learning a b o u t Pitt Countians who lived between 1760 and 1870 was likely never to find much of the pertinent information which was hiding away in the deed books. Whether he personally did the research, wrote a letter of inquiry to the very efficient staff in the office of the Register of Deeds, or hired a genealogist to search for him, much of the information was not likely to be discovered. This difficulty in locating many of the recorded deeds was occasioned by the fact that many of the deed books were not indexed at all, others were inaccurately indexed, and still others were not completely indexed, even for grantor and grantee.

If you wished to know, for example, if and when a certain Oliver Smith lived in Pitt County, the only source of information readily available from deed books would be the indexes, such as they were. Some very revealing deeds might well have been omitted from the Index; deeds involving more than one grantee or grantor were usually indexed only by the first name appearing in the deed. If Mary Jones, Sarah Brown, and Oliver Smith were grantors, only "Mary Jones et al" would appear in the Index; Sarah Brown and Oliver Smith would not appear at all. If Oliver Smith was not a property owner during his stay in Pitt County, his name did not appear in any Index, yet his name may have been mentioned in the bodies of deeds as a friend or relative or he may have witnessed a deed.

The only way a person might ferret out the information in such instances was to make a tedious search, page by page and line by line—and few persons have either the time or patience for this. A *complete* Index has been a neccessity. This series of books is a Complete Index to the Deeds of Pitt County, North Carolina, from 1761 to 1870, and includes all legible names mentioned in the 17,972 pages included in these 37 deed and grant books. There are over 60,000 entries. Included are names of grantees, grantors, former owners of property, adjoining property owners, witnesses, and other family members mentioned.

This set of books should be equally useful to the attorney, to the professional genealogist, and to the amateur genealogist. Great pains have been taken to avoid errors. However, some of these early deed books, now repaired and preserved by the Department of Archives and History, were badly faded and worn. As a result, the writing is not always legible. Any errors in reading or copying these deed books are honest errors; there has been no conscious effort to alter any name, date, or fact.

HOW TO USE THIS BOOK

The formats used in the Index and Abstracts sections were agreed upon by Dr. H. G. Jones, State Archivist, and myself as perhaps the most concise and simple to use. This set of books is *primarily an Index*. It is our feeling that anyone using it for any sort of authoritative research will want to go to the actual record or photostatic copies for final proof, since most lawyers and genealogists believe that no one else can research quite as accurately as they themselves can! The explanation and samples which follow should make it easy for the reader to understand the format.

THE ABSTRACT SECTION

(Numbers correspond to those used in Sample following.)

1 PAGE refers to page in deed book.

2 Capital letters after a name denotes home county or state of grantee or grantor.

3 Numbers following name denote year in which person acquired property

4 When *D* precedes numbers after name, it indicates that the person involved received the property by deed from the previous owner.

5 If *Pat.* precedes numbers after a name, it indicates he was the original owner, having received it by grant or patent.

6 If a sheriff or constable is the grantor, it denotes a Sheriff's Sale.

7 In the case of a Sheriff's Sale, the person whose property was sold is listed as the former owner.

8 Where no occupation is shown, person is usually a planter; where another occupation is given, that occupation is indicated after the person's name.

9 DATE refers to actual date of deed.

10 The inclusive dates at top of the abstract pages show period in which deed was recorded.

11 *Adj.* indicates owner of adjoining property.

12 First and second entries in Additional Information show amount of acreage and price paid.

13 Where the number of acres is not specified or is illegible, — A is used.

14 Where the type of property is not specified, — is used in the first position.

15 Where the amount of money is illegible, £ — is used.

16 Where there is no mention of money or other consideration, — is used in the second position.

17 *Wit.* denotes witness.

EXAMPLE

DEED BOOK Z (1750-1753)[10]

PAGE				
421[1]	10-15-1774[9]	John Simpson, (DOB)[2] (Pat.-1760)[5]	Ichabod Simpson, mariner[8]	100 A;[12] £40[12]. Adj.[11]: John Blount.
423	11- 3-1774	John Simpson, (D-1770)[4]	James Tison	— A;[13] —.[16] Wit.:[17] Samuel Cherry.
425	1-15-1775	John Simpson, Sheriff[6]	James Tison	—[14]; £—[15]. Former owner[7]: Joseph Meeks (1750)[3]

THE INDEX SECTION

In the Index section, each reference to a name is listed, together with the deed book and page on which it may be found and the kind of reference which is made. Abbreviations used are listed below:

1	(ee)	— grantee
2	(or)	— grantor
3	(W)	— witness
4	(M)	— mentioned
5	(F)	— former owner of property
6	(A)	— adjoining property owner

EXAMPLE

JOHNSON, WILLIAM: (ee)[1]C-146; (or)[2]D-52; (W)[3]D-198; (F)[5]H-365; (A)[6]M-234; (M)[4]R-23.

It must be remembered that all transactions for one first name and last name are listed together, but *do not necessarily mean that they indicate the same person.*

HELPS FOR THE AMATEUR GENEALOGIST

FORMATION OF COUNTIES

Pitt County records go back to 1760, the year the county was formed. Yet there were some property owners in the area over fifty years prior to 1761. Records of grants in the office of the Secretary of State will show many of these owners, and references to others abound in these early Pitt County deeds. However, actual records of others are to be found in the deed books of Beaufort, Craven, and Johnston counties, of which present-day Pitt was once a part. In order to do thorough research in any state, one must know the history of the counties involved.

The most complete yet concise information I have found concerning the formation of counties in North Carolina is included in the *North Carolina Genealogical Reference*, Second Edition, by Draughon and Johnson. I heartily recommend it to anyone doing genealogical research in North Carolina.

UNDERSTANDING MIGRATIONS

Migrations of families were almost continuous until all free land in the country had been taken up. Eldest sons usually fell heir to lands owned by their fathers, and other sons in the family often moved on, in company with sons of neighboring families, to take up new lands as they were opened. Bounty lands and land lotteries were also rsponsible for many native sons' leaving the land of their birth.

Migrations from North Carolina were usually south and west. During the early 1800's, hundreds of families moved into Georgia and through Georgia on to Mississippi, Alabama, Louisiana, and Texas. Hundreds more moved to Tennessee and Kentucky and on to Ohio and Indiana. Migrations to North Carolina were, for the most part, from Europe and Pennsylvania and Virginia.

Knowing the migration trends for a given section is helpful to the amateur genealogist who is seeking preceding or succeeding generations of a family.

In my own research in counties of southern Virginia, I have found a number of family names which subsequently appeared in records of Pitt and Edgecombe counties. They are listed below with the hope that persons working on these lines may find them useful.

ISLE OF WIGHT, VIRGINIA (1662-1758):

John Brooks	William Bryan
William Ruffin	Richard Jordan
William Sugg	Theophilus Joyner
Henry King	Thomas Drake

ISLE OF WIGHT, VIRGINIA (1662-1758): (Continued)

Roger Novill
Joseph Bridger
George Hardy
Arthur Skinner
John Askew
Christopher Holliman
Thos. Woodward
Thos. Pitt
Samuel Davis
Nicholas Cobb
James Manning
Robert Flake
Richard Williamson
James Blunt
John Ross
Harmon Joynor
James Powell
John Hardy
Robert Daniell
Thomas Williams
Wm. Andrews
John Sympson
Wm. Cooper
Peter Hines
Joshua Barnes
John Williams

William Murfrey
Barnabe Mackinne
John Corbitt
Wm. Spivy
Edward Cobb
John Allen
Richard Atkisson
Thomas Gay
Thomas Rives
William Gwaltney
Wm. Baldwin
John Frizzell
Jacob Dickinson
James Arthur
Will Kinchen
Benjamin Evans
George Green
Ambrose Hadley
James House
Will Salter
Henry Pope
Samuel Blow
Thomas Hardy
Richard Williams
John Proctor

BRUNSWICK COUNTY, VIRGINIA (1735-1830):

Michael Wall
Benjamin Lanier
William King
Hollun Sturdivant
Thomas Jeffrys
Benjamin Bynum
John Blunt
Sterling Dupree
James Dupree
Benjamin Dupree
James Wall
Wm. Gwaltney
David Hinds
John Willis
John Andrews
Absalom Atkinson

John Peebles
Wm. Renn
Thomas Rives
James Judkins
Ephraim Peebles
William Hines
James Lanier
William Atkinson
Stephen D. Watkins
Green House
John F. May
James Renn
Charles Sullivant
Thomas Lawrence
John King
Henry Williamson

There are also many Pitt names in Southampton, Surry, and Sussex counties. The Virginia State Archives in Richmond has excellently catalogued records, and the personnel there are most interested and solicitous of your needs.

VARIATIONS IN SPELLING

Often we hear people say, "Oh, that's not our family. We spell ours with one 't'." Little do they know until they start searching old deed books that they often *were* the *same* family! The spelling variations for one surname are more likely to be due to the poor spelling ability of the recorder or the inability of the clerk who copied them to read the original deeds. There will frequently be as many as three different spellings of a name within the body of *one* instrument. When you see such spellings in old deeds as *akers, eacors,* and *acurs* (acres), *patten* and *patern* (patent). *proklemation* (proclamation), *meshage* (message), *devedant* (dividend), *sarting* (certain), *acnolege* (acknowledge) and *whrite onebrable* (right honorable), you can easily understand the possibility of surnames' having been misspelled.

When looking up a surname in the Index, be sure to look for spellings other than the one with which you are familiar. Perhaps the most glaring examples of mispelling are *Marodef Corbet* for Matthew Corbitt, and *Mathew Studefin* for Matthew Sturdivant. Another unusual error, difficult to understand, is the continual interchanging of Pearson Tuten and Pearson Tutle, sometimes in the same document. Three surnames frequently confused are May, Mayo, and Moye; the *a* and *o* are often confused and the flourish at the end of the *y* in May seems to have been read as an *o* or *e* on occasion. Records of these families must be researched very carefully.

Here are samples of other names which have more than one spelling. There are many more.

Flanekin, Flanagan, Flannagan, Finnekin
Spear, Spier, Speir
Drake, Drack
Wallace, Wallis
Whittaker, Whiteacre
Hadduck, Hattock, Haddock
Kittrell, Citterl, Kittrel, Kittral
Hardee, Hardie, Hardy
Tison, Tyson
Herrington, Harrington, Henninton, Herenton
Sherrod, Sharod, Sherwood, Sharrod
Mooring, Moreing, Moring
Robson, Robeson, Roberson, Robinson
Duffil, Duffield
Jenkins, Jinkins
Knox, Nox
Albritain, Albrittain, Albritton, Albriton, Albriten
Blount, Blunt
Llewelling, Lewellen, Lewallen
Shirley, Shearley, Shurley

Sterling, Starling
Bird, Byrd
Dupree, Duprey, Dupray, Dupris, DuPree
Averitt, Everitt, Evritt, Evitt, Averrett, Averith
Kennedy, Kenedy, Canaday, Kenaday
Hatway, Hattaway, Hathaway, Hatheaway
Leggitt, Legate, Legett
Whitchard, Whichard, Witchard
Wheatley, Whitley, Wheatly

PEOPLE WITH SAME NAMES

One pitfall for the amateur geneaologist is the assumption that the same name (first and last) indicates the same person. However, it was not unusual for four or five persons with the same name to be living at the same time in the same town. The isolation and identification of each individual requires careful and painstaking research, and sometimes cannot be done with certainty.

A common method of naming children in the 18th and 19th centuries was as follows: the first son was named after the father's father, the second son was named after the mother's father, and subsequent sons were named after uncles and friends; the first daughter was named after the mother's mother, the second daughter was named after the father's mother, and younger daughters were named after aunts and friends. Following this procedure in an example, then, produces this very confusing situation.

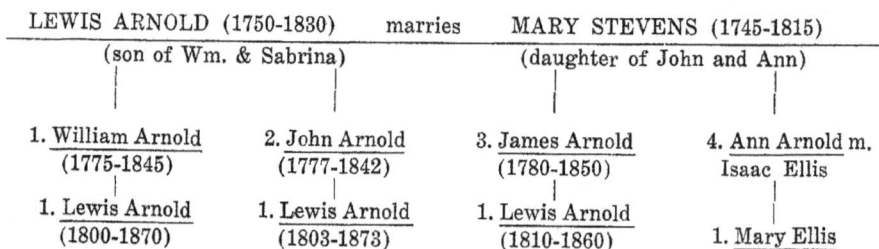

LEWIS ARNOLD (1750-1830) marries MARY STEVENS (1745-1815)

(son of Wm. & Sabrina)		(daughter of John and Ann)	
1. William Arnold (1775-1845)	2. John Arnold (1777-1842)	3. James Arnold (1780-1850)	4. Ann Arnold m. Isaac Ellis
1. Lewis Arnold (1800-1870)	1. Lewis Arnold (1803-1873)	1. Lewis Arnold (1810-1860)	1. Mary Ellis

Thus, between the years of 1824 and 1830, there are three Lewis Arnolds living, all 21 years and over. Between the years of 1831 and 1860, there are also three Lewis Arnolds living; however, these three are not the as the previous three just mentioned. The problem of the genealogist is to determine if a particular Lewis Arnold is the Lewis, son of William (1750-1830), or Lewis, son of the younger William (1800-1870), or Lewis, son of John, or Lewis, son of James. Aiding him in this effort are marks used in signing papers, names of brothers and sisters, occupations, and middle names, which began to appear about the turn of the nineteenth century. Names of wives are sometimes helpful in making identifications, although here again names are often duplicated. There were many Susannahs, Sarahs, Annes, and Elizabeths in those days!

This Index does not purport to be the work of a genealogist, and therefore does not attempt the identification of persons of the same first and last name, other than to report that identification which is offered in the deeds themselves. In the Index a listing of one first name and surname may actually refer to several persons and may span a century; i.e., *DUPREE, JAMES* includes all deeds for that name: for a James Dupree born in Virginia ca 1720, for a James Dupree born in Pitt County, N.C., in 1772, as well as for a James Dupree born in North Carolina in 1810. Information in the abstracts assists in differentiating between the individuals having the same name.

IMPORTANCE OF WITNESSES

Witnesses' names are very important for several reasons. One is, of course, that sometimes the discovery of a person as a witness furnishes the *only* record of a person who did not own property, appear in court, record a will, or stay in a county long enough to be included in a Federal Census.

Another reason witnesses are important is that witnesses were frequently neighbors. These neighbors were usually close friends and were often relatives. It is important to realize that plantations and farms were not always squares or rectangles as we perhaps envision them. They were most apt to be irregular in shape, following the bank of a stream and having perhaps six or eight other unequal sides. Instead of building the manor house in the center of the tract, the early settlers would build their houses where several plantations came together. These families of necessity did everything together, and records of one family would reveal records of the others. A witness who lived on an adjoining plantation could well be a son-in-law or other relative. The discovery—or even the suspicion—of such a relationship frequently points the way for further research. Many of these genealogical "jig-saw puzzles" have been solved by searching allied lines for a missing ancestor.

AMOUNT PAID FOR PROPERTY

The amount paid for each tract of land has been included in the abstracts, not to reflect upon the wealth of the purchaser, but because this too often provides a clue to relationship. *Deeds of gift* ("in consideration of the love, good will and affection I bear toward my son, etc.") almost always specify the relationship. However, there are numerous occasions where money changes hands between relatives, even between father and son. The only clue is that the amount is far less than the current market price. It is wise to pay attention to the prices paid and compare them to prices of other parcels of the same date. If the price paid in a particular deed is significantly less than the "going rate," a family relationship is likely. Searching records for the other party may provide information which will be helpful.

A NOTE TO PITT COUNTIANS . . .

All of my roots are in North Carolina. I have always known my ancestors bore the names of DuPree, Morton, Darden, Hardison, Andrews, Deans, Whitley, Boone, Tyner, Perry, Carraway, and Gainer. We had secured some scant information on some of these lines for membership in the Daughters of the American Revolution, Colonial Dames of the XVII Century, the Mayflower Society, and the Huguenot Society, but, like most North Carolinians, paid little attention to it. There were allied families whom we called "Cousin," but I never knew nor bothered to find out why we did so.

Several years before my father died, he became exceedingly interested in his forebears. Perhaps his having moved from North Carolina a number of years before had piqued his interest in his forebears, for he was not prompted by any sort of arrogance to research; it was simply a matter of curiosity. We had planned to spend the summer of 1961 in Pitt County to piece together the family story. He thought his branch of the family small, and, typically, thought himself unrelated to other families of the same name in Pitt County. (Imagine his surprise if he could know that they are all related and most of them third cousins, having had the same great-grandfather!)

My father died in March, 1961, and was unable to complete the research. I decided to attempt it, little realizing to what lengths it would lead me. My sister, Ysobel DuPree Litchfield of Beaufort County, and I have devoted every available moment since then to researching the DuPree family. We have traveled to courthouses all over the South and discovered Pitt County names and descendants in Georgia, South Carolina, Virginia, Mississippi, Alabama, Tennessee, Kentucky, Louisiana, Florida, Texas, Arkansas, Indiana, Ohio, Delaware, and California.

In the course of such wide-spread experiences I became painfully aware of the inadequacy of the existing Index for Deed Books in Pitt County, home base for our branch of the DuPree family since 1771. It was necessary to examine each book page by page in order to secure accurate and complete information. This was a tremendous task, time-consuming, tedious, and costly for those of us who live at some distance. It seemed ridiculous to think that everyone who wished information from Pitt County would have to duplicate my efforts and expense. I mentioned to Mrs. Allred, Register of Deeds, that I would someday provide an accurate and comprehensive Index for Pitt County as my tribute to my birthplace.

The opportunity came soon thereafter. Dr. H. G. Jones and Admiral Patterson of the State Department of Archives and History agreed that I could have access to the records in 1965. I started working on the Index in my spare time, since I was regularly employed as an assistant principal in the public schools of Dade County, Florida. As I came nearer to the completion of the project, I became impatient and was granted a personal leave for this year.

The task has been long and tedious, but it has been filled with affection and pride. And so, Pitt County, here is your Index—from me to you, with love.

JUDITH DuPREE ELLISON
February, 1968

ABSTRACTS
OF
DEEDS

DEED BOOK B (1762-1764)

Page	Date	Grantor	Grantee	Additional Information
1	2-18-1761	Earl Granville	James DeLoach (BEAU)	530 A; 10 sh. Adj.: John Williams; Wit.: Alex. Stewart
5	8- 6-1761	Earl Granville	Thomas Travis	285 A; 10 sh.
10	——-1761	Earl Granville	James Bonner (BEAU)	320 A; 10 sh. Wit.: Wm. Matthews
14	8- 6-1761	Earl Granville	John Chalcraff	320 A; 10 sh. Adj.: Benjamin Ellis, Thomas Gwaltney, Jr., Peter Reeves
19	8- 7-1761	Earl Granville	Amos Adkinson (BEAU)	700 A; 10 sh. Adj.: Francis Hobson
22	8- 6-1761	Earl Granville	John Shannon	220 A; 10 sh. Adj.: William Stafford
28	3- 5-1761	Earl Granville	Robert Land (BEAU)	370 A; 10 sh.
32	10-16-1761	Earl Granville	Caleb Wallis	700 A; 10 sh.
36	8- 7-1761	Earl Granville	Caleb Wallis	400+ A; 10 sh. Adj.: John Wooten
40	8- 7-1761	Earl Granville	Henry Ellis (BEAU)	173 A; 10 sh. Adj.: Thomas Gwaltney
44	8- 6-1761	Earl Granville	Abraham Tyson	700 A; 10 sh. Adj.: Matthias Tyson
48	10-16-1761	Earl Granville	Joshua Tucker	77 A; 10 sh.
52	11- 9-1761	John Holland	William Speir	1700 A; £560. Former owners: Capt. Richard Smith (pat. 1706); John Porter (ALB), father of Joshua Porter (1718); John Lillington, son-in-law of John Porter and husband of Sarah Porter; John Alexander Lillington, son of John and Sarah Lillington. Mentioned: Sarah Porter Pilkington. Wit.: John Speir, Jr., Arthur Council.
56	3- 1-1762	Thomas Travis 1759)	John Holland	340 A; £180. Former owner: Joseph Hardee (Pat. 1758)
57	2-10-1762	John Price (Pat. 1761)	Nesby Mills	50 A; £20.
61	1-29-1762	Robert Land	John Norris	200 A; £20.
63	3- 8-1762	Amos Atkinson	Nathan Mayo	210 A; £10.
65	——-1761	William Stansell	Jesse Sparkman (TYR)	220 A; £40
67	5-27-1762	Caleb Wallis	David Power	150 A; £—.
69	——-1762	Lannard Ray	William Stansell, Jr.	320 A; £20. Former owner: Daniel O'Quinn
71	3- 9-1761	John Mercer (DOB)	Thomas Moore	100 A in Dobbs; £24. Wit.: Joseph Mercer.
73	5-26-1762	William Mace	Benjamin Pollard	100 A; £26. Wit.: William Gwaltney, Peter Rives
75	1-31-1755	Earl Granville	Richard Barrow	640 A; 3 sh. Wit.: James Campbell, Edmund Tison
79	5-26-1762	Caleb Wallis (Pat. 1761)	Thomas Wallis, tailor	145 A; £40.
81	12-30-1761	Denniss Glisson	William Lewis (TYR)	150 A; £40. Adj.: James Glisson. Wit.: Robert Ward, Joseph Glisson
82	4-25-1762	Walter Bryant	Robert Ballard	210 A; £16. Wit.: John Ballard, Jr, Joseph Ballard, Jr., Arthur Ols, William Dew. Adj.: Jesse Jolley
85	11-24-1761	Walter Bryant	Jesse Jolley	210 A; £30. Wit.: Joseph Whitfield

DEED BOOK B (1762-1764)

Page	Date	Grantor	Grantee	Additional Information
88	5-22-1762	John Chalcraft	Peter Rives	100 A; £7. Adj.: William Braddy. Wit.: Thomas Gwaltney, Elizabeth Rives
90	5-25-1762	Simon Burney	William Burney, son	Negroes; love & aff. Mentioned: Elizabeth Burney, wife of Simon Burney
91	3- 5-1762	James Blunt	Benjamin Blunt, son	Personal goods, animals; love & aff. Wit.: Jacob Blunt, Samuel Spencer.
92	3-26-1762	John Hardee	Joseph Eastwood	2 A; £5. Adj.: Capt. James Ellison
93	1- 5-1762	William Daniel Pinkett	Zachariah Pinkett	120 A; £ 30. Former owner: Thomas Pinkett, dec. (Pat. 1740), father of William Daniel Pinkett. Wit.: Alexander Barnhill, John Hodges, Thomas Pinkett
95	5-25-1762	Archibald Adams (D-1757)	Levi Adams, son	50 A; love & aff. Former owner: William Baldwyn. Wit.: Edmund Williams, John Cason
96	5-25-1762	Archibald Adams (D-1750)	Archibald Adams, Jr., son	100 A; love & aff.
97	5-20-1762	Thomas Nobles	John Nobles	— A; £5. Wit.: Nathaniel Nobles, Benjamin Bowers
99	4-10-1762	Solomon Wright (EDG) (Pat. 1761)	Peter Mayo	112 A; £12. Wit.: Francis Hobson
100	5-24-1762	Moses Tison (Pat.)	George Dickes	— A; £10. Wit.: Aaron Tison
102	1-25-1762	Thomas Little	Daniel Rogers (HERT)	500 A; £110. Former owner: Josiah Little (Pat. 1735)
103	12-28-1761	Dennis Glisson	Isaac Glisson	100 A; £—. Wit.: Joseph Glisson, Robert Ward
104	3- 8-1762	Amos Atkinson	Peter Mayo	145 A; £14. Wit.: Andrew Gofford
106	4——1762	Walter Bryant	Arthur Olds	100 A; £11.
108	3-25-1762	James Blunt and Katherine Blunt, wife	Benjamin Blunt, son	100 A; maintenance
111	5-26-1762	John Joyner	John Moore	½ of grant; £10. Former owner: Abraham Tison (Pat. 1761)
113	——-1762	William Archdeacon	Henry Jenkins	160 A; £12. Adj.: Godfrey Stancil. Wit.: James Mayo
115	4- 9-1762	William Parker	Thomas Bond	200 A; £40. Wit.: Robert Ballard, John Bond
116	2——1761	Daniel Oquim (Pat. 1750)	Lanard Ray	320 A; £15.
119	11- 9-1761	William Speir (Pat. 1755)	John Holland	150 A; £65.
121	8-27-1762	John Wooten, hatter	James Johnston, Sen.	100 A; £10. Wit.: Thomas Harper
123	8-27-1762	John Speir, Jr. (Pat. 1762)	William Daniel Pinkett	200 A; £20. Wit.: William Moore, Elias Bergeron
126	3- 3-1761	Earl Granville	Thomas Little (BEAU)	100 A; 10 sh.
129	6-26-1762	Earl Granville	Abraham Tyson	420 A; 17 sh.
133	11- 7-1761	Earl Granville	Thomas Moore	205 A; 10 sh.
137	11-17-1762	Earl Granville	Thomas Noble	540 A; 10 sh.

DEED BOOK B (1762-1764)

Page	Date	Grantor	Grantee	Additional Information
141	6-20-1761	Earl Granville	John Mayo	700 A; 10 sh.
145	6-26-1761	Earl Granville	John Williams	685 A; 10 sh. Adj.: Edward Williams, Barwell Evans, Robert Williams, Sen., Nathan Johnston
149	11- 9-1761	Earl Granville	Joseph Mercer	690 A; 10 sh.
153	2-20-1761	Earl Granville	Capt. William Speir	249 A; 10 sh. Adj.: John Whichard
157	3-10-1761	Earl Granville	Jonathan Hennington	— A; 10 sh.
161	6-26-1762	Earl Granville	William Clark	185 A; 10 sh.
165	11- 9-1761	Earl Granville	Simon Prescott and John Prescott	— A; 10 sh. Adj.: Bennett Britton and Arthur Flake
169	11- 7-1761	Earl Granville	Edmund Williams	65 A; 10 sh. Adj.: Stephen Mundin
173	6-20-1761	Earl Granville	Isaac Eason	520 A; 10 sh.
177	11- 7-1761	Earl Granville	Thomas Little	695 A; 10 sh.
181	9-22-176–	Earl Granville	William Speir (BEAU)	98 A; 10 sh.
185	11- 7-1761	Earl Granville	George Cannon	200+ A; 10 sh.
189	10-16-1761	Earl Granville	William Harris (BEAU)	400 A; 10 sh.
193	3-10-1761	Earl Granville	Jesse Jolley (BEAU)	450 A; 10 sh. Adj.: Solomon James
197	3-28-1760	Earl Granville	Walter Bryant	520 A; 10 sh.
201	11-16-1761	Earl Granville	George Moye	220 A; 10 sh.
205	8- 7-1761	Earl Granville	Timothy Harris	382 A; 10 sh.
210	6-26-1762	Earl Granville	John Speir, Jr.	— A; 10 sh.
214	6-26-1762	Earl Granville	Samuel Stokes	411½ A; 10 sh. Adj.: Richard Stone, Richard Williams
218	3-24-1758	Robert West (BERT) (Pat. 175-)	Robert West, Jr.	600 A; £30. Wit.: Robert West, Jr.
220	8-27-1762	John Wooten, hatter	James Crafford	100 A; £14. Wit.: Samuel Swearingen, James Johnston
222	5-20-17—	Alexander Stewart	Thomas Harper	100 A; £5. Former owners: Patrick Maule (Pat. 1726), father; Sarah Bryan and Joseph Bryan, daughter and son-in-law of Patrick Maule. Wit.: David Perkins
223	8-31-1762	Robert Hardee	James Latham, millwright	Negro boy; love & aff. Wit.: John Hardee, William More
224	———-176–	Abraham Giddins	John Hardee, Jr., son	100 A; £10. Former owner: Phillip Trapree
226	8-28-1762	William Smith (TYR)	Joseph Barber	160 A; £20. Wit.: Jacob Atkinson, John Chalcrafft, James Cobb
			Edward Cobb	
228	8——-1762	John Hodges, Jr.	Edmond Kenedy	200 A; £60. Former owner: Ebenezer Folsom (Pat. 1761). Wit.: Robert Hodges, Howel Hodges
230	8- 4-1762	Thomas Nobles	Jonathan Jolley	— A; £40. Wit.: George Porter, Joseph Jolley

B 141-230

DEED BOOK B (1762-1764)

Page	Date	Grantor	Grantee	Additional Information
232	3-15-1762	Henry Kent-(EDG)	Thomas Hattaway	100 A; £11. Wit.: Amos Atkinson, Edmond Hatheaway, Cornelius Church
234	8- 7-1762	Thos. Coomes, physician	James Brooks	— A; £20. Wit.: John Simpson, Elizabeth Simpson
236	2-17-1760	Thomas Bonner (BEAU)	Henry Bonner, son	100 A; love & aff. Mentioned: Simon Jones
237	2- 7-1763	Thos. Bonner, Jr. (BEAU)	Henry Bonner	150 A; £25. Wit.: Thomas Bonner, Edward Salter, Jr.
238	2—22——	Michael More	John Brooks	— A; £60. Former owner: Peter More (Pat. 1742)
240	2-16-1763	William Stansell, Jr.	William Willis	100 A; £10. Former owners: Leonard Rae, Daniel Oquin (Pat. 1755). Wit.: James Handcock, Mark Hardin
242	2-23-1763	John Mayo (Pat. 1763)	George Walston	100 A; £7+. Wit.: Benjamin Mayo, Mary Mayo
244	10-26-1762	William Barber and Dinah Barber, wife	John Kelley	— A; £24. Wit.: Samuel Tindall, Benjamin Kelly, Mark Hardin
245	8-31-17——	Frederick Becton (CRAV)	Mark Hardin and Elizabeth Hardin	One-half of plantation. Former owner: Richard Becton ½ grant; £10.
247	7- 6-1762	Thomas Coomes	William Gerrald	Negro girl; love & aff. Wit.: John Speir, Jr., William Jones
249	2-24-176—	Robert Hardee	William Moore, son-in-law	
250	2-22-1763	Caleb Wallis (Pat. 1762)	David Powers	150 A; £5+. Wit.: Peter Johnston, Abraham Tison
252	11-30-1762	John Mayo	William Wilson Coats (EDG)	100 A; £2. Wit.: Jesse Baggett, Alexander Autry
254	2-25-1763	Henry Cannon and Mary Cannon, wife (DUP)	Patrick Quoturmas, Jr.	200 A; £50. Former owners: Simon Burney, William Mitchell. Wit.: William Moore, Abraham Barrow
256	2-22-1763	Joseph Mercer	Samuel Davis	100 A; £40+. Former owner: Joseph Lambard. Wit.: Elias Bergeron, William Moor
257	——-1763	Edward Williams, sadler	Robert Williams, father (Pat. 1738)	100 A; love & aff.
259	1——1763	Jacob Evans (Pat. 1738)	Robert Williams, Jr., merchant	270 A; £100.
261	2-25-1763	Samuel Stokes	Richard Williams	205½ A; £7+
263	——1762	William Ellitt (Pat. 1755)	William Cannon	152 A; £16.
264	7-14-1762	John Cooper	Robert Gremmer	70 A; £10. Former owner: Michael O'Neal. Wit.: James Cobb
266	——29-1762	John Hodges, Jr.	Stephen Munden	50 A; £—. Former owner: William Cason, Sen. (Pat. 1740); Edward Cannon. Wit.: Edmund Williams, Lucretia Williams

DEED BOOK B (1762-1764)

Page	Date	Grantor	Grantee	Additional Information
268	11-20-——	Benjamin Bowers	Henry Barnhill	200 A; £42+. Wit.: William Osborn, John Barnhill
270	——1763	Joshua Mercer	Samuel Davis	— A; £75. Former owner: William Galloway (Pat. 1745)
271	10- 6-1762	William Giddins (Pat. 174-)	George Dyks	100 A; £—.
273	12-23-1762	John Williams, millwright (Pat. 1762)	Edward Williams, saddler	183 A; £—.
275	9-25-1762	John Wichard (D-1750)	John Barber	128 A; £—. Former owner: William Stafford (Pat. 1740)
277	1-21-1763	John Williams, miller	Nathan Johnson	9 A; £2 +
279	10-——1762	John Averett (EDG)	John Edwards	320 A; £12
280	2-20-1763	Edward Williams, sadler (Pat. 1760)	Michael Oldshe, tailor	135 A; £—.
283	——1763	David Averrett	William Wright	100 A; £8. Former owner: Richard Mayo
285	——1763	John Brown (HAL)	Richard Mayo	640 A; £65. Former owner: Samuel Ward.
287	1-——1763	Nathan Johnson, shoemaker	Richard Williams	20½ A; £40. Former owner: Jacob Evans
289	2-19-1763	William Mitchell and Mary Mitchell, wife (DUP)	Mary Cannon	D of G; Mentioned: Henry Cannon, husband of Mary Cannon. Wit.: Edward Cannon, David Cannon
289	12-23-1762	John Williams (Pat. 1762)	Roderick Williams	153 A; £—. Adjoining: Richard Allen, George Suggs. Wit.: Edward Williams, Richard Williams, Cornelius Church
292	5-——1762	William Daniel, sadler	Ebenezer Folsom, sadler (EDG)	Power of attorney
292	12-11-1762	Simon Burney	Abraham Barrow and Elizabeth Barrow, wife	Negroes; love & aff. Men: Elizabeth Barrow is daughter of Simon Burney. Wit.: Isaac Stocks, John Stocks
294	10- 6-1762	George Dyks	William Giddins	100 A; £20. Former owner: Moses Tison (Pat. 1761). Wit.: Samuel Albertson, Jacob Giddins.
296	2-22-1763	Thomas Moor	Samuel Davis	60 A; £30. Former owner: Thomas Mercer (Pat. 1746). Wit.: William Moor, Elias Bergeron
298	2-22-1763	Robert Williams (Pat. 1738)	Richard Williams, son	100 A; love & aff.
299	2-25-1763	Caleb Wallis	George Every, ship carpenter	100 A; £4υ. Adj.: Thomas Wallace
300	11-22-1762	Richard Allen, yeoman	Abraham Breeler, yeoman	80 A; £10. Former owner: George Sugg
303	11- 4-1762	Joseph Whitfield	John Barnhill	150 A; £35. Adj.: Robert Knox. Former owner: Jesse Jolley (Pat. 1761)
304	3-28-1760	William Taylor (BEAU)	John Taylor, son	Negro; love & aff.
305	10-20-1762	Robert Ballard	Thomas House (BERT)	200 A; £—. Wit.: William Bryan, Henry Cross, Thomas Cross

DEED BOOK B (1762-1764)

Page	Date	Grantor	Grantee	Additional Information
307	11-19-1762	Richard Allen, yeoman	John Stocks, yeoman	180 A; £20. Adj.: Samuel Truss. Wit.: Samuel Smyth, Allen Sugg, George Tison
310	2-21-1763	John Highsmith	John More	75 A; £5. Wit.: William Moore, Edward Moore, Major Harris
312	8- 6-1761	Earl Granville	William Baldry	300 A; 10 sh
316	6-16-1762	Earl Granville	John Munden	100 A; 10 sh
322	6-26-1762	Earl Granville	William Moore	700 A; 10 sh
326	10-16-1761	Earl Granville	Thomas Hewell	96 A; 10 sh
330	2- 7-1763	Earl Granville	John Tison	442 A; 10 sh
335	6-26————	Earl Granville	John Highsmith	170 A; 10 sh
339	6-26——	Earl Granville	Laurance Kirwin	650 A; 10 sh
344	6-26-1762	Earl Granville	John Joyner	555 A; 10 sh
349	6-26-1762	Earl Granville	Joseph Whitfiel (BEAU)	100+ A; 10 sh
354	6-26-1762	Earl Granville	John Cook	321 A; 10 sh
359	5-25-1761	Ebenezer Folsom, sadler (Pat. 1761)	Solomon Whichird	— A; £—.
361	—————	Earl Granville	William Stafford	440 A; 10 sh
366	5-30-1763	Laurance Kirwin	John Slaughter	150 A; £10. Adj.: David Williams. Wit.: Abraham Tison, Thomas Cooms
368	5——-1763	Israel Baxter	Children: Stephen Baxter, Sarah Baxter, David Baxter, Theophilus Baxter, Rebecca Baxter	All goods; love and aff.
370	5-20-1763	Jonathan Tison (D-1755)	John Kelley	300 A; £10. Wit.: Samuel Tison, Isaiah Quatermus
372	7——-1762	William Osburn	Andrew Gofford	330 A; £—.Adj.: Ephram Jones. Wit.: Francis Hobson, Godfrey Stansell
374	5-17——-	John Stocks	Isaac Hardee	140 A; £10. Wit.: Isaac Stocks, Joseph Parker
376	12-28-1762	John Meeks	John Drake, (Southampton, Va.)	100 A; £—.Wit.: James Barrow, Benjamin Pollard, Robert Gremmer. Adj.: David Hatway
378	2-28-1763	Joseph Mercer (Pat. 1761)	Samuel Davis	230 A; £35. Wit.: Elias Bergeron
379	1-3-1762	John Swinson, Sen.	John Swinson, Jr., son	200 A; love & aff. Wit.: Elizabeth Camell
380	4- 1-1763	John Chalcraft	John Pope (Southampton, Va.)	400 A+ 225 A; £200. Wit.: James Lanier
382	5- 2-1763	Joseph Eastwood	John Hardee	100 A; in Dobbs Co.; £75. Former owner: George White. Wit.: Isaac Hardee, Robert Hardee, Jr.

DEED BOOK B (1762-1764)

Page	Date	Grantor	Grantee	Additional Information
384	2-28-1763	Joseph Mercer	Samuel Davis	233 A; £6
385	8——1762	John Stocks, Sen.	Samuel Truss	160 A; £30
387	——1763	John Kelley and Mary Kelley	James Quatermus	—A; £—. Former owners: Mathew Kelley, Edward Salter
388	4- 8-1763	James Shields	John Simpson	— A; £20. Adj.: David Cannon. Former owner: John Mills (Pat. 1743)
391	3- 7-1763	Joseph Eastwood	John Hardee	2 A; £10. Adj.: Capt. James Ellison
392	3-2 1763	William Autry	Thomas Wallis	120 A; £7+. Wit.: John Mayo, Benjamin May
394	3-19-1763	Benjamin Cordin	James Brooks	100 A; £20. Former owner: John Wane (Pat. 1752) Wit.: William Baldwyn, John Hardee, Jr.
396	——1763	John Moye	John Jones	129 A; £30. Adj.: John Moye, Jr., John Noble, William Proctor. Wit.: Matthias Moor, George Moye
398	——1763	Abraham Tison and Aquilla Sugg (EDG) exec.	Amos Atkinson	200+ A; £30. Former owner: George Sugg, dec. Adj.: Samuel Swearinggane. Wit.: William Scarborough
400	3-15-1763	Robert Land	Samuel Smyth	100+ A; £32. Wit.: Charles Edwards, Philip Wilson, Allen Sugg
402	10-28-1762	William Gareld and Mary Gareld	Lewis Williams	100 A; £36. Former owners: Joseph Jackson, William Cotes, James Gareld, father of William Gareld. Adj.: James Blunt. Wit.: Edward Cannon, John Prise, Sen.
404	9-23-1762	Bennet Britten	John Fleming, Sen.	250 A; £100. Adj.: Wm. Prescott. Former owner: John Prescott (Pat. 1741). Wit.: John Nobles, Thos. Pinkett, Simon Prescott
406	5-22-1763	Larrance Kirvin	John Hardee	100 A; £—. Wit.: William Moor, Daniel Wilson
408	——1763	William Gwaltney	Benjamin Evans	213 A; £7. Former owner: William Stevens (Pat. 173-). Wit.: James Thain, Robert Gremmer
410	——1763	Thomas Littel (Pat. 1761)	James Littel, son	50 A; love and aff. Adj.: Seth Pilkington. Wit.: Josiah Littel, John Knowis, Alex. Stewart
412	1- 8-1763	Moses Tison	Simon Burney	300 A; £50. Moses Tison, legatee of Cornelius Tison (Pat. 1738), former owner. Wit.: William Denmark, Isaac Stocks
414	8-31-1763	Simon Jones	James Jones, son	175 A; love & aff. Former owner: Edward Vale. Wit.: William Jones
415	8-31-1763	Simon Jones	William Jones, son	175 A; love & aff.
416	——1763	William Willis	Moses Dean	100 A; £35. Wit.: Hillery Elligood, Thomas Williams
418	10-10——	Joseph Jolley, Sen. (1761)	Lawrence McNemar	200 A; £20. Wit.: Joseph Jolley, Jr., William Beaman
420	2-28-1763	Joseph Mercer	Nathan Moor	230 A; £7

B 384-420

DEED BOOK B (1762-1764)

Page	Date	Grantor	Grantee	Additional Information
421	——1763	William Stafford	Malachi Dickinson	320 A; £100. Former owner: William Ham
423	5——	William Autry	Simon Nusom	400 A; £33
425	7-20-1763	John Dixon, inholder	Mathew Albritton, houseright	100+ A; £60. Former owners: Charles Finnakin, John Hodges. Mentioned: Edward Salter (Pat. 1761) Wit.: George Moye, Isaac Hardee
428	7-27-1763	Isaac Hardee	Robert Hardee	140 A; £10. Former owner: John Stocks (Pat. 1761). Wit.: John Hardee, Peter Hull
430	7-16-1763	William Clark	Edward Salter	1 A; £10. Former owner: Thos. Farmer. Wit.: William Braddy, James Braddy
432	——	William Autry	John Autry	100 A; £11. Wit.: Thomas Duffield, Simon Nusom
434	4-15——	Simon Taylor (D-1755)	Martin Nelson, Jr.	61 A; £30. Former owner: William Taylor (Pat. 1737). Wit.: John Simpson, Peter Nelson
436	8-25-1763	George Bland	Joseph Pendercuts	200 A; £—. Wit.: John Joyner, Charles Macclain
438	6- 3-1763	Richard Mayo	William Mace	— A; £—. Wit.: Richard Dudley
440	4-30-1763	George Duncan and Abraham Duncan (N.H.)	Charles Price	320 A; £10. George Duncan and Abraham Duncan, legatees of Abraham Duncan (Pat. 1752), former owner
441	7- 7-1763	Thomas Albritton	John Brooks	140 A; £—. Adj.: John Edwards. Wit.: Henry Cooper
443	8-29-1763	Nathan Johnson and Elizabeth Johnson, wife	Matthew Sturdivant of Sussex Co., Va.	700 A; £180.
445	——1763	John May (1763)	Richard Gay	— A; £25. Wit.: Benjamin Mayo
447	9- 1-1762	Mark Harden and Elizabeth Becton Harden	Frederick Becton (CRAV)	⅓ of 416 A + ⅓ of 640 A; £—. Former owners: Richard Becton (BEAU), former husband of Elizabeth Becton Harden and brother of John Becton (dec.) and uncle of Frederick Becton, John Becton. Mentioned: Arthur Moor, Benjamin Barrow. Wit.: Frederick Isler, Wilmoth Johnston
450	7-26-1763	Matthew Albriton (D-1760)	John Dixon	100 A; £60. Adj. David Kennion. Former owners: Robert Callahan (Pat. 1741), David Cannon (1752), his son Edward Cannon (1756)
452	1- 7-1763	Earl Granville	Nathan Johnston	102 A; 10 sh.
457	1- 7-1763	Earl Granville	Thomas Albritton	325 A; 10 sh. Adj.: John Edwards
462	6-20-1761	Earl Granville	Moses Tyson (BEAU)	700 A; 10 sh.
466	11- 7-1763	Earl Granville	Abraham Glisson	270 A; 10 sh.
471	——1763	John Price	James Mayo	100 A; £30

DEED BOOK B (1762-1764)

Page	Date	Grantor	Grantee	Additional Information
473	11-30-1763	John Williams, Sr.	Isaac Stocks	100 A; £55. Former owner: Shadrach Allen (Pat. 1752)
475	12- 2-1763	Richard Mayo, sadler	William Mace	200 A; £18. Wit.: Abraham Tyson, Robt. Williams
477	—-1763	John Edwards	Wenefret Edwards, dau.	Negro; —. Mentioned: Son, Andrew Edwards. Wit.: Martin Nelson, Mary Nelson
478	9-24-1763	Caleb Wallis and Ann Wallis, wife	Nathan Johnston	120 A; £40. Wit.: James Lanier, Simon Pope, Richard Williams
480	11-26-1763	Caleb Wallis, and Ann Wallis, wife	Joseph Evans	100 A; £15. Former owner: William Brantly (Pat. 1755). Wit.: Richard Williams, Merryman Allen
482	9- 1-1763	William Gwaltney	Marcus Stokes of Sussex, Va., carpenter	219 A; £53. Former owner: William Steavens (Pat. 1735), his son, John Steavens. Wit.: John Pollard, Charles Dinkins
484	11-25-1763	William Baldwyn, school-master (Pat. 1757)	William Baldwyn, son	100 A; love & aff. Adj.: Archabald Adams
485	6——-1763	John Brown, Jr. (BEAU)	Robert Rogers	200 A; £10. Wit.: James Latham, Alex Stewart
487	———	Simon Burney	Thomas Daniell, son-in-law, of HAL	2 negroes; love & aff.
488	8- 7-1763	Joseph Jolley, Sen. (D-1757)	Isaac Knox	100 A+ 200 A; £35. Former owners: Lemuel Cherry (Pat. 1745), Charles Cherry. Wit.: Larence MacNemar, William Congleton
490	8-13-1763	Abraham Giddens and Margreat Giddens	Jacob-Blount	200 A; £—
492	8-24-1763	Benjamin Evans and Lucy Evans	Joseph Hickman	200+ A; £35+. Former owner: William Stevens (Pat. 1735). Wit.: Wm. Gwaltney, Benjamin Pollard
494	7- 1-1763	Elias Hodges (D-1740)	Henry Hodges	150 A; £30. Adj.: Thos. Pilkinton, John Hodges, Richard Smith. Former owner: Seth Pilkinton. Wit.: Matthew Hodges, John Cherry
496	3-22-1763	Alexander Stewart (D-1757)	James Latham	200 A+ ¼ saw mill and grist mill; £126. Adj.: Francis Roundtree, Anthony Whitchard
497	1- 7-176-	Earl Granville	Simon Taylor	216 A; 10 sh.
501	——-176-	Earl Granville	David Averett (BEAU)	700 A; 10 sh. Adj.: William Pollard
506	1- 7-1763	Earl Granville	Isaac Giddings	325 A; 10 sh. Adj.: Joseph Sullavan, John White
510	6- 6-1763	Earl Granville	Simon Jones	231 A; 10 sh. Adj.: William Watkins
514	6- 6-1763	Earl Granville	John Brown	388 A; 10 sh. Wit.: Jno. Savage
519	11- 9-176-	Earl Granville	William Osburn	670 A; 10 sh.

B 473-519

DEED BOOK B (1762-1764)

Page	Date	Grantor	Grantee	Additional Information
524	1- 7-1763	Earl Granville	John Noble	102½ A; 10 sh.
528	1- 7-1763	Earl Granville	Thomas Mercer	540 A; 10 sh. Adj.: Abraham Pettipool
533	1- 7-1763	Earl Granville	William Autrey	700 A; 10 sh. Adj.: Thomas Wallace
537	1- 7-1763	Earl Granville	Elias Bergenum	690 A; 10 sh.
542	1- 7-1763	Earl Granville	Thomas Moore	605 A; 10 sh.
546	1- 7-1763	Earl Granville	Edward Serman	50 A; 10 sh.
550	12-12-1763	Thomas Mercer	Jacob Mercer	100 A; £4. Wit.: Elias Bergeron, Joseph Sullivant
551	2-28-1764	John Pope	Simon Pope	400 A; 5 sh. Wit.: Benjamin Ellis, Henry Ellis, Former owner: Joseph Barrow (Pat. 1741)

DEED BOOK C (1764-1767)

Page	Date	Grantor	Grantee	Additional Information
1	1-26-1764	Arnal Hopkins	Andrew Gofford	50 A; £10. Wit.: William Hopkins
2	1- 5-1764	Richard May and Bathaia May, wife	Archabald Patterson, (formerly Md.)	440 A; £70. Former owner: John Brown (Pat. 1734). Wit.: Charles Forbes, James Cowpland, James Lanier
5	12-19-1763	David Smith (TYR)	John Mobley	125 A; £15. Former owner: John Holland (Pat. 1760). Wit.: Francis Hobson, John Smith, Middleton Mobley
6	2-17-176—	William Teel (D-1761)	Joseph Brierly, son-in-law	50 A; love & aff. Former owner: James DeLoach (Pat. 1761). Wit.: William Baldwyn, William Baldwyn, Jr.
7	2-15-1764	Thomas Littel	Josiah Littel, son	300 A; love & aff. Wit.: George Littel
8	9-11-1750	Henry Snoad (BEAU)	Jacob Anderson	320 A; £26. Adj.: James Bonner. Wit.: William Watkins
10	12- 9-1763	Edward Salter	John Perritt (EDG)	640 A; £200. Former owners: Lewis Devall, (Pat. 1715), Martha Devall, extx., Edward Salter (dec.). Wit.: John Speir, Jr, Robert Salter
12	1-23-1764	John Mills (Pat. 1762)	John Mills, Jr.	150 A; £30. Wit.: Thos. Daniel, Edward Salter, Jr.
14	2-18-1763	John Norris	John Brinson	70 A; £20. Wit.: William Edward
16	2-29-1764	John Fulford (Pat. 1752) & Sarah Fulford, wife	Thomas Allen	100 A; £—. Adj.: Abraham Tison, Philip Riland. Wit.: Moses Tison, Edmund Tison, Jr.
18	2-20-1764	Andrew Gofford	Middlton Mobley	100 A; £30. Former owner: Mickle King (Pat. 1757)
20	2-27-1764	William Speir (Pat. 1760)	Henry Anderson	98 A; £45. Wit.: John Speir, Jr, Major Harris
22	3- 1-1764	James Everitt (D-1755)	Martin Nelson, Jr.	220 A; £4. Adj.: Peter Nelson. Former owner: Seth Pilkington (Pat. 1744). Witness: John Nelson
24	2-28-1764	Israel Baxter	Children: Stephen, David, Sarah, Theophilus	Furn., negro, horse, goods; love & aff. Wit.: John Hardee, James Lanier
25	2-28-1764	George Cannon	Edward Moore	150 A; £10. Wit.: Samuel Barrow, Zachariah Pinkett
27	2-15-1764	Thomas Littel (Pat. 1741 and 1761)	George Littel, son	90 A+ 150 A; love & aff.
28	2-29-1764	John Fulford (Pat. 1752) and Sarah Fulford	Roger Allen	100 A; £—.
30	10- 7-1763	William Smith (TYR)	David Smith	125 A; £21. Former owner: John Holland (Pat. 1760). Wit.: Wm. Archdeacon
32	2-16-1764	John Keneday	Francis McNemar	220 A; £21.
34	2- 3-1764	John Norris (DUP)	John Brown	200 A; £15.
36	10-24-1763	John Ball	Mary Knowis and Sadock Knowis	90 A; £12. Former owner: Thomas Williams (Pat. 1743)

DEED BOOK C (1764-1767)

Page	Date	Grantor	Grantee	Additional Information
38	1-30-1764	Moses Moor	George Cannon	300 A; £50. Former owner: Jacob Moor (Pat. 1739). Wit.: Zachariah Pinkett
40	12-12-1763	Thomas Mercer	Joseph Sulavant	240 A; £8. Wit.: Christopher Mercer
42	2-28-1764	Edward Salter	Robert Salter, son	326A+ 350 A; love & aff.
44	2-20-1764	Edward Salter	Robert Salter, son	4 negroes; love & aff. Wit.: John Speir, Jr., William Jones
45	1-16-1764	William Speir	Matthew Parramore	170 A; £—. Wit.: Solomon Whichard, Alex Stewart
47	4——1764	Ephraim Allen (HYDE)	Caleb Spivy	640 A; £10. Former owners: Col. John Snoad, Timothy Allen, father of Epraim. Wit.: Francis Roundtree, Christien Roundtree
48	12- 3-1757	William Baldwyn	Archabald Adams	293 A; £5. Adj.: Richard Harris. Wit.: Levi Adams
51	——1763	Jacob Little (EDG)	Joseph Little	— £30. Adj.: John Little. Former owner: John Williams (A; Pat. 1760). Wit.: Edward Cobb, James Little
53	3-20-1764	John Edwards	Daniel Edwards, son	Negro; love & aff.
54	7-14-1763	John Nobles	Jonathan Taylor	100 A; £6.
56	5-30-1763	Daniel Willson	John Hardee	50 A; £10. Former owner: Larrance Cirvin
58	5——1764	James Brooks	Michael More	250 A; £50.
60	4——1764	Robert Williams, Jr. (D-1763)	Richard Evans	270 A; £150. Former owner: Jacob Evans (Pat. 1738)
62	2-17-176—	Jacob Little (EDG)	John Little	100+ A; £30. Former owner: John Williams (Pat. 1760)
64	——1764	John Hardee (1760)	Solomon Robson	57 A; £40.
66	——1762	Joseph Wall (D-1761)	Thomas Daniel	5 A; 1 sh. Former owners: John Worseley, Thos. Worsley, Jr., Thomas Worsley. Men.: Thomas Blount (Pat. 1719)
68	3——1764	Edmund Kenedy	John Hodges, Jr.	100 A; £—. Adj.: Lemuel James. Former owner: Ebenezer Folsom (Pat. 1761). Wit.: Archabald Adams, Jr.
70	——1764	Larance Cirvin	Daniel Wilson	200 A; £10.
72	5-18-1764	John Simpson	Paul Herrington	200 A; £10.
74	5-27-1764	William Moore	William Butler	150 A; £6. Wit.: Benjamin May, Jesse Baggett
75	4-13-1764	James Bonner (BERT)	Warren Andrews (TYR)	150 A; £40. Former owner: Joseph Wimberly (Pat. 1745). Wit.: Etheldred Andrews, Levy Andrews
77	5-25-1764	Joseph Jolley, Sen.	Francis McNemar	200 A; £12. Wit.: William Congleton, William Jolley, Elizabeth Smith
79	——1764	James Blount, taylor	William Moore, cooper	500 A; £—. Former owner: James Blount, (1745). father of grantor. Wit.: John Hardee, Isaac Hardee
81	5-29-1764	John Simpson (Pat.1764)	Adam Laughan	200 A; £10.
83	5-30-1764	Joseph Wall	Thomas Daniel	250 A; £. Wit.: Larence McNemar, Lazarus Pearce

DEED BOOK C (1764-1767)

Page	Date	Grantor	Grantee	Additional Information
84	3- 8-1764	Isaac Stocks (Pat. 1755)	John Moy, Jr.	100 A; £60.
86	5-28-1764	John Willson	William Willson, son	186 A; £—.
88		John Edwards	John Nelson	320 A; £20. Former owner: Isaac Buck (Pat. 1743)
94	2-10-1764	Lawrence McNemar	William Smith	100 A; £50.
96	1- 7-17—	Earl Granville	Samuel Edwards	200+ A; £10.
101	5-12-1764	William Smith	Francis McNemar	100 A; £50. Wit.: Henry Cooper, Jesse Barbre, William Jolley
103	9-17-1764	Thomas Tison	Archibald Paterson	150 A; £35. Former owner: Sabree Tison (Pat. 1756). Wit.: James Lanier
106	8-24-1764	William Stafford (Pat. 1763)	Edmund Tison, Jr.	200 A; £7.
108	2 ——1764	James Barnet	Samuel Stansell	150 A; £30.
110	——1764	Thomas Richard	Reading Blount (BEAU)	— A; £80. Wit.: Reading Blount, Jr., Joseph Nathaniel Blount
112	3-30-1764	Isaac Knox (D-1763)	John Griffin	200 A; £45. Adj.: William Congleton. Former owners: Lemuel Cherry (Pat. 1745), Charles Cherry, Joseph Jolley (D-1761)
114	4- 1-1764	James Bonner (BEAU)	Elijah Harris	150 A; £—.
115	8——1764	Abraham Pettypool	Hardy Griserd	125 A; £15. Wit.: Elias Bergeron, Isaac Giddins
117	6-30-1764	Thomas Daniel, (Pat. 1764)	James Mancor	250 A; £20. Wit.: Robert Salter, John Bonner
119	3- 9-1764	John Moye, Jr.	Edward Williams, wheelwright	100 A; £45. Adj.: William Harris, George Moy, Former owner: Ebenezer Folsom. Wit.: William Baldwyn, William Baldwyn, Jr.
121	6-20-1764	James Mancor	Nathan Godley	80 A; £20. Adj.: Thomas Daniel. Wit.: Edward Salter, Robert Salter
123		Richard Williams	Meryman Allen	80 A; £3. Former owner: Samuel Stokes (Pat. 1762). Wit.: George Moye, John Smith
125	——1764	George Dikes	Abraham Pettipool	100 A; £35. Wit.: John Tison, Ephraim Pettipool
127	8——1764	Anthony Whichard	James Latham	200 A; £—. Former owner: Patrick Maubly (Pat. 1726)
127	8-27-1764	John Hardee	Benjamin Smith	100 A; £20. Former owner: George White (Pat. 1737)
130	——1764	Joseph Little and Elizabeth Little, wife	Benjamin Brown	100 A; £40. Adj.: John Little, Thomas Farmer
132	——1764	Absalum James	Jesse Sparkman (TYR)	185 A; £11. Adj.: John Butler, Moses Deane

C 84-132

DEED BOOK C (1764-1767)

Page	Date	Grantor	Grantee	Additional Information
134	6-20-1764	Francis Buck	Peter Albritton	200 A; £20. Adj.: John Taylor. Former owner: Capt. Isaac Buck (Pat. 1757). Wit.: John Simpson, Elizabeth Simpson
136	———	Batson Whitrust and Elizabeth Whitrust	Joseph Little	100 A; £40. Wit.: Francis Hobson, Charles Cox, Abia Cox
137	8- 6-1764	Isaac Giddings	Abraham Pettypool	125 A; £27. Wit.: Elias Bergeron, Hardy Grisard
139	1-20-1761	John Church	Richard Mayo	50 A; £—. Adj.: Isaac Church. Wit.: David Averrett, Susanna Averrett
141	8-18-1764	James Averrett	William Edwards	224 A; £10. Former owner: Seth Pilkington (Pat. 1744)
143	1-25-1764	John Mills (Pat. 1762)	Isaac Mills, son	150 A; £30. Wit.: Edward Salter, Robert Daniel
145	11——1764	Francis Hobson	Abia Cox	350 A; £15. Adj.: William Crisp, John Brown
146	2- 5-1763	John Norris, Sen. (DUP)	Francis Hobson	500 A; £—. Wit.: James Mayo, Arnal Hopkins, Rachel Gofford
147	2-10-1762	William Archdeacon	Francis Hobson	250 A; £—. Former owner: Samuel Wiggins (Pat. 1738)
148	9-11-1764	James Cason (Pat. 1761)	James Albritain, Jr.	200 A; £59.
150	11- 7-1764	Edward Stafford	Richard Williams	229 A; £—.
152	——1764	Edward Stafford	Thomas Wallis	412 A; £36.
154	11-21-1764	William Moor and Thomas Ward	Mikel Ward	150 A; good will to friend. Wit.: Elias Bergeron, David Ward
155	11-30-176	George Avorey, ship carpenter	James Blount, taylor	100 A; £50. Wit.: Abraham Tison, Robert Salter
157	——1764	Richard Williams (D-1763)	Demcy Allen	— A; £5. Wit.: Edward Williams, John Williams
159	——1764	James Blount	Allis Blount, dau.	Personal goods; love & aff. Men.: Benjamin Blunt, son
160	8-31-1764	Joseph Bryan and Sarah Bryan	William Lanier	50 A; £5. Former owner: Patrick Manle, dec. Wit.: Joseph Worsley, John Lanier
161	11-19-1764	Valentine Brown (Lunenburg, Va.) and Richard Brown (HAL) and John Brown (HAL)	Archibald Paterson	640 A; £—. Wit.: James Lanier, John Colwell Brown, Gary Brown, Lewis Brown
163	10-16-1764	Simon Jones (Pat. 1762)	James Cason	131 A; £—. Adj.: William Watkins. Robert Boyd, Wit.
165	———	John Williams (Pat. 1762)	Richard Williams	58 A; £2. Wit.: John Stokes
167	———	John Williams	Joshua Williams	120 A; £—. Wit.: William Robson, Thomas Williams

C 134-167

DEED BOOK C (1764-1767)

Page	Date	Grantor	Grantee	Additional Information
169	—1764	Isaac Noble	John Jones	130 A; £16. Former owner: Ebenezer Folsom, Men.: John Noble, father of Grantor. Wit.: Edmund Williams, Archibald Adams
171	11-27-1764	James Everitt	John Everitt, son	100 A; love & aff.
172	11-12-1763	Francis Hobson, Jr., (D-1761)	Arnald Hopkins	100 A; £7+. Former owner: John Norris. Wit.: James Mayo, Nathan Mayo
173	9-25-1764	James Howl	John Persey	50 A; £5. Former owner: Benjamin Sanders, Sen. Adj.: John Frier. Wit.: John Swinson, John Swinson, Jr, Levi Swinson
174	11-15-1764	William Moor	John Slaughter, Jr.	150 A; £30.
176	11-—1764	Amos Atkinson	William Nickols	145 A; £14. Wit.: Francis Hobson, Godfrey Stansell
177	8- 8-1764	Thomas Moor (Pat. 1763)	Abraham Moor	100 A; £—. Wit.: Elias Bergeron, Nathaniel Moore
179	3- 5-—	James Brooks	Richard Richardson	100 A; £5. Former owner: John Wane. Wit.: John Moye, Sen., John Hardee, Jr.
181	11-27-—	Thomas Moore	Jacob Giddins	— A; £12. Wit.: Elias Bergeron, Christopher Mercer
183	9- 8-—	Thomas Moor (Pat. 1763)	—Mercer	240 A; £—. Wit.: John Washington
185	—1764	Thomas Tyson (Pat. 1756)	James Lanier	100+ A; £25. Wit.: Charles Forbes, Malachi Dickinson, William Slaughter
187	9-11-1764	James Albritton, Jr.	Matthias Moor	— A; £30. Adj.: Samuel Moor. Wit.: John Cason, Thos. Pinkett, James Cason
189	6- 6-1762	Earl Granville	William Judkins	135 A; £10.
193	1-28-1765	James Barrow and Nathan Mayo and Mary Mayo, wife	Simon Pope	200 A; £20. Former owner: Joseph Barrow (Pat. 1741). Wit.: John Pope
194	6- 8-1764	Francis McNemar	John Kenady, Sen.	120 A; £20. Adj.: Robert Hodges. Wit.: William Jolley
196	2-—1765	Simon Pope	John Pope	150 A; £20.
198	8-28-1764	John Swinson	Joseph Jolley	— A; £—. Wit.: Peter Jolley
199	8-—1764	Walter Dixon, Sen.	Charles Tindale	160 A; £12. Former owner: Seth Pilkington (Pat. 1738). Wit.: John Munden
200	11-13-1764	Malachi Dickinson	William Baldwin	300 A; £100.
202	2-13-1765	Silvanus Pumphrey	Nathan Pumphrey, son	100 A; love & aff. Former owner: Israel Joyner (Pat. 1738). Wit.: Robert Thomson
203	12-24-1764	Archibald Adams. Jr.	William Baldwin, Sen. (Pat. 1757)	100 A; £8+. Former owner: Archibald Adams, Sen.

DEED BOOK C (1764-1767)

Page	Date	Grantor	Grantee	Additional Information
204	———————	William Harris, Sen.	William Harris, Jr., son	150 A; love & aff.
205	12-22———	Richard Mayo	Thomas Sumerling	50 A; £14. Former owner: John Church. Wit.: David Averitt, David Hathaway, David Hathaway, Jr.
207	12-26-1764	Thomas Sumrall	David Hatway, Sen. (Pat. 1756)	100 A; £30.
208	2- 2-1765	Abraham Barrow (Pat. 1755)	Moses Tison, Sen.	100 A; £75.
210	2———1765	Richard Williams, doctor	Edward Williams	210 A; £40. Former owners: Robert Williams, John Williams, Nathan Johnson. Wit.: Newton
213	1-12-1764	Isaac Giddins	Isaac Giddins, son	200 A; love & aff.
214	2———1765	Howell Wall	James Cason	300 A; £50. Former owner: Joseph Gadd (Pat. 1749)
216	2-14-1765	Elias Hodges (Pat. 1716)	Reading Blount	600 A; £160.
217	2-15-1765	Nathan Godley	Anthony Kinnin, schoolmaster	40 A; love & aff. for friend. Men.: James Blount
219	2-20-1765	Edward Salter	Edward Salter, Jr., son	300 A; love & aff. Former owner: Lewis Duvall. Wit.: John Lesslie, Lazarus Pearce
220	12-25-17——	Jeremiah Rhame	————Parker, taylor	— A; £—.
222	2-22-1765	John Brooks	James Brooks, son	100 A; £—. Former owner: Samuel Vine
223	11-24-1762	John Meeks, Sen.	John Meek, Jr.	100 A; £14. Wit.: John Averrith, Richard Botten, Nathan Mayo
225	2———1765	Nathan Godley	Reading Blount	80 A; £20. Wit.: James Jones
226	2-26-1765	Caleb Wallis (Pat. 1761)	Thos. Duffield	100 A; £25.
228	11-13-1764	Thomas Crandell	Moses Harrell	200 A; £—. Former owner: Charles Cherry (Pat. 1761)
229	———1765	Mark Powell	James Brooks	150 A; £15. Wit.: Joshua Putnal, Joseph Stevens
230	2———1765	Daniel Wilson	John Kenedy	— A; £25.
232	10- 8-1764	Thomas Tison	Samuel Smyth (CRAV)	200A + 450 A; £100. Former owner: Thomas Tison, father of grantor (Pat. 1739)
234	5-17-1765	William Taylor	Sarah Taylor, dau	Negro; love & aff. Wit.: Martin Nelson, Mary Edwards
234	5-25-1765	William Taylor and Dinah Taylor, wife	Charles Taylor, son, Liscomb Taylor, dau Nancy Taylor, dau	Negro; love & aff.
235	1- 1-1765	Luke White (DOBBS)	Phillip Pipkin	150 A; £150. Wit.: Mark Hardin, Daniel Pipkin, George White
237	4- 1-1765	John Taylor (Pat. 1757)	John Simpson	280 A; £80.
239	5-11-1765	Samuel Moor		100 A; love & aff.
240	12-12-1764	James Baggett	John Ingrim (NORHN)	160 A; £66.

DEED BOOK C (1764-1767)

Page	Date	Grantor	Grantee	Additional Information
241	5-29-1765	John Kenedy and Apsley Kenedy, wife	Nehemiah Wooten and Henry Wooten	436 A; £140. Former owners: Wm. Adams (Pat. 1740), George Lewis (D-1741), John Speir, (dec.) (D-1756). Men.: Apsley Speir Kenedy, heir. Wit.: Richard Evans, Peter Richardson
243	3-30——	William Gwaltney	Drury Spain	213 A; £35. Former owners: William Stevens (Pat. 1735), John Stevens, heir of William Stevens. Wit.: Marcus Stocks, Nathan Mayo, Joseph Hickman
244	1-11-1765	Luke White (DOBBS)	Phillip Pipkin	360 A in Pitt and Dobbs; £—.
246	5- 1-1765	Benjamin Saunders	Hardee Teel	85 A; £30. Wit.: William Whiteacre, Simon Saunders, John Persey
247	———1765	David Green	Levi Adams	200 A; £40. Wit.: William Clark, John Robson, Sampson Pittman
248	5-23-1765	Edmund Tison	Thomas Goff	117 A; £100
250		John Williams, Sen.	John Mayo	300 A; £20. Adj.: Joseph Hardee. Wit.: Henry Ellis, John Williams
251	9-28-1764	Joseph Loyd	Jesse Cooper	200 A in Pitt (formerly Tyrrell); £—. Men.: James Smith (Pat. 1755). Wit.: James Kenedy, Jesse Peine, John McCaskey
252	1- 1-1765	Jonathan Jolley	John Jolley	200 A; £15. Former owner: Thomas Nobles
254	5-17-1765	Simon Presscott and John Presscott	Abner Proctor	230 A; £50
255	8-26-1765	David Averett	John Barrow	90 A; £10. Wit.: James Barrow, Benjamin Evans, Robert Gremmer
257	6- 1-1765	William Giddings	George Dikes, Jr.	— A; £40. Wit.: Jesse Moore, Aurther Moore, Jr.
258	9-18-1764	Thomas Tyson (Pat. 1738 and 1748 and 1753)	Thomas Cooper	920 A; £130
260	8-——1765	Henry Ellis	Simon Pope	162 A; £50. Adj.: Thomas Gwaltney
262	12- 6-1764	John Swindell (HYDE)	John Knowis, Jr.	440 A; £20. Adj.: George Beck. Wit.: Christ Respess, Edward McSwain
263	8-26-1765	David Averett	Robert Gremmer	40 A; £10. Wit.: James Barrow, Benjamin Evans
264	1-15-1764	John Meeks	Walter Meeks (Pat)	50 A; £20. Adj.: William Wright
266	———1763	William Archdeacon	Elexandrew Wheatley	— A; £100. Men.: Thomas and Mary Wheatley, mother and father of grantee, Elexandrew

C 241-266

DEED BOOK C (1764-1767)

Page	Date	Grantor	Grantee	Additional Information
266	10-30-1764	Francis Buck and Sarah Buck, wife	Robert Webb (BER) and John Land (BER)	200 A; £—. Wit.: Isom Webb, John Perritt
268	4- 1-1765	John Worsley	David Daviss, cordwinder	120 A Pat. in Edgecombe; £60. Former owner: John Holland
269	6- 7-1765	Charles Fineehan and Christian Fineehan, wife	Warren Andrews (TYR)	300 A; £80. Former owner: David Smith. Wit.: Benjamin Bowers, Jno. Rial, Levi Adams
271	6-26-1762	Earl Granville	Joseph Sullivan	296 A; 10 sh
274	4-30-1763	Abraham Duncan and George Duncan (N.H.)	John Cannon	120 A; £40
276	——1765	Thomas Moor	Samuel Davis	— A; £20. Wit.: Elias Bergeron, John Ingram
277	4-30-——	Robert Ward	William Smith (TYR)	— A; £45. Wit.: Ed. Moor, Edward Smith. Former owners: Dennis Glisson (Pat), James Glisson
278	——1765	John Barber	Lemuel James	128 A; £75. Former owners: William Stafford (Pat), James Albriton(D), John Whichard(D). Wit.: John Jones, Thomas Pinkett
280	11- 4-1765	James Mayo	Nesbe Mills, Jr.	100 A; £40. Former owner: John Price, Sen. Wit.: John Smith, Henry Smith
282	3-17-17——	James Edwards (BEAU)	William Mosely	125 A; £10.
283	———————	John Tison	Samuel Tison, son	200 A; love & aff. Wit.: Benjamin May, Jacob Giddins. Adj.: Jacob Giddins
285	8-22-1765	Absolum Rogers	William Rogers	100+ A; £20. Adj.: Daniel Rogers. Wit.: Abner Proctor, James Cobb
286	11——1765	John Ingram	Samlel Davis	160 A; £66. Former owner: John Ward, Sen. (Pat.)
288	10- 2-17——	John Moye	John Price	— A; £20. Former owners: David Cannon, Peter Conway
289	8-27-1765	Lazarus Pearce	David Chadwick	— A; £5. Wit.: Thomas Pearce, Hezekiah Pearce, James Mancor
292	10-29-1765	Thomas Coomes, physician	John Mayo, cooper	320 A; £—. Adj.: Isaac Buck. Wit.: John Simpson, John Parker
292	5- 1-1765	William Denmark, batchelor	Thomas Coomes	320 A; £23. Wit.: Samuel Tison, Jr, Robert Hardee, Jr., William Folsom
294	2-15-1765	Arthur Olds (ONSW)	Joseph Whitfield	100 A; —. Former owner: Walter Bryant (Pat. 1757)
295	——1764	William Archdeacon	Elexander Wheatley	160 A; love & aff. for friend. Wit.: Thomas Wheatley, Mary Wheatley, Samuel Wheatly, Jr.
296	6——1765	John Knowis, Jr. (D-1764)	Richard Holland	220 A; £30.

DEED BOOK C (1764-1767)

Page	Date	Grantor	Grantee	Additional Information
297	1- 3-1766	William Willis (EDG) (Pat. 1740)	John Fullingham, Jr.	— A; £—.
300	12——1765	John Pollard (Pat. 1761)	Benjamin Pollard	78 A; 40 sh. Adj.: Peter Rives
301	9-26-1765	Daniel McLam	William McLam, son	All goods; —.
302	2- 1-1765	John Stocks (Pat. 1760)	Peter Moss	140 A; £50.
303	1-28——	William Wilson Coats	James Williams (EDG)	100 A; £25. Adj.: John Mayo, dec. Wit.: Roderick Williams, Shadrack Williams
304	2- 2-1766	Edward Ward and Maryon Ward	Samuel Ward	200 A; —.
306	1- 3-1766	William Willis (EDG) (Pat. 1763)	Benjamin Hull	180 A; £15.
308	5-24-1766	William Watkins, Sen. (Pat. 1758)	William Watkins, Jr., son	412 A; love & aff.
310	1-18-1766	Jesse Sparkman (TYR)	William Hays	100 A; £20. Former owner: Caleb Howel (1743); Adj.: Thomas Williams. Wit.: John Cherry
312	2- 1-176	Joseph Burkett (1756)	John Hardee	100 A; £30. Wit.: Peter Johnston, Joseph Donaldson, John Nelson
315	1- 7-1763	Earl Granville	William Willis	180 A; 10 sh.
316	——176	John Simpson, merchant (Pat. 1764)	James Brooks	— A; £—.
318	3-15-1766	Levy Adams (1782)	Joshua Tucker, shoe maker	50 A; £15. Former owners: Archabald Adams, Sen, William Baldwyn, Sen. (Pat. 1757)
321	3- 1-1766	John Windom and Elizabeth Windom	John Nickol, grandson, and Jean Nickol, daughter	100 A; love & aff.
322	——-1766	William Prescott and Elizabeth Prescott, wife, and John Prescott, Sen.	Thomas Davis	50 A; £35. Wit.: Wm. Bryan, John Nobles, William Moore
324	———	William Archdeacon	James Mayo, Jr.	— A; £—. Wit.: William Hopkins, James Mayo, Sen.
325	2-15-1766	John Moy, Sen.	Samuel Dunbar	— A; £—.
327	5- 7-1766	Robert Salter and Clare Salter, wife	Thomas Nobles	190 A; £65. Wit.: Benjamin Burney, James Jones. Former owner: Capt. John Speir (Pat.)
329	10-15-1766	Richard Richardson, inholder	John Simpson, merchant	100 A; £30. Former owner: John Wane (Pat. 1752), John Benson, Charles Price, Benjamin Cording, James Brooks.

C 297-329

DEED BOOK C (1764-1767)

Page	Date	Grantor	Grantee	Additional Information
331	5-14-1766	Richard Barrow	Joseph Barrow, tupper	50 A; £—. Wit.: James Barrow
333	4——1766	John James	Henry Couper	71 A; £20. Wit.: Hillery Cason, John James, Thomas Pinkitt
335	4——1766	Lemuel James	Henry Couper	29 A; £20. Former owner: James Cason (Pat)
337	————	Thos. Hardee	John Stocks	150 A; £30. Former owner: Joseph Hardee, father of Thomas Hardee, (Pat. 1755)
340	2-26-1766	Samuel Stansell and Robert Ward	Joseph Gray	150 A; £50. Wit.: Samuel Ward, Daniel Smith, Ed More, John Kaney
341	————	David Averrett	Benjamin Evans	72 A; £10
343	3-12-1765	William Mace, Jr.	Benjamin Jordin	200 A; £—. Former owner: William Mace, Sen. (Pat. 1738)
345	————	Caleb Spivey	Benjamin Hull, blacksmith	170 A; £40. Wit.: James Cremean. Former owner: Patrick Maule
347	6-22-1765	George Becton (CRAV)	Frederick Becton	116 A (formerly in Craven and Johnston); £25. Former owners: Richard Becton, (dec.), uncle of grantor and grantee; John Becton, brother of Richard. Men.: Edmund Becton and Michael Becton, also nephews of John and Richard
350	9-21-1766	William Crisp	Simon Prescott	100 A; £15
352	11-18-1766	William Jolly	Hugh Tross	230 A; £—.
354	11- 6-1766	William Clark	Edward Salter, merchant	2 A; £—;
358	———1766	Moses Tison	Abraham Tison	150 A; £25. Former owner: Cornelius Tison, (Pat. 1745)
360	11-25-1766	John Moy and Ruth Moy, wife	William Brierly	154 A; £50
362	7-20——	John Averett (EDG)	Peter Nelson	200 A; £—. Former owner: Seth Pilkington
364	12-14-1765	John Dowdin	John Ingram	100 A; £—. Men.: Edward Dowdin
366	1-19-1765	Robert Boyd	Robert Boyd, Jr., son	200 A; love & aff.
368	————	William Mizell	Thomas Wolfenden and Thomas Cooper	320 A; £50.
370	8——1766	William Stansell, Jr.	Joseph Barrow	220 A; £60. Former owner: Daniel Oquin (Pat.)
372	———1766	Benjamin Warner	John Simpson	— A; £—. Former owners: John Warner, father of grantor; John Hardie
374	2-27-1766	William Burnett	Joseph Gray	90 A; £12.
376	12- 2-1765	David Averett (Pat. 1761)	Isaac Church	112 A; £5.
378	4- 5-1766	Elijah Harris	Lemuel Harris	175 A; £—.

DEED BOOK C (1764-1767)

Page	Date	Grantor	Grantee	Additional Information
380	——————	John Price	Joseph Rogers, grandson; John Rogers, grandson; John Price, son; Mary Rogers, daughter	50 A; horse, all goods; love & aff. Men: Mary Price, now Mary Rogers
381	8——1766	James Cason (1762)	Robert Salter and Edward Salter, Jr.	231 A; £28. Former owner: Simon Jones (Pat. 1762). Wit.: Thomas Salter
383	10——1766	Thomas Wallis, taylor (1763)	Caleb Wallis, son	122 A; love & aff. Former owner: William Autry. Wit.: Abraham Tison, Lucy Tison, Joel Sugg
384	10——1766	Thomas Wallis and Affiah Wallis, wife	William Wallis, son	159 A; love & aff.
387	10——1766	Thomas Wallis, taylor, and Affiah Wallis, wife	Thomas Wallis, Jr., son	140 A; love & aff. Former owner: Samuel Swearingen, Jr.
389	8-15-1766	Philip Riland	John Fulford	100 A; £—. Former owner: Sary Allen
392	——1766	Moses Hare (BEAU)	Simon Jones	200 + A; £20.
394	1-16-1766	Joseph Sullivan (Pat. 1762)	Benjamin May	296 A; £16.
396	8-26-1766	Robert Hardee	Josias Hardee, son	100 A; love & aff. Adj.: William Williams
398	1-12-1764	Jacob Anderson, mariner (D-1750)	Richard Evans Bath Towne)	320 A; £83. Former owner: Henry Snoad (Pat.) Wit.: Robert Knox, George Evans, Thomas Williams
400	3-24-1766	Nathan Moore	Samuel Davis	230 A; £40. Former owner: Joseph Mercer (1761) Wit.: Nathaniel Moore, John Gay
402	——————	Amos Atkinson	Nathan Mayo	200 A; £15.
404	1-22-1767	John Hadduck, Jr. (1767)	John Simpson	200 A; £100. Former owner: Simon Burney, William Taylor, Sen. and son, William Taylor, Jr. (1731)
406	1-22-1767	William Taylor, Jr.	John Hattock, Jr.	200 A; £120.
408	12- 1-1766	Laurence Kirvin	John Simpson	200 A; £15.
410	12-17-1766	Mary Rogers	John Price, brother	Goods from father; £180. Wit.: Mary Price
411	10-31-1766	Edmund Tison (D-1764) and Mary Tison, wife	Philip Ryland	220 A; £25. Former owner: William Stafford (Pat. 1763). Wit.: George Tison, William Tison
413	——1767	Benjamin Wilkinson	Solomon Cherry, carpenter	200 A; £—. Wit.: Samuel Cherry, Arthur Olds
415	11-17-1766	Thomas Halleman (Isle of Wight, Va.) and Elizabeth, Halleman, wife	Charles Reeks	200 A; £—. Adj.: James Mayo, Jr. Former owner: James Mayo, Sen. (Pat.) Wit.: Benjamin Little, Benjamin Edwards, William Hart
417	2-27-1767	Benjamin Warner	John Moye	99 A; £20. Former owner: Col. John Hardie. Wit.: George Moye, Matthias Moore
419	7-28-1766	William Taylor	Isaac Edwards	248 A; £50

DEED BOOK C (1764-1767)

Page	Date	Grantor	Grantee	Additional Information
422		Robert Boyd (BEAU)	Joseph Boyd	— A; £25
423	12-11-1766	William Willis	Joseph Platts, shoemaker	100 A; £15. Former owner: Daniel O'Quin
426	2- 5-1767	Edmund Tison, Jr. (Pat 1755)	Philip Riland	120 A; £25
428	—1767	William Brady	James Brady	150 A; £5
430	8-12-1766	William Smith (TYR) and Benjamin Smith	Mary Buntain	125 A; £—. Former owner: John Holland (1760)
432	—1767	Ebenezer Folsom (EDG) (Pat. 1761)	Solomon Whitchard	130 A; £13
433	2-13-1767	Solomon Robson	William Robson	100 A; 1 sh. Wit.: Sovereign Robson
435	—1766	Thomas Pugh (BERT)	Lewis Hudson	150 A; £25. Wit.: William Junkeson, Wm. Bryan, Samuel Grymes
437	1-25-1767	Benjamin Ellis (D-1753)	Henry Ellis	200 A; £15. Former owner: William Ham (Pat 1752). Adj.: Cornelius Tison. Wit.: Robert Grimmer
440	—1763	Thomas McKnight (PASQ), merchant	Jacob Elligood, mariner	500 A; £50
442	12- 4-1761	Nathaniel Newton and Anne Newton, wife	Thomas McKnight	500 A; £40. Former owner: Doctor Robert Kingman, Princess Anne, Va. (Anne Newton, heir) Wit.: Anne Elmsley
445	9- 7-1764	James Cales	Richard Evans	510 A; 5 sh. Former owner: Dr. Robert Kingman, Princess Ann, Va., (dec.)
446	9-26-1764	Jacob Elligood (CHOW)	James Cales (BEAU)	510 A; £200. Wit.: Will Cumming
448	9-28-1764	James Cales (BEAU)	Margaret Cales, wife, John Cales, son, and Robert Cales, son	510 A; love & aff
450	6-27-1764	Jacob Elligood	Alexander Elmsley	Power of Attorney
451	11-21-1766	Thomas Ward	Frances Ward, mother	Plantation; love & aff. Former owner: Mikel Ward, father (dec.)
452	11-21-1766	Thomas Ward	John Ward	160 A; £20
453	1- 7-1763	Earl Granville	William Stansell	695 A; 10 sh
458	1-19-1767	John Lesslie	George Evans and William Pratt	Estate; £500. Men.: Ann Holland, intended wife
462	4-10-1765	Edward Buck	Benjamin Buck	640 A; £30. Former owners: Capt. Isaac Buck, father of Edward (D-1757); Capt. James Ellison
464	4-20-1767	Jacob Taylor (DUP)	Mathew Albriton	½ of tract; £5+. Former owner: Simon Burney. Men.: William Taylor, father of Jacob (D-1749)

DEED BOOK C (1764-1767)

Page	Date	Grantor	Grantee	Additional Information
466	1-12-1767	William Field	William Turnage	200 A; £—. Former owner: George Pettit (Pat) Wit.: James Barr, William Peoples
469	3-——-1767	William Gerald (Pat. 1751) and Susanah Gerald, wife	David Garald (BEAU)	107 A; £75. Wit.: James Jones, William Travis
471	3-——-1767	Shadrack Allen (Pat. 1753)	Isaac Stocks	100 A; £30. Wit.: William Burney, John Stocks
473	3- 3-1767	Jacob-Blount (CRAV)	William Dunmarke	100 A; £18. Wit.: Anne Blount, Joseph Allen
475	10-——-1766	John Drake Of Southampton, Va. (1762)	Thomas Drake	100 A; £—. Wit.: George Evans, Robert Gremmer
477	——-1767	William Garrald and Susannah Garrald, wife	David Garrald (BEAU)	50 A; £20
477	——-1767	Warren Andrews (TYR)	Levi Andrews	100 A; £5. Wit.: Etheldred Andrews. Former owners: David Smith, Charles Fineehan
481	1- 1-1761	John Holland (TYR) (Pat. 1760)	Aquila Sugg (EDG), merchant, and Abraham Tison	240 A; £20. Wit.: William Osborn
483	7- 7-1767	William Speir (Pat. 1758)	John Newton	250 A; £80. Wit.: William Newton, Walter Newton
485	8-17-1767	William Smith (TYR)	John Mayo	100 A+; £25. Wit.: Jacob Atkinson, Amos Atkinson, Edward Cobb
489	8-26-1767	Archibald Adams, Sen., shoemaker (1757)	George Williams, taylor	— A; £20
491	8-22-1767	Henry Bonner (BEAU)	Lazarus Pearce	300 A; £53. Former owner: Thomas Bonner. Wit.: Joshua Pearce, John Grist
493	5-20-1767	Isaac Giddins	Benjamin May	200 A; £90. Wit.: Abraham Pettipool
496	3-——-1766	William Barnett (DOB)	John Knox	100 A; £20
498	5- 5-1767	Henry Cannon (CRAV)	Dennis Cannon	120 A; £10. Wit.: Brittain King
500	8-26-1767	William Stansell	Benjamin Barrow	440 A; £50. Wit.: Joseph Barrow
502	5- 5-1767	Abraham Pettypool	Benjamin May, saddler	100 A; £75. Wit.: John Sanders
505	8- 6-1767	Williams Stansell, Jr.	James Turnage	250 A; £22
507	5- 5-1767	Abraham Pettypool	Benjamin May	290 A; £45
510	7-20-———	William Archdeacon	William Mobley	50 A; £15. Wit.: Edward Smith
511	——-1767	Thomas Harper	Daniel Johnson	100 A; £—. Wit.: Robert Williams, James Johnston
513	8-12-1767	William Gerrald	Isaac Mills	100 A; £30. Former owner: Thomas Coomes (Pat)
514	4-17-176	Moses Hare (1762)	John Maule	200 A; £—. Wit.: John Keel

DEED BOOK C (1764-1767)

Page	Date	Grantor	Grantee	Additional Information
517	8——1767	Daniel Rogers	Richard Evans and George Evans	1 A.; 20 sh
518	8-27-1767	George Moy	Major Harris	100 A.; £25. Former owner: Richard Harris (Pat) Wit.: Richard Moye, William Travis
519	9- 9-1766	Middleton Mobley	William Archdeacon	100 A.; £50. Former owner: Michael King. Wit.: Bigars Mobley
521	1——1767	John Williams, Jr.	Abraham Tison	100 A.; £50. Adj.: Abraham Tison, father of grantee. Former owner: Thomas Allen (Pat. 1752) Wit.: Roger Allen, John Fulford
524	——1752	Earl Granville	Solomon Robinson (BEAU)	100 A.; 3 sh
529	11- 6-1766	John Benson, dec. (D-1752)	Richard Evans	120 A.; £40. Former owner: Henry Bradley (Pat); John Becton (D-1738). Wit.: Speir Holland
531	9-28-1767	Thomas Hardee (D-1761)	John Simpson	100 A.; £67. Former owners: Shad Allen (Pat); John Williams, wrestler; John Williams, Jr. Wit.: John Moye, Sen., Rolen Dixson
533	11-10-1766	Richard Evans	Ichabod Simpson	120 A.; £40. Former owners: John Benson, Henry Bradley (Pat. 1738)
535	7-28-1767	John Moye	John Simpson	Mtg. household goods; £117.
536	4- 4-——	William Archdeacon	Godfrey Stansell	100 A.; £45
537	5-25-1767	John Brinson	Samuel Smyth (CRAV)	70 A.; £17. Wit.: Henry Williamson
539	9- 2-176—	David Averrett	Cornelius Church	207 A.; £—. Adj.: William Pollard. Wit.: Isaac Church, William Averett, Thomas Hathaway
540	4- 7-1767	John Moye (D-1767)	John Simpson	100 A.; £70. Adj.: Capt. James Ellison. Former owners: Col. John Hardee (Pat); John Warner, Benjamin Warner
542	11-20-1767	Thomas Allen	John Fulford	Binding; £200+. Wit.: James May

DEED BOOK D (1768-1771)

Page	Date	Grantor	Grantee	Additional Information
1	3- 9-1767	John Bartlett (ONSL)	Arthur Olds	190 A; £20. Wit.: Henry Cross, Enoch Ward
2	1——1768	Eleazer Hodges	Roger Hodges (CRAV)	200 A; £5. Former owner: Elias Hodges, dec. (Pat. 1762). Wit.: Edward Salter, Jr., William Moore
3	1-16-1768	Charles Price	Thomas Hardee	320 A; £70. Wit.: James Handcock, Abel Dail
4	1-19-1768	Joseph Rogers	Abel Deel, Jr.	50 A; £10. Wit.: Charles Hardee
5	9-28-1767	Lewis Handson	Benjamin Bowers	150 A; £30. Wit.: John Bowers, John Nobles, Nathaniel Nobles
5	1-11-1768	William Baldery (1761)	Jesse King	100 A; £40. Wit.: John Hardee, Thomas Goff
7	1-27-1768	George Moye, Sheriff	Edward Salter	160 A; £6. Former owners: Charles Tindall, Walter Dixon
7	4- 1-1768	Thomas Nobles	Nathaniel Nobles	100 A; £40. Adj.: Francis Pugh. Wit.: John Nobles, John Bowers, James Nobles
8	3-12-1768	Elamlidge Peninton	Joseph Briley	50 A; £30. Wit.: Jonas Shivers, William Teel, Edmund Smithwick
9	4- 4-1768	Thomas Pugh (BERT), merchant	William Bryan	120 A; £20. Wit.: John Whitehurst, William Junkason
10	10- 1-1767	William Gwaltney and Thomas Gwaltney	Micajah Lancaster	200 A; £250. Wit.: Benjamin Ellis, Richard Stafford
11	2-10-1767	David Hathaway	Edmond Hathaway, son	200 A; £250. Wit.: Thomas Hathaway, Francis Hathaway
12	6-20-1767	Benjamin Blunt (1765)	Thomas Garrett	63 A; — . Wit.: Jeremiah Rhame, Charles Hardee
13	2-19-1768	Nathan Johnston and Elizabeth Johnston, wife	John Wooten	120 A; £69. Wit.: Mathew Sturdivant, George Evans. Former owner: Caleb Wallace
16	4- 5-1768	Samuel Trus and Mary Trus, wife	John Kenedy	150 A; £30. Former owner: John Forbes, father of Mary Trus, (Pat. 1710). Wit.: Richard Allen, James Quartermus
17	9-12-1767	James Brooks	Joshua Putnell	150 A; £30. Former owner: Mark Powell (Pat. 1764). Wit.: Joshua Hull
18	12——1767	William Willis (EDG)	George Moye	220 A; £37. Former owners: William Stansill; his son, William Stansill; Benjamin Mathis. Wit.: John Moye, Richard Moye
19	6-13-1768	William Watkins, Jr.	William Moore	Negro; £40. Former owner: Benjamin Hodges
19	7-28-1768	Edward Salter	Matthew Scott, merchant	3 A; £100. Former owners: William Clark; Thomas Farmer; Edward Salter, father of grantor (1763, 1776). Wit.: Thomas H. Hall

DEED BOOK D (1768-1771)

Page	Date	Grantor	Grantee	Additional Information
20	3-30-1768	Roger Hodges (CRA)	William Grist	100 A; £13. Former owners: Elias Hodges, dec.; Eleazer Hodges, heir of Elias. Wit.: Nathan Godley, Lazarus Pearce
21	1-23-1768	Nathan Mayo	Jacob Atkinson	120 A; £25. Former owner: William Mayo, father of Nathan Wit.: Amos Atkinson, John Bullock, Drury Spain D 1-21
22	2- 9-1768	Lemuel Harris (D-1766)	Richard Reed	50 A; £10+. Adj.: Robert Rogers. Former owners: James Bonner, Elijah Harris. Wit.: John Hooks, Caleb Spivey
23	1- 1-1768	Abraham Breeler, yeoman	Joel Truss	80 A; £25. Adj.: Thomas Bonner. Wit.: Allen Sugg, Arthur Forbes, James Breeler
24	7-25-1768	James Mancor	Richard Grist (BEAU)	250 A; £20. Adj.: Thomas Worsley. Former owner: Thomas Daniel (Pat. 1764). Wit.: Major Slade
25	6- 7-1768	William Archdeacon	John Wheatley (TYR)	320 A; £10. Adj.: Godfrey Stancill, Benjamin Wilkinson. Wit.: Middleton Mobley, Edward Smith, Thomas Wheatley
26	6- 7-1768	John Hodges, Sen. (D-1744)	John Whichard, Sen.	75 A; £46. Former owners: Seth Pilkington (Pat. 1739). Elias Hodges. Wit.: Robert Hodges, Matthew Hodges
27	2-19-1768	Nathan Johnston	Mathew Sturdivant	— A; £5. Former owner: Jacob Evans, Sen.
28	2-29-1768	Richard Evans and Susannah Evans, wife	James CharlesCraft	100 A; £30. Former owner: Thomas Sellars (Pat. 1739)
29	10-17-1767	Joseph Platts	James Barr (DOB)	100 A; £28. Wit.: Mark Hardin, Wm. Handcock
30	3-15-1768	Joseph Boyd (BEAU)	James Armstrong	110 A; £65. Former owners: Robert Boyd, Sr., Robert Boyd, Jr. Wit.: William Dixon
31	4- 8-1768	Robert Webb (TYR) (1764)	Peter Albritton	200 A; £25. Wit.: John Perritt
32	6-27-1765	John Perritt (D-1763)	William Speir	225 A; £50. Former owners: Lewis Duvall, dec. (Pat. 1715); Martha Duvall, dau. of Lewis Duvall. Wit.: John Speir, Isom Webb, Abner Brown
33	2-26-1768	William Taylor	Martin Nelson, Jr.	165 A; £70. Wit.: George Baldree, Nathan Nelson
34	2-16-1768	John Hattock, Jr.	John Hattock, Sen.	100 A; £15. Wit.: Nesby Mills
35	2-27-1768	Richard Stone (1761) and Prudence Stone, wife	Timothy Harris	200 A; £100. Former owners: John Stokes, Joshua Stafford (1752), Wit.: Abraham Tison, Samuel Tison, Moses Tison
37	12-27-1767	John Price (D-1741)	John Simpson	100 A; £40. Former owner: Nezby Mills (Pat. 1738) Witness: Mary Smith, Mary Rogers

DEED BOOK D (1768-1771)

Page	Date	Grantor	Grantee	Additional Information
38	10-27-1767	William Edwards (D-1758) and Clary Edwards, wife	John Tison	— A; £65. Former owner: Thomas Tison (Pat. 1715), Major Tison (D-1752). Wit.: Samuel Tison, John Tison, Jr.
39	7- 5-1765	John Baul	James Latham	100 A; £27. Former owner: Thomas Williams (Pat. 1743)
40	10-22-1768	Caleb Spivey	James Latham	192 A; £3. Wit.: Obed. Rountree, Micajah Hart
41	11-14-1768	Thomas Daniel	Benjamin Barney	192 A; +250 A; £100. Former owner: Joseph Wales (Pat. 1762)
42	1-30-1768	Joseph Barrow	Caleb Tripp	120 A; £19. Witness: Charles Hardee
43	11-10-1768	Thomas Daniel	Benjamin Barney	100 A; £200. Former owner: John Worsley (Pat. 1723)
44	3- 7-1768	Isaac Wimberly (BERT)	James Bullock	110 A; £25. Wit.: Thos. Bullock, Elizabeth Wimberly
45	2- 8-1768	Jacob-Blunt	Jeremiah Ram	100 A; £50. Wit.: Daniel Bates, Joseph B. Barber
46	10-30-1767	Jacob Giddins	Samuel Tison	240 A; £20. Wit.: John Tison, John Tison, Jr. Jacob Tison. Former owner: Thos. Moore
47	4- 7-1767	John Hardee, Sheriff	James Barr (DOB)	— A; £15. Former owners: Peter Stancil; William Stancil, his father; Benjamin Mathews. Wit.: Jno. Leslie, James Hall
49	1- 7-1767	James Little (DOB) (1760)	John Mooring, Jr.	100 A; £45. Former owner: Robert Flake. Wit.: William Bell, Abner Proctor, Isaac Little; Adj.: William Mitchel
50	3- 7-1769	William Taylor, Jr. (1767)	William Taylor, son	200 A; £20. Men.: Simon Taylor; William Taylor is minor son of William Taylor, Jr.
50	2-22-1769	John Simpson (D-1767)	Isaac Stocks	100 A; £40. Former owners: Shadrich Allen, John Williams, Jr., Thomas Hardee. Wit.: Apsley Kennedy, Benjamin Randall
51	3-10-1768	Hillery Elligood (D-1757)	Thomas Williams	150 A; £50. Former owners: Richard Grist; John Grist, his son. Wit.: James Cranford
52	9-30-1768	Edward Williams and Elizabeth Williams, wife	James Williams	210 A; £50. Former owners: Robert Williams, Richard Williams. Wit.: Thomas Wallis, John Williams, Shadrach Williams
54	3-11-1769	John Brown (1762)	Henry Hodges	94 A; £15. Wit.: James Bonner, Matthew Hodges
55	2-21-1768	Archibald Paterson	James Lanier	640 A; £80. Former owner: John Brown. Wit.: Simon Pope, Henry Williamson, James Degge
56	5-17-1768	Abraham Tison	John Cannon	150 A; £35. Former owner: Cornelius Tison (Pat. 1745). Wit.: Henry Cannon, Jr., James King, Thos. Mebill
57	1-24-1768	John Meeks, Sen.	Francis Meeks	100 A; £8. Witness: Nathan Meeks

DEED BOOK D (1768-1771)

Page	Date	Grantor	Grantee	Additional Information
58	3-11-1769	John Brown (1762)	Matthew Hodges	94 A; £15.
59	2-16-1769	James Brooks (1762)	John Blackstone	200 A; £20.
60	4-17-1769	Anthony Mills (Pat. 1760)	Samuel Smith	100 A; £50. Wit.: William Burney
61	4-28-1769	James Barr (DOB)	William Turnage	— A; £50. Wit.: Owen Griffin, David Ellis. Former owners: Benjamin Mathews, William Stancils, William and Peter Stancil, his sons
61	3-15-1769	Thomas Drake	Edmond Hathaway	— A; £17. Former owners: John Meeks, Benjamin Pollard. Wit.: William Oliver, Hanner Church
63	1-27-1769	Jacob Giddens	John Harrel	125 A; £45. Men.: William Giddens, sons of Jacob. Wit.: Samuel Tison, Banjan May
64	1-29-1769	Adams Laughan (1764)	Thomas Blackstone	100 A; £10. Wit.: Thomas Maning, John Brackstone
65	2-10-1769	Matthew Albriton (D-1767)	Nathaniel Pettit	200 A; £25. Former owner: Simon Burney (1749)
66	2-10-1769	William Watkins (D-1730)	William Ormond, son in law, (DOB)	All possessions; love & aff. Former owner: Edward Salter. Wit.: Abigail Jones, William Jones, Simon Jones
67	3- 4-1769	James Albrittain (D-1756), saddler	John Simpson	500 A; £300. Adj.: John Mills, Jr. Former owner: David Cannon (1740). Wit.: George Albritton
68	3- 4-1769	John Simpson, merchant (1764)	James Albrittain	100 A; £15.
71	3- 4-1769	John Simpson (1765)	James Albrittain	280 A; £80. Former owner: John Tayler (Pat. 1757)
72	3-30-1769	Stephen Harding	John Simpson	— A; £10. Former owner: Israel Harding (1745), Father of Stephen Harding. Wit.: Ebenezer Fuller
72	10-25-1768	John Knowis, Sen.	Zadock Knowis	90 A; love & aff. Former owner: John Ball. Wit.: Demsy Moss
73	2-10-1769	William Watkins	James Cason,-son-in-law	Negro + ½ estate; love & aff. Former owners: Moses Dean (1745), Jesse Sparkman, dec. Adj.: John Johnston. Men.: George Jackson, Wit.: Mathew Scott
74	8-10-1768	John Hardee, Sheriff	Alex Stewart	100 A; £13.
75	8-10-1768	John Hardee, Sheriff	Alex Stewart	— A; £4+. Former owner: Jesse Sparkman
76	10-24-1767	John Hardee, Sheriff	Charles Bondfield (CHOW)	200 A; £1+. Former owners: Robert Ward, Edward Ward, John Ward
78	8-10-1768	John Hardee, Sheriff	Joseph Gainer	100 A; £15+. Former owner: Jesse Sparkman
79	3- 8-1769	Benjamin Evans	Samuel Atchison & Co.	72 A; £25. Former owner: David Everitt. Wit.: Benj. Berston, David Averitt, Thomas Cooper

DEED BOOK D (1768-1771)

Page	Date	Grantor	Grantee	Additional Information
80	4- 7-1769	Benjamin Evans (1765)	Samuel Atchison & Co.	200 A; £75. Former owner: James Conner, George Walston
81	2-10-1769	William Watkins (D-1730)	James Jones, son-in-law	Slave + 74 A; love & aff. Wit.: Abigail Jones, William Jones, Simon Jones. Former owner: Edward Salter
82	2-12-1769	William Burney and Mary Burney, wife	John Hardee, Jr.	200 A; £96. Former owner: Simon Burney, father of William Burney. Wit.: Aney Keela Hardee
84	7-24-1769	James Crandell, Sen. (1762)	Samuel Crandell	276 A; £5. Adj.: James Crandell, Jr. Wit.: Thomas Willis, Alex Stewart
84	2-24-1769	James Crandell, Sen.	James Crandell, Jr.	400 A; £50.
85	2-13-1769	John Braxton (Blackston)	Francis Roundtree	100 A in Pitt and Craven; —. Wit.: Moses Maning
86	2-10-1769	William Watkins	William Watkins, son	Negro man; 10 sh.
87	1- 5-1769	George Walston	Thomas Cooper, merchant	100 A; £15. Former owner: John Mayo (1763). Wit.: James Barr
88	5-21-1768	David Garrall	Isaac Buck	50 A; £10. Former owner: John Pain (1761)
89	12- 5-1768	Frederick Becton (CRAV)	Shadrack Moore	190 A; £60. Former owner: Richard Becton (1753). Wit.: Levi Moore, Mark Hardin
90	2-22-1769	John Ingram	Richard Barrow	100 A; £25. Wit.: Simon Pope, John Dowden, Cornelius Church
91	2- 9-1768	David Garrall	Isaac Buck	200+ A; £90. Adj.: Thomas Sutton. Former owner: John Paine, Sen. (1751). Wit.: William Buck, James Averitt
92	6-23-1768	Richard Mayo	David Averett	— A; £1. Former owner: Thomas Sumerell, Jr., John Church. Wit.: Isaac Church, William Averett, John Church
93	3- 6-1769	Peter Harget (1762) and Barbara Harget	Richard Proctor (BUTE)	400 A; £140. Former owners: George Sugg (Pat. 1756), Frederick H. Harget, Frederick Harget, Jr. Wit.: George Evans, William Hull
94	6-15-1769	Speir Holland	Parker Lacy	150 A; £45. Former owners: William Speir (Pat. 1755); John Holland, father of Speir Holland, (1761). Wit.: Samuel Atchison, Edmund Williams
95	1-21-1769	Walter Session	William Knox	100 A; £20. Dennis Glisson. Wit.: Edmund Andrews, John Ward
96	11-29-1768	Jesse Moore (1752)	Levi Moore	75 A; £22. Wit.: Arthur Moore, Shadrack Moore
97	2-26-1769	Joseph Barrow	Reuben Barrow	50 A; £8. Wit.: Moses Tison, Jr, Richard Barrow

D 80-97

DEED BOOK D (1768-1771)

Page	Date	Grantor	Grantee	Additional Information
97	10-24-1769	Thomas Allen	John Fulford	4 A; £2. Former owner: Sarah Allen (1752), now Sarah Fulford, wife of John Fulford. Wit.: Poll Allen, Zachariah Allen
99	2-23-1769	William Brady	John Brady	100 A; £5. Adj.: John Pollard. Wit.: James Sugg, Sampson Pittman, James Brady
100	10-24-1768	William Mobley	Benjamin Wilkinson	50 A; £33. Adj.: Michael King. Wit.: Godfrey Stansell, Bray Crisp, Bigers Mobley
100	——1769	Solomon James, Jr. (BLAD)	Richard Smith (BLAD)	150 A; £50. Former owner: John Johnson (1740). Wit.: Jacob Atford, James Pace
102	1-25-1769	Abia Cox (BEAU)	Robert Williams	350 A; £40. Adj.: William Crisp. Wit.: Francis Hobson, James May, Jr., Joseph Little
102	1- 4-1770	Edward Harris	Mathew Scott	290 A; £50. Adj.: Samuel Burton. Former owner: Timothy Harris, Jr. Wit.: Elizabeth Spear, Samuel Smithwick
103	10-14-1769	John Kennedy	Speir Holland	300 A; £125. Wit.: Sally Wolfenden, Richard Evans
104	1-11-1770	John Simpson (D-1766)	Thomas English, Jr., Bricklayer	200 A; £25. Former owner: Laurence Kirvin (1762). Wit.: Charles Forbes, William Moore
105	12- 8-1768	Joseph Sullivant (D 1755 & 1763)	Thomas Mercer	125 A; £40. Former owner: John Lamberson. Wit.: Shadrack Mercer
106	1——1770	Henry Gindraw (GRAN) and Selah Gindraw, wife	Nathaniel Moore	180 A; £26. Former owner: John May, dec, father of Selah Gindraw. Wit.: Benjamin May, Samuel Stafford
106	1- 6-1770	James Barrow	Peter Rives	200 A; £60. Former owners: John Vernon, Joseph Barrow (D-1746), father of James Barrow
108	9-24-1768	John Joyner	Jesse Jorden	100 A; £35. Wit.: John Tyson, Jacob Tyson
108	1-20-1768	William Mosley (EDG)	Christopher Edwards	125 A; £45. Adj.: James Edwards
109	1-28-1770	Matthias Moore	John Legate	50 A; £40. Wit.: George Cherry, Thos. Pinkitt, John Cason
111	3-16-1770	George Moye (1761) and Elizabeth Moye, wife	William Moore	220 A; £40.
112	3-16-1770	George Moye (1758) and Elizabeth Moye, wife	William Moore	300 A; £160. Former owners: John Wilson (Pat), John Moye (D-1741), Geo. Moye, Sen., dec. (D-1743)
114	3-30-1770	John Hardee	John Stocks	150 A; £60. Former owner: Joseph Hardee (Pat. 1755), father of John Hardee, grantor. Adj.: William Elliott
115	4- 4-1770	Richard Barrow (1755) and Reuben Barrow	Benjamin Randall, blacksmith	280 A; £60.

DEED BOOK D (1768-1771)

Page	Date	Grantor	Grantee	Additional Information
116	4-29-1769	Philip Ryland	John Simpson	Animals, goods; £30. Wit.: William Pratt, Benjamin Randall
117	4-29-1769	Philip Ryland (1767)	John Simpson	120 A + 120 A; £40. Former owners: Edmund Tison (Pat. 1755), Edmund Tison, Jr. (D-1764), William Stafford (Pat. 1763)
119	3- 8-1770	John Mayo, Jr., cooper (1743)	John Lesslie	320 A; £60. Adj.: Isaac Buck. Witness: Thomas Mayo
120	10-14-1769	Mathew Whitfield (TYR)	Geo. Clements (BERT)	100 A; £30. Adj.: Abraham Glison. Wit.: Alexander Brown, Stephen Swain
121	3-15-1770	Drury Spain and Mildred Spain	Marcus Stokes	— A; £72. Former owners: William Stevens (Pat. 1735), John Steavens, his son; Wit.: Richard Barrow, Jr., Mary Godwin, Mary Barrow
123	4- 2-1770	John Williams, Jr.	William Travis	220 A; £70. Former owner: Daniel O'Quin (Pat.), Wit.: John Williams, Edge Williams
124	8- 6-1769	Caleb Tripp	John Wiliams, Jr.	220 A; £20. Former owner: Daniel O'Quin (Pat.), Wit.: Charles Hardee, Thomas Hardee
125	12- 1-1769	William Nickols, Sen. (D-1764)	William Nickols, Jr.	95 A; love & aff. Former owner: Amos Atkinson (Pat.). Wit.: Richard Ellis, Thomas Cooper
127	10- 3-1769	John Moore	Mark Moore	— A; £100. Former owner: Abraham Tison (Pat. 1761)
128	7-17-1769	William Moore, Sen. (1762)	William Moore, Jr.	200 A; £10. Wit.: Nathaniel Moore, Abraham Moore
132	——1770	John Salter	William Judgkins	300 A; £27. Former owner: Edward Salter, dec. (Pat. 1760). Wit.: Josiah Hardee
133	9-11-1770	George Moye Jr. (D-1752)	Robert Daniel	200 A; £80. Former owner: George Moye, Sr. (Pat. 1738). Wit.: Anthony Degge
134	10- 3-1770	Thomas Salter	Jacob Palmer	200 A; £25. Former owners: Edmund S. Pearce (Pat. 1743), Edward Salter, dec., father of Thomas Salter. Wit.: Robert Salter, Edward Salter.
135	1-29-1770	John Swinson (DUP)	Levi Swinson (TYR)	350 A; £40. Adj.: John Butler. Wit.: Joseph Joiner
136		Robert Hardee	Geo. McGounds	140 A; £70. Former owner: John Stocks (1761)
137	10-11-1770	William Judgkins (1762)	John Munden	135 A; £40. Wit.: Thomas Judgkins
138	10-16-1770	Henry Cooper	John Hodges	160 A; £100. Adj.: Robert Daniel. Former owner: William Cannon (Pat. 1740). Wit.: William Cooper
140	11-21-1769	William Harris	John Moreing	75 A; £5. Former owner: Timothy Harris (Pat). Wit.: Richard Evans, Thomas Cooper

DEED BOOK D (1768-1771)

Page	Date	Grantor	Grantee	Additional Information
141	5-12-1770	John Slaughter	Samson Slaughter, son	100 A; love & aff. Adj.: David Williams. Men: Charity Slaughter, wife of John Slaughter. Wit.: Benjamin King
141	12-14-1768	Winifred Wilson (BEAU)	Walter Dixon, Jr. and William Baldwyn, Jr. exrs.	320 A; £13. Men.: Walter Dixon, dec. Former owner: Seth Pilkington, (Pat. 1738), father of Winifred Wilson
143	10-16-1770	John Nelson (D-1764)	John Simpson	320 A; £20. Former owners: Isaac Buck (Pat. 1743), Benjamin King, John Evitt, John Edward. Wit.: George Cherry, Roslin McKenney
144	10——1770	Thomas (Tuten (D-1769)	John Simpson	300 A; £25. Former owner: William Taylor, (Pat. 1769)
146	9-26-1769	Abraham Pettipool (DOB) (D-1764)	Thomas Giddins	100 A; £20. Former owner: George Dikes. Wit.: John Harrell, Isaac Giddins
147	1-29-1770	John Cooper (EDG) (1761)	Thomas Drake	104 A; £30. Former owners: Michael O'Neal (Pat. 1735), Benjamin Evans. Wit.: Robert Grimmer
148	2-24-1770	Richard Williams, doctor and Mary Williams, wife	Benjamin Ellis	Adj.: William Harris, John Forbes. Wit.: Henry Ellis, Robert Williams, Tabitha Williams
150	3-19-1770	Benj. Jordan, Sen.	Benjamin Jordan, son	200 A; love & aff.
151	4-26-1770	John Harrell (DOBB)	Josiah Askew	125 A; £75. Men.: William Giddins and Jacob Giddins, his father. Wit.: Benjamin May, John Sanders
153	——1770	William Wilson (D-1764)	Joshua Putnell	100 A; £20. Former owner: John Wilson (Pat 1764)
154	5- 1-1770	William Wilson (1764)	John Blackstone	86 A; £20.
155	5-11-1770	Joshua Putnell (1767)	James Brooks	150 A; £30. Former owner: Mark Powell (1764)
156	1——1771	Robert Flake	Wiliam Mitchell	12 A; £4. Adj.: William Flake. Wit.: Isaac Nobles, Jacob Little
157	4- 6-1768	James J. Quaturmas	John Kennedy	150 A; £100. Former owner: John Forbes (1740)
159	3-20-1770	Wiliam Smith	Samuel Warren	100 A; £27. Adj.: Edward Cobb. Wit.: Abraham Legett, Amos Atkinson, James Meeks
160	6——1769	Wiliam Buck	John Kennedy	435 A; £190. Former owner: Capt. Isaac Buck, father of William Buck. Wit.: Nehemiah Tuten, Henry Moore
161	4-23-1770	Samuel Grandell (1762)	James Crandell, Sen.	276 A; £15. Wit.: James Crandell, Jr, Josiah Little, William Grimes
162	8- 4-1770	Thomas Mercer (1764)	Samuel Davis	240 A; £70. Former owner: Thomas Moore. Wit.: Nathaniel Moore, William Moore
164	10- 5-1770	Roger Ormond (BEAU)	Jacob Brown	100 A; £35. Former owners: Andrew Conner, Henry Ormond, brother of Roger Ormond. Wit.: Wyrriott Ormond.

D 141-164

DEED BOOK D (1768-1771)

Page	Date	Grantor	Grantee	Additional Information
165	1- 3-1771	Benjamin Evans and Mary Evans, wife	Sterling Dupree (Brunswick Co., Va.)	200 A; £80. Wit.: David Hines, Peter Hines, Henry William-son
166	1-18-1771	William Bray	Reuben Brady, son	100 A; love & aff. Adj.: Thomas Gwaltney, Shadrach Pope, John Pope, Emanuel Teel, Benjamin Brown. Wit.: John Evans, Thomas Gwaltney, Jr.
167	3-12-1771	Benjamin Evans and Mary Evans, wife	James Dupree (Brunswick Co., Va.)	200 A; £200. Wit.: David Hines, James Hines, Peter Hines
168	3-12-1771	Benjamin Evans and Mary Evans, wife	James Dupree (Brunswick Co., Va.)	300 A; in Edgecombe; £60. Wit.: Peter Hines, David Hines, James Hines
169	3-14-1771	Benjamin Evans and Mary Evans, wife	Sterling Dupree (Brunswick Co., Va.)	455 A; in Edgecombe; £30. Wit.: David Hines, Richard Botten, Jr, Chas. Evans, Jr.
170	3-27-1771	Caleb Spivey	James Latham	448 A; £30. Former owner: John Snoad (Pat.) Wit.: Alex Stewart

DEED BOOK E (1771-1774)

Page	Date	Grantor	Grantee	Additional Information
1	3-28-1771	John Simpson (D-1769)	William Peebles	120 A+ 220 A; £46. Former owners: Edmund Tyson, Jr. (Pat. 1755), Philip Ryland (1767), William Staffords (Pat). Wit.: John Fry, William Johnston
2	4- 1-1771	Joseph Hardee, dec. (Pat. 1755)	John Cannon	150 A; £20. Wit.: Thomas Alderson, Hardy Nelson
3	4-23-1771	Edward Sirman	Thomas Gwaltney, Jr.	50 A; £13. Wit.: William Baldwin
4	4-24-1771	George Williams	Archibald Adams, Sen.	143 A; £20. Former owner: William Baldwyn (Pat 1755). Wit.: Edmund Williams, Matthew Parremore
5	4- 2-1771	Joseph Pendercuts	Thomas Allen	200 A; £30. Former owner: Moses Tison (1761). Wit.: Arthur Forbuck, John Joyner
6	2- 2-1771	James Crandell	David Perkins	220 A; £15. Wit.: James Crandell, Jr., James Latham
7	3-25-1771	John Cherry	Joseph Holiday	398 A; £27. Former owners: Lemuel Cherry (Pat 1745), William Cherry. Wit.: Elijah Harris, Peter Floyd
8	2- 3-1768	James Tunnage	Daniel Pipkin	150 A; £30. Former owner: William Stansill, Jr. (Pat 1763). Wit.: James Handcock, Thomas Simmons, Mark Hardin
9	12- 2-1770	John Barenhill	Alexander Brown, taylor	250 A; £31. Adj.: Dinnes Glison, Solomon James. Former owner: Jesse Jolly (Pat 1761). Wit.: James Haus, Mathew Paremore
10	5-19-1768	Absalom A James	Francis Hobson	150 A; £10+. Wit.: Mark Jolly
11	3-12-1770	Edward Sumerell	Benjamin Womwell	100 A; £5. Adj.: John Dowdin, James Mayo. Wit.: James Barrow, Cornelius Church, Hnery Anderson
12	9----1771	John Cook, Sen.	Edmon Andrews	100 A; £20. Men: William Cook. Wit.: Francis Hobson
13	2- 6-1769	William Butler	Elicksander Autry	150 A; £25. Adj.: Michel Ward. Wit.: William Moore, William Moore, Sen.
14	12- 3-1770	Robert Knox and Ellenor Knox	Simon Everett	200 A; £50.
15	4-27-1771	John Knowis, Sen.	John Knowis, Jr.	950 A; £50. Wit.: Josiah Little, John Wallice
16	9----1771	Mathew Sturdivant and Tabitha Sturdivant, wife	James Lockhart	— A; £205. Adj.: Osborn Jeffrey. Wit.: John Williams, John Sugg
18	10- 2-1771	Benjamin Windham	Samuel Warren	½ A; —sh. Wit.: Amos Atkinson
19	7-24-1771	John Simpson, Exr., Walter Dixon, exr. and William Baldwyn, exr.	Priscilla Dixon	100 A; £62+. Men: Walter Dixon, dec. (Pat. 1759). Wit.: John Leslie

DEED BOOK E (1771-1774)

Page	Date	Grantor	Grantee	Additional Information
20	7- 4-1771	John Simpson, Walter Dixon, and William Baldwyn, exrs.	George Fleming	100 A; £62. Former owner: Walter Dixon (Pat. 1739)
21	7- 8-1771	Martin Nelson	Samuel Nelson, brother	60 A; —sh. Former owner: Martin Nelson, father of Martin and Samuel Nelson (Pat. 1745). Men.: Sarah Nelson, mother of Martin and Samuel
23	11-11-1769	James Williams	John Autry	100 A; £21. Adj.: John May, dec.
24	9-15-1771	Shadrach Moore	Elisha Moore	100+ A; £60. Former owner: Richard Becton (Pat. 1753). Wit.: Jesse Moore, Levi Moore
26		Joshua Putnell, Sen.	John Braxstone	100 A; £—. Former owners: John Willson (Pat.), William Willson (D-1761). Wit.: Sampson Powell.
27	11-24-1770	John Perritt (1763)	Demsie Grimes (EDG)	415 A; £207+. Former owners: Edward Salter, father; Edward Salter, son. Adj.: William Speir. Wit.: Alexander Stewart, William Speir
29	1-28-177—	James Lanier	Nathaniel Lanier, son	248 A; love & aff.
29	12-27-1771	Peter Rives	James Little (DOB)	200 A; £—. Former owner: Joseph Barrow (1746) Wit.: John Little, Jacob Little, Robert Rives
30	1——1772	Francis McNamar	Zachariah Pinkitt	200 A; £30. Adj.: William Congelton
31	11-11-1771	John Cooper	James Meeks	50 A; £10. Adj.: Thomas Drack. Wit.: David Averrett, William Averrett, David Averrett, Jr.
32	10-26-1771	Thomas Bond (BERT)	Jesey Barberree	200 A; £60.
33	1-28-1772	John Munden (D-1770)	Stephen Munden	60 A; £20. Former owner: William Judgkin. Wit.: William Baldwyn, Isaac Munden
34	6-14-1762	Samuel Poyner	James Dudley	— A; £28. Wit.: Griffith Howell, John Whiteacre
35	4-20-1771	John Braxstone and Mary Braxstone, wife	Abell Dial, Jr.	200 A; £30. Wit.: Sampson Powell, Samuel Powell
37	1-20-1772	Benjamin Barrow and Elizabeth Barrow	John Moye, Jr.	300 A; £60. Wit.: Richard Moye, George Cherry
38	1-22-1772	John Meeks	James Meeks	100 A; £5. Adj,: Frances Meeks, Walter Meeks. Wit.: David Averrett, David Averrett, Jr.
39	1-24-1772	Peter Nelson	James Nelson	100 A; £20. Former owner: Seth Pilkington (1740). Wit.: John Nealson, Giles Nealson
40	1-28-1772	George Moye	Richard Moye	100 A; £40. Wit.: William Bryan, John Mundin

E 20-40

DEED BOOK E (1771-1774)

Page	Date	Grantor	Grantee	Additional Information
41	9- 3-1770	Priscilla Johnston (EDG)	Lemuel Bullock	100 A; £20. Adj.: John Wooten, John Williams. Wit.: Matthew Sturdivant, Shadrack Williams
42	12-17-1771	James Shields (Ga., formerly Pitt Co.)	John Simpson	100 A; £35. Adj.: David Cannon, John Mills. Wit.: Mary Hardee, Elizabeth Enloe
43	12-13-1768	John White	Joseph Sulevant	100 A; £20. Wit.: Thomas Mercer
44	12-31-1771	William Stafford (S.C.)	Moses Hart	161 A; £60. Adj.: Moses Tyson, Edmund Tyson, Jr. Wit.: Samuel Stafford, John Tison, Mary Mallet
45	1- 2-1771	James Turnage (DOB)	Benjamin Barrow	100 A; £12. Former owner: William Stansell, Jr., (Pat. 1763)
46	12-31-1771	William Stafford (Granvile, S.C.)	Moses Hart	220 A; £65.
46	12-20-177–	Silvanus Pumphry (DUP)	John Barber	— A; £63. Adj.: George Collins, George Smith. Former owner: Israel Joyner (Pat. 1738)
47	8- 7-1771	Benjamin Buck	Roland Dixon	— A; £5. Wit.: James Buck, Wirks Chapman
48	10- 4-1771	Edward Salter	John Simpson	4 A; £10. Former owners: Alexander Salter (D-1754), father of grantor, Edward Salter; Robert Hardee
49	12-22-1771	Priscilla Johnson (EDG)	Mary Williams, daughter; Merryman Allen, son; Charles Allen, son; Gabriel Allen, son; Hardee Maun, grandson	Goods and all lands; love & aff. Former owners: David Averritt, Daniel Johnson. Wit.: James Lanier
50	2-21-1772	John Whichard	Jemima Whichard, wife, and Philip Whichard, infant son	All goods; love & aff. and £20. Men.: Henry Hodges. Wit.: Robert Hodges
51	7-27-1772	John Barrow and James Barrow	Ricchard Rives, Jr.	200 A; £115. Wit.: Samuel Cherry, Batson Whitclif
52	8-10-1771	Francis Hobson	Henry Irwin (EDG)	225 A; £163. Former owner: John Holland. Wit.: John Sikes, Samson Sikes
55	7-29-1772	John Little	Daniel Rogers	500 A; £100. Former owner: Josiah Little (Pat. 1735). Wit.: Richard Barrow, Samson Pittman, David Averrett
56	4- 3-1772	William Archdeacon and Bigars Mobley	Samuel Wheatly	76 A; £60. Wit.: William Bryan, Thomas Wheatley
58	5-26-1772	Benjamin Wilkinson	Thomas Wheatley	50 A; £45.
60	2-27-1772	William Nelson (HALI) and Martha Nelson, wife	William Osborn	400 A; £100. Former owner: Ephraim Jones. Adj.: Samuel Eldridge

DEED BOOK E (1771-1774)

Page	Date	Grantor	Grantee	Additional Information
64	——-1772	John Salter and Henry Jones	Benjamin Ellis, Jr.	— A; £15.
66	——-1772	Arthur Forbes	William Baldwin, taylor	— A; £124.
67	4-21-1770	William Moore	William Dixon	248 A; £15. Former owners: William Taylor, Isaac Edward. Wit.: James Armstrong, Arch Campbell
69	1-10-1771	Samuel Smyth (CRAV)	John Wolfenden	200A+ 450 A; £155+. Former owner: Thomas Tison (Pat.). Wit.: Charles Crawford, Alex Stewart
71	5-15-17——	John Price (1765)	James Moye	100 A; £30. Former owners: Peter Conway, John Moye. Wit.: Samuel Danby
72	5- 4——	James Appolas Averett (1764)	John Simpson	100 A; £—.
73	3-28-1768	John Williams, wrestler (Pat. 1764)	John Simpson	200 A; £20. Wit.: Mathew Alberton
75	——-1770	Nesby Mills, Jr.	John Simpson	100 A; £30. Former owner: John Moye
76	10- 1-1761	Nathaniel Pettit	Anna Pettit	— A; —.
77	4-20-1772	William Travis (Pat 1767)	William Hancock	— A; £15. Wit.: Simon Burney, Elizabeth Burney
78	4-29-1772	James Lockhart and Hannah Lockhart, wife	Matthew Sturdivant	700 A; £205. Adj.: Osborn Jeffrey. Wit.: Sterling Dupree
80	12- 9-1770	James Inglis (S.C.) and Mary Inglis	William Gay	— A; £20+. Former owner: John May (Pat. 1761)
81	2-17-1772	Osborn Jeffreys (BUTE) (Pat. 1726)	Matthew Sturdivant	300 A; £125. Wit.: James Lockhart, Simon Jeffreys
83	——-1772	Thomas Allen	Arthur Forbes	100 A; £25. Former owner: Sarah Allen (1752)
84	——-1771	Richard Evans and Susannah Evans, wife	James Lockhart	270 A; £100.
85	5- 5-177–	Thomas Hardee	James Handcock	160 A; £20. Former owners: Abraham Duncan (Pat. 1752), George Duncan, legatee of Abraham Duncan. Wit.: Mark Hardin, Elizabeth Hardin
87	4-29-1772	Nathaniel Moore	Benjamin May	180 A; £35. Former owners: John May (Pat. 1770), dec., and father of Selah May Gindraw; Henry Gindraw. Wit.: Samuel Stafford, James May
88	2- 6-1771	John Thompson	John Worseley	120 A; £80. Wit.: William McClellan
90	4-10-1772	William McHenery	William Bryan (DOB)	200 A; £85. Former owner: ——— Turnage (Pat. 1738)

Page	Date	Grantor	Grantee	Additional Information
91	4-27-1772	Amos Atkinson	Hugh Cravy (EDG)	215 A; £50. Former owners: John Snoad, William Snoad, William Snoad (Pat.). Wit.: Richard Proctor, Edward Cobb
93	———	Thomas Bonner and Sarah Bonner, wife	Susannah Evans	—; £100.
94	10-20-1771	Robert Salter, Sheriff	George Evans	640 A; £—. Former owner: Lillington Lockhart (BERT). (Pat. 1761), dec.
96	3-21-1772	John Slator	Michael Coutanche Evans	150 A; £48. Former owner: Francis Blount (Pat.)
97	8—1771	Winifred Wilson, widow	Richard Evans	500A + 500A + 300 + A; £300. Former owner: Seth Pilking-ton (Pat. 1735, 1752)
100	1-26-17—	William Moore, Sheriff	John Thompson	320 A; £53. Former owner: William Mizell
102	4-15-1769	Samuel Tison (Pat. 1751) and Elizabeth Tison	John Tison	200A + ; £86.
104	——177-	William Travis	John Sirman	220 A; £20. Former owner: Daniel O'Quin (Pat. 1750). Wit.: Edward Sirman
105	10- 3-1772	George Duncan and Abraham Duncan, exrs. (N.H.)	Ichabod Simpson, marriner	150 A; £45. Former owner: Abraham Duncan, dec. Wit.: Stephen Holland, James Betton, John Duncan, Thomas Taggart
106	7-23-177-	Daniel Rogers	John Little	500 A; £110. Former owner: Josiah Little (Pat. 1735)
108	2-22-1772	Dove Morgan Williams	Thomas Shingleton Williams	75 A; £15. Wit.: John Cherry, James Stuart
109	9-12-1772	Joseph Jackson (CRAV)	John Herenton	100 A; £20. Former owner: John Hover (Pat. 1753)
110	2-21-177-	John Whichard, Sen., and Jemima Whichard	Henry Hodges	5 A; £40. Former owner: Seth Pilkington, Elias Hodges, John Hodges
111	10- 1-1772	Comm. of Martinborough	Isaac Eason	2 (½A) lotts, #3 & 77; £4.
112	1-30-1772	Joseph Evans and Mary Evans	Richard Williams	100 A; £60. Former owner: William Brantley
113	——1757	John Wane (Pat)	Jeremiah King	100 A; £—. Men.: Edward Salter. Wit.: Edward Gatlin
115	2-20-177-	John Simpson	John Slator	112 A; £37. Wit.: Simon Jones, John Leslie
116	1- 7-1772	Meriman Allen	Demsey Wright Allen	80 A; £18. Former owner: Samuel Stokes (1762)
117	11-12-1768	John Wooten (Pat) and Mary Wooten	Richard Jordan (EDG)	214 A; £25. Wit.: George Evans, Benjamin Jordan
118	4-25-1772	Samuel Green	Moses Cocks	75 A; £5.
120	10-26-1772	Ann Shannon	Arthur Forbes, son	220 A; love & aff. Wit.: Nathaniel Lanier, Allen Sugg

DEED BOOK E (1771-1774)

Page	Date	Grantor	Grantee	Additional Information
121	10-19-1772	Samuel Stokes	James Stokes, brother	— A; love & aff. Men.: Elizabeth Stokes
122	10- 1-1772	Comm. of Martinborough	William Ormond	½A lott, #117; 40 sh.
123	1-25-1773	Andrew Hardee (Pat. 1772)	Ann Ferguson	100 A; £5.
125	1-16-1772	James May, Jr.	Henry Anderson	175 A; £55. Wit.: Cornelius Church
127	3-17-1773	Ichabod Simpson, marriner	John Hardee	150 A; £—. Former owner: Abraham Duncan. Wit.: Robert Salter, Elizabeth Enloe
131	6- 2-1773	John Kennedy (BEAU)	Samuel Cherry	— A; £20. Adj.: John Hardee. Wit.: James Quatermus, Isaac Hardee
133	12- 4-1772	John Simpson	John Stocks	— A; £—. Adj.: Matthew Pollard. Former owner: John Williams (Pat. 1764). Wit.: Mary Hardee, Anna Jonson
135	11- 4-1772	Jeremiah King (CRAV)	James Brooks	100 A; £—. Wit.: Edward Salter, Thos. Hardee
137	1 —1772	Nehemiah Wootten	John Mooring	82 A; £3. Adj.: William Mitchell, James Little, William Flake. Wit.: Alex Stewart, Thomas Pinkett
139	—1772	Thomas Allen	Zachriah Allen	140 A; —. Adj.: Abraham Tison. Former owner: Sarah Allen (Pat. 1752). Wit.: Pitt Allen
141	3-13-1772	George Evans	Alexander Stewart	320 A; £150. Former owner: Joshua Porter (Pat), John Lillington (D), Alexander Lillington (D)
143	—1772	Mikel Ward	Solomon Ward	160 A; £7. Wit.: Elias Bergeron, John Ward
145	7-25-1771	Edmund Tison and Mary Tison, wife	Susanna Tison, daughter	Negro; love & aff. Wit.: Abraham Tison, Moses Tison, Lucy Tison
146	—1771	Winifred Wilson (BEAU), extx.	Dove Morgan Williams	240 A; £48. Former owner: Seth Pilkington (1748), dec., father of Winifred Wilson. Wit.: John Kennedy, James Crandell
148	4-27-1772	Benjamin Buck	Simon Jones	640 A; £25. Wit.: William Buck, Joseph Boyd
150	12- 2-177–	Thomas Allen	Samuel Hussey	100 A; £40. Former owner: Moses Tison (Pat.) Wit.: George Tison
153	—1772	William Brierly	John Heninton, Sen.	50 A; £4+. Former owners: William Jones (Pat. 1740); Ruth Jones Moye, daughter of William Jones; John Moye, husband of Ruth Jones Moye
155	12- 5-177–	David Chadwick (CRAV) (Pat. 1751)	Samuel Green	75 A; £—.
157	1- 4-1773	Solomon Whichard (D-1767)	Nathan Cherry	100 A; £13. Former owner: Ebenezer Folsom
159	6-26-1773	Andrew Hardee (Pat. 1772)	Samuel Smith	150 A; £5.

DEED BOOK E (1771-1774)

Page	Date	Grantor	Grantee	Additional Information
162	8- 8-1772	John Nicols and Jean Nicols	Able Thomas (HALI)	100 A; £—.
164	3-20-1772	Eleazar Hodges	Robert Hodges	150 A; £30. Former owner: Benjamin Hodges, Benjamin Hodges (Pat. 1745), father of Eleazar Hodges, grantor. Wit.: Mathew Hodges, John Hodges, Floyd Hodges
166	3-20-1772	Eleazar Hodges	Mathew Hodges	150 A; £30. Former owner: Benjamin Hodges
169	—1773	William Baldery	Starkey Bell	200 A; £35.
172	—1770	David Sutton (CRAV)	John Hattuck	100 A; £20.
174	11-19-1771	Comm. of Martinborough	Thomas Hathaway	½ A lott #8; 40 sh.
176	11-19-1771	Comm. of Martinborough	David Powers	½ A lott, #104; 40 sh.
178	11-19-1771	Comm. of Martinborough	William Robson	2 (½ A lotts) #55, #121; £4.
181	2-19-1774	Moses Hart	George Tison	70 A; £20. Former owner: William Stafford (Pat)
184	—1773	Spear Holland and Elizabeth Holland	Susanna Evans	300 A; £170.
185	6- 4-1773	James Blount	John Williams ,Jr.	— A; £30. Adj.: Thomas Wallace
187	5-23-177—	Benjamin Randall, blacksmith	James Lockhart	280 A; £—. Former owner: Richard Barrow (Pat. 1735)
190	2-19-1773	John Barrow	Richard Rives	90 A; £20. Wit.: Christopher Edwards, William Miller
192	—1773	Henry Ellis	William Ellis	229 A; £40. Wit.: James Lanier, William Baldwin, Lucy Ellis
194	12-29-1772	William Stafford (S.C.) (Pat. 1756)	Samuel Stafford (S.C.)	180 A; £—.
197	7-21-1773	James Dupree	Benjamin Chaplain Dupree, son	2 slaves; love & aff. Wit.: Nathaniel Lanier
198	—1773	William Ormond (D-1769)	James Jones	74 A; £150. Former owners: William Watkins, dec., Edward Salter. Men.: Christian Watkins, widow of William Watkins. Wit.: James Cason, Simon Jones, William Watkins
201	1-23-1771	John Hardee	Green Windom	100 A; £30. Former owner: David Hathaway (Pat. 1756), Joseph Burkett. Wit.: Robert Daniel, John Tison
203	3-31-177—	Christopher Edwards	Robert Sanders	125 A; £50. Wit.: Jacob Atkinson, Daniel Rogers, Benjamin Jordan
204	9-21-177—	Thomas Pugh (BERT)	Reuben Manning (Norfolk County, Va.)	640 A; £—. Wit.: Noah Hinton, Jonathan Carr
207	4-21-1774	Robert Flake	Fitzh Harris	111 A; £—. Wit.: John Presson, Arthur Flake, William Flake

DEED BOOK E (1771-1774)

Page	Date	Grantor	Grantee	Additional Information
209	————	Richard Barrow and Mary Barrow	Nichols Bynum (EDG)	150 A; £120. Wit.: Samson Pittman, Luke Bates, Drewry Bynum
211	3-24-1773	Benjamin Ellis, Jr.	Nichols Bynum	200 A; £100.
213	1-16-1774	John Fulford	Benjamin Smith	100 A; £65. Former owners: Sarah Allen (1752), now Sarah Allen Fulford; Thomas Allen
215	2-13-1774	John Stocks, Sen.	Simon Burney	150 A; £30. Former owner: John Williams, Sen (Pat)
218	2-11-1774	John Cooper (EDG)	William Perry	356 A; £120.
220	———1774	Nathan Mayo (HALI)	Mathew Luter	400+A; £130+. Adj.: Francis Hobson, Peter Mayo. Former owner: Amos Atkinson
222	12-28-1773	Elijah Harris	Henry Hodges	300 A; £24. Former owner: James Bonner
224	———1772	Alexander Lillington (NEW HAN)	George Evans, nephew	320 A; love & aff. £—sh. Former owner: Joshua Porter. Wit.: Sarah Lillington, John Fry
227	12-29-1772	John Smith (CRAV) (Pat. 1771)	William Denmark	100+ A; £25. Wit.: William Burney, Alexander Bass
229	2-19-1774	Richard Allen (D-1756) and Martha Allen	James Williams	175 A; £55. Men.: George Sugg. Wit.: Mary Mosely
232	1- 9-1773	George Evans	Edmun Andrews	300 A; £30. Adj.: Warren Andrews. Former owner: Linington Lockhart (1761). Wit.: Joshua James
234	2-19-177–	George Moore	Keley Tucker	100 A; £65. Former owner: George Moye (Pat.) Men.: Samuel Moore, Sen. Wit.: Edmund Williams, Matthias Moore, Samuel Barrow
237	1-11-1774	William Stokes	Benjamin Cooper	200 A; £100. Wit.: John William, James Lockhart
239	11-22-1773	Thos. Giddens	Hardy Grisard	159 A; £50.
241	3- 8-1773	Nathan Mayo	Jacob Atkinson	170 A; £60. Former owner: William Mayo, father of Nathan and John Mayo. Adj.: John Mayo, brother of Nathan Mayo. Wit.: Amos Atkinson, Edward Cobb, Jr, James Hearn
244	2- 4-1774	Michael Oldsue, taylor	Edward Williams, saddler	80 A; £225. Adj.: Daniel Lockhart
247	2- 1-176–	Henry Ellis (D-1761)	Micajah Lancaster	10 A; 40 sh. Adj.: Thomas Gwaltney
250	10———1772	Joseph Whitfield	Jesse Jolley	35 A; £7. Former owner: Arthur Olds. Wit.: Edmun Andrews
252	———1773	Thomas Giddens (D-1769)	Hardy Grisard	100 A; £55. Former owner: Abraham Petpool. Wit.: Nathaniel Moore, Jacob Mercer

DEED BOOK E (1771-1774)

Page	Date	Grantor	Grantee	Additional Information
254	——1772	Solomon Alberson (Pat. 1764)	Elizabeth Alberson, mother (DOB)	100 A; £16. Wit.: John Joiner, Josiah Askew
257	7-29-1773	Joseph Jolley, Sen.	John Jolley	100 A; £3+. Wit.: Alexander Brown
258	9- 4-1773	Mark Moore	James Moore	— A; £64. Former owner: John Joyner. Men.: John Moore. Wit.: Mark Hardin, Richard Daniel
261	1——1774	John Fillingham	William Hayes	84 A; £40. Former owner: William Willis (Pat. 1740). Wit.: Griffeth Howell, James Latham
263	12-24-1773	John Mayo	John Stokes	300 A; £—. Adj.: Joseph Hardee. Former owner: John Williams, Sen. (Pat. 1764). Wit.: Jacob Atkinson, John May, Hardy May
265	11- 1-1773	Benjamin Barney (BEAU)	Nathan Godley	100 A; £250. Former owners: Thomas Worseley (Pat. 1723), Thomas Daniel (D). Wit.: Edward Salter
266	2- 8-1773	Benjamin Barney (BEAU)	Nathan Godley	200+ A; £40.
269	11-24-1772	John Simpson, merchant (Pat. 1762)	John Fulford	185 A; £40. Wit.: George Moye, Matthew Albritton
271	4-27-1774	George Evans	Joseph Page	380 A; £20. Former owner: Linninton Lockhart
273	4-27-1774	Samuel Stafford	Timothy Harris	100+ A; £35. Former owner: William Stafford (Pat. 1756). Wit.: Samson Pittman, Jacob Tison, Henry Ellis
276	2-18-1773	Richard Rives	Samuel Stafford	195 A; £150.
279	4-20-1774	John Hattock, Sen. (D-1768)	William Hattock	100 A; £15. Former owner: John Hattock, Jr. (Pat. 1764)
282	——1774	John Simpson	John Nelson	320 A; £20. Former owners: Isaac Buck (1743), John Evitt, John Avery, Jo—hn Edwards. Wit.: John Leslie, James Nelson
284	10-23-1773	James Brooks	Nesby Mills, Jr.	150 A; £20. Former owner: John Simpson (1764). Wit.: William Williams
286	——1772	John Bonner, mariner (BEAU)	William Speir	160 A; £70. Former owners: Thomas Roper (Pat.); William Little (1721); John Snoad, father of William Snoad, John Snoad, Henry Snoad; Anne Bonner, mother of John Bonner (D-1748)
289	11-19-1771	Comm. of Martinborough	Edmund Williams	½ A lott, #85; 40 sh. Wit.: Benjamin May, George Williams
292	1-27-1773	Comm. of Martinborough	Samuel Colhoon	½ A lott, #122; 40 sh. Wit.: Peter Hines, Jr., Nathaniel Moore
294	10——1772	Comm. of Martinborough	Micajah Lancaster	½ A lott, #108; 40 sh. Wit.: Joel Sugg, Thos. Wolfenden

DEED BOOK E (1771-1774)

Page	Date	Grantor	Grantee	Additional Information
296	1-25-1773	Comm. of Martinborough	John Williams	½A lott, #59; 40 sh. Wit.: Nathaniel Moore, Peter Hines, Jr.
299	10- 1-1772	Comm. of Martinborough	George Williams	½A lott #89; 40 sh.
301	10- 1-1772	Comm. of Martinborough	Simon Pope	½A lott, #15; 40 sh.
304	10- 1-1772	Comm. of Martinborough	Hardy Grizzard	½A lott, #46; 40 sh.
306	10- 1-1772	Comm. of Martinborough	Levey Andrews	½A lott, #28; 40 sh.
308		Comm. of Martinborough	John Pope	½A lott, #102; 40 sh.
311	10- 1-1772	Comm. of Martinborough	Edward Williams	½A lott, #84; 40 sh.
313		Comm. of Martinborough	David Perkins	½A lott, #66; 40 sh.
315		Charles Roach and Elizabeth Roach, wife	Godfrey Stancel	— A; £20. Wit.: William Robson, James Barnhill
315	——1774	Jeremiah Ream (S.C.)	Benjamin Blount	100 A; £30. Former owner: Jacob Blount (Pat. 1754)
317	3-15-1773	John Simpson	Frederick Mills	100 A; £—. Former owners: John Moye (Pat. 1765); John Price; James Mayo (D-1767); Nesby Mills, Jr. (D-1771)
318	7-24-1774	Richard Allen and Martha Allen	Shadrack Williams	130 A; £—.
320	4-15-1771	Samuel Ward	Charles Bondfield (Edenton)	200 A; £10.
322	10-13-1771	John Averitt (D-1764) and James Averitt	John Simpson, merchant	100 A; £26. Wit.: Robert Hardee
324	6-22-1774	Nathaniel Pettit	James Anderson, mariner	200 A; £55. Former owners: Simon Burney (Pat. 1719); William Taylor; Jacob Taylor, Mathew Averitt. Wit.: Joseph Boyd, Elizabeth Boyd
326	10- 1-1772	Comm. of Martinborough	William Tison	2 (½A) lotts, #151 & #158; £4.
328	1-22-1774	James Lockhart and Hannah Lockhart	Benjamin Dupree	270 A; £300+. Wit.: Sterling Duprey, Henry Sturdivant
329	5-18-1773	Abraham Glison and Sarah Glison, wife	Stephen Swain	276 A; £50. Adj.: Solomon James. Wit.: William Clements, Peter Joly
331	4-11-1774	Paul Herrington (D-1764) and Sarah Herrington, wife	Joseph Jackson	100 A; £5. Former owner: John Simpson

DEED BOOK F (1774-1801)

Page	Date	Grantor	Grantee	Additional Information
1	——1774	Jonathan Taylor	William McClellan (EDG)	100 A; £24. Wit.: James Hill
3	11——1773	William Congleton	Abraham Congleton	— A; —. Adj.: Zachariah Pinkett. Wit.: William Griffen
4	5-21-1774	William Edwards	Joshua Putnall	100 A; £30. Wit.: Simon Taylor
6	10- 1-1772	Comm. of Martinborough	Benjamin Randall	½ A. lott, #109; 40 sh.
8	10- 1-1772	Comm. of Martinborough	John Nobles	½ A. lott, #73; 40 sh.
10	6-26-1771	Absalom Kitterell (DOB) (1770)	John Frizel	290 A; £25. Wit.: Obed Rountree, Moab Rountree
11	12-10-1773	John Kenneday (Beaufort)	Frederick Gibble (DOB)	— A; £167+. Former owner: Isaac Buck, dec Wit.: Anthony Degge, Elizabeth Simpson
14	10- 1-1772	Comm. of Martinborough	Benjamin May	½ A. lott, #144. 40 sh.
18	7- 2-1774	John Cooper (EDG)(D-1761)	Robert Grimmer	60 A; £12. Former owners: Michael O'Neal (Pat. 1735), Benjamin Evans (1761). Adj.: Thomas Drake. Wit.: James Lockhart, Benjamin Cooper
26	7-26-1774	David Averett	David Averett, Jr.	125 A; £5. Wit.: William Averett, Barshabea Nichols
22	2- 3-1770	John Jolley	John Dearman	200 A; —. Former owners: Thomas Nobles (Pat.), Jonathan Jolley. Wit.: David Perkins, James Smith, Joseph Jolley
24	11-30-1773	James Meeks	Joseph Little	150 A; £87. Former owner: John Meeks, father of James Meeks, grantor. Adj.: Frances Meeks, Walter Meeks, John Church, Thomas Drake. Wit.: Amos Atkinson, James Little, Mathew Meeks
26	7-25-1773	William Dixson and Anne Dixson	Walter Dixson	102 A; £90. Wit.: Robert Boyd, Joseph Boyd. Former owners: Walter Dixson, Sen. (1735), Caleb Granger and Mary Granger, his wife
27	1- 1-1773	Jessey Barbre	Benjamin Wilkinson	200 A; £100. Wit.: William Bryan, Frederick Bryan
29	9-10-1773	John Autry and Ann Autry	Thomas Downs	100 A; £26+. Adj.: John May. Wit.: Benjamin May, Thomas Duffield
31	2-23-1773	Arthur Olds	John Highsmith	140 A; £25.
32	3-15-1773	Richard Barrow and Mary Barrow, wife	Nichols Bynum (EDG)	100 A; £30. Adj.: Joseph Burket. Wit.: Drewry Bynum, Luke Bate
34	11-18-1773	Samuel Davis	Joshua Barnes	160 A; £66. Adj.: Michael Ward (dec). Former owner: John Ward, Sr. Wit.: James Barrow
35	7-22-1774	Micol Moss	Harry Smith	150 A; £40. Wit.: Benjamin Sutten
37	2- 3-1774	James Brooks (Pat. 1771)	Frederick Mills	200 A; £5.
39	7-25-1774	Hardy Grisard (D-1764)	Lewis Davis	125 A; £61. Wit.: Benjamin May, Nathaniel Moore

DEED BOOK F (1774-1801)

Page	Date	Grantor	Grantee	Additional Information
41	11-19-1771	Comm. of Martinborough	Benjamin Ellis	½ A. lott, #145; 40 sh.
43	5- 4-1774	Isaac Buck	Benjamin Sutten	45 A; £15.
45	9-15-1771	Peter Lewis	William Clements	70 A; £40. Adj.: James Smith. Wit.: Stephen Swan, Geo. Clements
47	10-24-1772	John Fillingine, Jr.	Thomas Williams	10 A; £6. Wit.: John Whiteacre, Griffith Howell
48	10- 1-1774	John Swinson, bricklayer, and Elsie Swinson, his wife	John Holaday Hudson, bricklayer	300 A; £100. Adj.: Benjamin Sanders. Wit.: Mark Mizell
50	8-20-1774	Stephen Mundin (D-1761)	Isaac Carril, bricklayer	160 A; £60. Former owners: William Judkins (1762), William Cason (Pat. 1740). Wit.: Edmund Williams
52	4-11-1772	William Brady, Sen.	William Brady, Jr.	100 A; £10. Adj.: James Brady, John Pollard. Wit.: Henry Ellis, John Robberson, John Little
54	1-28-1772	Isaac Carril, bricklayer	Edward Dixson	60 A; £25. Former owners: William Judkins (Pat. 1762), John Mundin (1770), Stephen Mundin. Wit.: Edmund Williams
56	10-12-1774	John Autry (CUMB)	William Page	100 A; £16. Former owner: William Autry (1763). Wit.: Thomas Willias, George Stuart
58	9-16-1773	Mary Buntin, widow	Daniel Buntin	— A; £10. Wit.: James Rawlin, James Edminson, Peter Barbre
59	10- 8-1774	Susanna Evans	John Fry and George Evans, elder	2 tracts; 10 sh. John Fry and George Evans, trustees of estate of Richard Evans (dec), former husband of Susanna Evans. Wit.: James Charlcraft, Edward Sirman
61	3-29-1774	James Bullock	Josiah Bullock	110 A; £10. Adj.: Walter Session. Wit.: Alexander Brown, David Vance
62	10- 8-1774	Susanna Evans	Richard Evans, son	1400 A; love & aff.
63	5-10-1774	Henry Anderson	James Meeks	175 A; £46. Adj.: James May, Joseph Burket. Wit.: James DeLoach, Cornelius Church.
65	3-19-1774	Moses Hart	William Hart	100 A; £20. Former owner: William Stafford. Wit.: Robert Hart, George Tison, William Johnson
67	11- 2-1773	Joseph Little and Elizabeth Little, wife	Stephen Carter	100 A; £50. Wit.: George Carter, Edmun Andrews
68	10-26-1774	William Brierly	William Brierly, son	— A; —.
69		Francis Rountree	William Davis	160 A; £60. Former owners: Patrick Maule (Pat. 1726), Sarah Maule, his daughter, Sarah Maule Bryant (same), wife of Joseph Bryant

DEED BOOK F (1774-1801)

Page	Date	Grantor	Grantee	Additional Information
71	3-13-1771	Jeremiah Rhame (Pat. 1762)	George Dikes	100 A; £30. Wit.: Samuel Powel, Benjamin Blunt.
73	2-21-1774	Mathew Albritton, inholder (D-1763)	Benjamin Buck	Former owners: Edmund Salter (Pat. 1751), Charles Finnakin (D), John Hodges (D), John Dixson (D-1756). Wit.: John Salter, Edward Salter
75	5-21-1774	Thomas Albritton, James Albritton, Peter Albritton, (PITT) and Matthew Albritton (Onslow)	George Albritton	200 A; £90. Former owners: Simon Burney (Pat.), William Taylor, Sen, William Taylor, Jr. (D-1751), John Hattock, Jr.(D-1767), John Simpson (D-1767); also James Albritton, Sen. (D-1769), father of grantors. Wit.: Richard Albritton
78	4-22-1774	Comm. of Martinborough	John Hardee	3 (½A) lotts #103, 102, 90; 5 sh. For courthouse, pillory, and market house. Wit.: John Fry.
80	11-19-1771	Comm. of Martinborough	Edward Salter	5 (½A) lotts #14,113, 127, 148, 152; £10. Wit.: Joel Sugg
81	10-25-1774	Jesse Rountree	Thomas Williams	150 A; £7+. Former owner: Richard Grist (1745). Adj.: Hillary Elligood. Wit.: William Whitfield, John Frizzle
83	11-27-1774	Simon Gay (CRAV)	Richard Gay (EDG)	150 A; £40. Wit.: William Gay
84	5-15-1770	William Moore ((D-1770)	William Speir	220 A; £50. Former owner: George Moye (Pat. 1761). Wit.: John Jordan
86	7-24-1774	William Speir	Eleazar Cherry, cooper	79 A; £15. Adj.: John Whichard, Mathew Paramore. Wit.: John Doudna, Thomas Pinket
87	1- 6-1775	George Albritton	Francis Buck	200 A; £45. Former owners: David O'Brian (Pat. 1738), John O'Brian. Wit.: Sampson Pittman, Benjamin Bowers, Jr.
90	7-11-1774	Robert Daniel	Solomon Whichard	200 A; £85. Former owners: George Moye, San. (Pat. 1738), George Moye, Jr. (D-1752). Wit.: John Hodges, John Jones
92	10-10-1774	Martin Nelson (D-1768)	Thomas Angel	15 A; £5. Former owners: Jacob Taylor (1737), dec., William Taylor, heir of Jacob Taylor
94	11-16-1774	Henry Sumrell (EDG)	John Edwards	125 A; £90. Adj.: John Lee, James Hearn. Wit.: Jacob Atkinson, Mary Atkinson, John Hearn
96	12-17-1774	William Ellis	Nathaniel Lanier	229 A; £70. Adj.: John Forbes. Wit.: Allen Sugg, James Lanier, Jr.
98	11-26-1774	Zacariah Pinket (D-1762)	Ann Pinket	120 A; £50. Former owner: Thomas Pinket (Pat. 1742), father of William Daniel Pinket. Wit.: John Knowis, Jr., Jonath Taylor

DEED BOOK F (1774-1801)

Page	Date	Grantor	Grantee	Additional Information
99	1-23-1775	Andrew Hardee (1772)	Thomas Hardee, son	— A; £10. Adj.: David Mills, Pearson Tuten. Wit.: Pearson Tutle
101	12-17-1774	Benjamin Jordan	Thomas Jordan	100 A; —. Former owners: William Maul (Pat. 1738), Benjamin Jordan, Sr. (D)
102	11- 5-1774	Zachariah Pinket	Thomas James	200 A; £35. Adj.: William Congleton. Wit.: James Stewart, Jr.
104	1—-1775	Samuel Smith (CRAV) (1772)	Pearson Tuten	150 A+ 100 A; £60. Former owner: Andrew Hardee (Pat. 1772). Wit.: John Allen, Henry Cannon
108	5-15-1770	William Moore (D-1773)	William Speir	300 A; £100. Former owners: John Wilson (Pat.), John Moye (D-1774), George Moye, Sen. (dec.), John Moye, heir of George Moye, Sen., George Moye, Jr, brother of John Moye, and son of Geo.
110	9-26-1774	Moses Maning (Pat. 1773) and Lydia Maning	Samuel Maning	160 A; £8. Wit.: Caleb Tripp, Thomas Maning, Sarah Maning
111	2-18-1774	John Simpson (D-1770)	William Dixson	300 A; £30. Former owners: William Taylor (Pat. 1769), Thomas Tuten. Wit.: Thomas Alderson
113	11-15-1774	Wm. Harris, Sen.	John Mooring, Sr., Henry Barnhill, William Norcet	— A; love & regard. Men.: John Holland. Wit.: Samuel Colhoun, Hood Harris
114	12- 5-1774	Moses Maning (DOB) (Pat, 1773)	Samuel Powel	320 A; £20. Wit.: George Granbery, Moses Granbery
116	1-11-1775	William Hays	Thomas Williams	200 A+ 100 A; £40. Former owners: Caleb Howell (Pat. 1743), William Willis (Pat.). Wit.: William Crawford, John Whiteacre
118	4- 7-1774	James Wall	Richard Grist	100 A; £70. Adj.: William Grist. Wit.: Thomas Bartlet
119	12- 8-1774	Moses Maning (DOB) (Pat. 1773)	John Frizzell	160 A; £8. Wit.: Reuben Rountree
121	7- 8-1774	Alexander Brown (MART), taylor	Simon Evrett	250 A; £40. Adj.: Dennis Glison. Former owner: Jesse Jolley (Pat. 1761). Wit.: William Rodgers, John Barnhill
122	1- 5-1775	John Holaday Hudson, bricklayer (MART)	Joseph Gainer	300 A; £82. Wit.: William Mizell
124	1-23-1775	Sarah Washington	Joshua Barnes	145 A; £45. Former owner: John Washington (Pat. 1758). Wit.: Elias Bergeron, James Barrow

DEED BOOK F (1774-1801)

Page	Date	Grantor	Grantee	Additional Information
126	12-26-1774	Comm. of Martinborough	Charles Read	10 lotts (½ A each): #134, 135, 136, 144, 145, 146, 153, 154, 155, 160; £18. Men.: John Salter, Samuel Colhoun, George Evans, Jr., Joseph Ashmaid, Samuel Truss, Joseph Evans, Daniel Lockart
129	11-14-1774	John Haddock, Sen.	Zachriah Haddock, son	100 A; £50. Former owner: John Wain (Pat. 1752). Wit.: William Haddock
131	10-24-1775	Joseph Wall	Nathan Godley	100 A; £32. Former owners: Thomas Blount (Pat. 1719), Thomas Worsley (D), father of Thomas Worsley
132	2-20-1776	John Daniel (Greenville, S.C.)	Nathan Godley	195 A; £86. Men.: Elias Hodges, grandfather of John Daniel. Wit.: John Godley
134	1- 1-1775	William Speir (D-1770)	Stephen Munden	300 A; £100. Former owners: John Wilson (Pat.) John Moye, George Moye, Jr., William Moore. Wit.: John Munden, Major Harris, Thomas Pinkit
136	1-31-1775	William Spier	Stephen Munden	270 A; £50. Former: Geo. Moye (Pat. 1761), William Moore (D-1770)
137	10- 1-1772	Comm. of Martinborough	William Campbell	½ A. lott #82; 40 sh.
139	10- 1-1772	Comm. of Martinborough	George Falknier	2 (½A) lotts #88 and #97; 40 sh.
140	9-10-1775	John Robinson and Amay Robinson	George Albritton, guardian of Henry Albritton, minor	280 A; £20. Former owner: James Albrittain, dec. Men.: Ami Albrittain. Wit.: Thomas Tuten
142	12-30-1774	Samuel Stokes (Pat. 1756)	Richard Williams	20 A; £12. Wit.: Simon Pope, James May, Daniel Lockhart
144	1-23-1776	Allen Sugg (1758)	Roderick Williams	30 A; £15. Former owner: George Sugg, father of Allen Sugg (Pat. 1752). Wit.: Robert Williams
145	1- 7-1775	Richard William and Mary Williams	Joseph Culpeper	20 A; £13. Former owner: Samuel Stokes (1756). Wit.: Robert Williams, Priscilla Johnson, Mary Stokes
147	12- 6-1775	Hardee Grizzard (D-1773)	Nathaniel Moore	159 A + 259 A; £133 +. Former owner: Thomas Giddings. Wit.: Benjamin May, Josiah Askew
149	1-18-1776	Edmund Tison	Henry Tison	100 A; £5. Wit.: Aaron Tison, James Tison
150	1-18-1776	Edmund Tison	James Tison	100 A; £5.
152	——1774	Benjamin Blount	Reuben Powell	100 A; £40. Former owner: Jacob Blount (Pat. 1754). Wit.: Sampson Powell, William Whitfield
153	4- 5-1771	John Knowis, Sen. (D-1752)	John Doudie	50 A; £20. Former owner: Patrick Maule (Pat. 1723). Wit.: John Knowis, Jr., Alex Stewart
154	8- 1-1775	Thomas Salter (Pat. 1774)	Nathan Nelson	50 A; £5. Wit.: James Salter, Theofilus Crafton

DEED BOOK F (1774-1801)

Page	Date	Grantor	Grantee	Additional Information
155	——1774	Peter Diggens(DOB) (Pat 1770) and Elizabeth Digens	John Frizzle	200 A; £10. Wit.: William Morris
157	3-15-1775	Andrew Gufford (DUPL)	James May, Jr.	330 A; £100. Wit.: Jacob Atkinson, Samuel May, James May
158	2-10-1767	David Hattaway	Francis Hattaway, son	100 A; love & aff. Adj.: Edmund Hattaway, Thomas Hattaway, both witnesses
159	11-29-1775	James Moore	Abraham Joiner	200 A; £15. Wit.: John Joiner, Daniel Lockhart
161	3-29-1775	Jesse Cooper (MART)	Thomas Hattaway	200 A; £40. Former owner: James Smith (Pat. 1755). Wit.: William Mosely, Thos. Hattaway, Jr., Edmund Hattaway
163	4-24-1776	George Williams	George Falconeer	½ A. lott #89; £5. Wit.: Josiah Little
164	11-20-1776	Thomas Mercer	William Vines	175 A; £90. Former owner: Thomas Tison. Wit.: Nathaniel Moore
165	3- 7-1776	Thomas Mercer and Sarah Mercer, wife	William Vines (BEAU)	400 A; £200. Adj.: Jacob Mercer, brother of Thomas Mercer. Former owners: Thomas Mercer, father of Thomas Mercer, grantor, Christopher Mercer, bother of grantor. Wit.: Shadrach Mercer, William Brantly, Thomas Mercer
167	4-22-1777	Nathaniel Lanier	James Lanier	100 A; £50. Wit.: Isom Lanier
168	11-15-1776	Joseph Sullivant	Benjamin May	285 A; £100. Former owners: Thomas Tison, John White. Wit.: Henry Ellis, Nathaniel Moore
170	9-11-1776	Margaret Barnhill	Margaret Clarke, daughter, and husband, William Clarke	3 negroes; love & aff. Wit.: Geo. Evans, John Evans
171	11- 5-1774	James Williams and Ann Williams, wife	John Williams	210 A; £133. Former owners: Robt. Williams, Edward Williams, Richard Williams. Wit.: James Lanier, Ben Cooper, David Stokes
173	6- 3-1775	Henry Irwin (EDG)	Charles Waldrom	225 A; £200. Former owner: Francis Hobson. Wit.: Timothy Harrington, Robert Salter
174	11-17-1775	William Hart	Watkins Hart	100 A; £37. Former owners: William Stafford, Moses Hart. Wit.: George Tison, Rachel Tison
176	1- 4-1775	Samuel Stokes	Henry Stokes, brother	75 A; love & aff. Wit.: Edward Flannikin, Susannah Stokes
177	1- 4-1775	Samuel Stokes	Reden Stokes, brother	75 A; love & aff. Wit.: Darkis Williams
178	7-20-1776	John Pollard	Benjamin Wombwell	100 A; £25. Men.: Benjamin Pollard, father of John Pollard, grantor. Former owner: William Mace (Pat. 1743). Wit.: James Brady

DEED BOOK F (1774-1801)

Page	Date	Grantor	Grantee	Additional Information
179	4-13-1776	Thomas Wheatley	Samuel Wheatley	50 A; £60. Wit.: Samuel Crisp, Benjamin Crisp, Lydia Wheatley
181	1-22-1777	William Nichols (D-1764) and Mary Nichols, wife	Abel Thomas	95 A; £37+. Former owner: Amos Atkinson. Wit.: Simon Gray
182	10-24-1776	Lewis Davis	William Fatheree	125 A; £70. Adj.: John White. Wit.: William Vines, John Vines
184	6-17-1776	Reuben Manning	Thomas Cason, shoe maker	50 A; £25.
185	1-28-1777	William Hancock	Sampson Slaughter	80 A; £25. Wit.: Geo. Falconeer, Isaac Hardee
186	9- 9-1776	Jacob Blount (Pat. 1767)	John Willson and his mother, Sarah Willson	100 A; £5. Adj.: Joseph Slade. Wit.: John Sirman, Levi Sirman
187	12-27-1775	John Highsmith	Thomas Carson	140 A; £40. Adj.: Arthur Oles. Wit.: John Bowers
189	1-22-1777	Arthur Olds	Thomas Carson	150 A; £100. Wit.: Edmund Andrews
190	11-13-1776	William Peebles	Absalom Rogers	200 A; £36. Wit.: John Ellis, Henry Goff
191	———1777	Samuel Mannin	Elizabeth Winget (CRAV)	160 A; £30. Adj.: Dennis Cannon. Wit.: Cannon, Benjamin Warner
192	7- 1-1771	Hillery Cason	John Hennington	100 A; £41. Former owners: George Cannon, James Cason (Pat. 1761). Wit.: John Cason, Jonathan Hininton
194	———1775	Nathaniel Cannon (1774)	Solomon Sutton	— A; £5. Adj.: Benjamin Blunt. Wit.: William Whitfield, Sampson Powel
196	11- 9-1775	William Judkins	Betty Hare, daughter	150 A; —. Wit.: John Hill
197	11-16-1776	David Mills (Pat. 1774)	Joshua Putnal	300 A; £16. Wit.: Isaac Gardner
199	2-12-1777	John Mundin (1770)	Sothey Cobb	70 A; £35. Former owner: William Judgkins. Wit.: Robert Daniels, Samuel Barrow
201	12-14-1771	Thomas Shield (MECK) and William Shield, Jr.	James Crandell	130 A+ 70 A; £44. Men.: Wm. Shield, Sr., Father of William Shield, Jr., Former owners: Seth Pilkington (Pat. 1743), John Knowis. Wit.: James Crandell, Sen., John Lanier, Jr.
202	2- 8-1777	Philip Pipkin	Woodey Belcher	20 A; £7+. Wit.: Richard Moye, Phillaney Moye
203	8- 7-1776	Jessee Rountree	Randal McDonald	170 A; £20. Former owner: Francis Rountree. Wit.: Wm. Lanier, Jr., Reuben Rountree
205	8- 3-1776	Aaron Tyson	George Evans	90 A; - 2 A; £360. Adj.: Thomas Goff, Edmund Tison. Men.: Abraham Tison. Wit.: Arthur Forbes, Wm. Robson
206	3- 4-1777	Samuel Charlcraft	George Falconer	50 A; £100. Adj.: Michael Coutanche. Wit.: Mary Dixon
208	11-18-1776	Richard Albritton	Nehemiah Tuten	100 A; £20. Adj.: Peter Albritton

DEED BOOK F (1774-1801)

Page	Date	Grantor	Grantee	Additional Information
209	5-27-1777	Thomas Salter (Pat. 1774)	Simon Jones	100 A; £60. Wit.: Paul White, Christopher White
210	4-21-1777	Hillery Cason	Eleazar Cherry	6 A; £7+. Wit.: John Jones, Samuel Moore
211	——-1777	John Hardee	Edward Gatlin	300 A; £30.
212	3-22-1776	William Whitfield, taylor (Pat. 1774)	Sampson Powell	25 A; £5. Wit.: Avirileah Tripp
214	———	Sampson Powell (Pat. 1775)	Reuben Powell	320 A; £10.
217	2-12-1777	Jonathan Taylor (D-1763)	John Barber	100 A; £30. Former owner: John Noble. Wit.: William Barber
218	10- 1-1772	Comm. of Martinborough	Samuel Truss	½ A. lott #124; —.
219	2- 4-1777	Edward Travis	Thomas Travis	142 A; £5. Former owner: Thomas Travis, Sr. (Pat. 1761)
222	4- 7-1777	William Stancil	John Frizzle	150 A; £55. Former owner: John Lambardson (Pat. 1750). Wit.: Isaac Blount
224	5-13-1776	John Frizzle	George Granbery	200 A; £36. Adj.: Samuel Powel, Jeremiah Rame. Former owner: Peter Diggins (Pat. 1770)
226	10-27-1775	Thomas Nobles	James Nobles	100 A; £5. Wit.: Benjamin Bowers, John Bowers
228	1-23-1777	John Pope	Evritt Pope	250 A; £150. Former owners: Joseph Barrow, John Charl-craft. Wit.: James Brown, Simon Pope
230	1-23-1777	Evritt Pope	James Brown	125 A; £60.
232	2-10-1777	Thomas Nobles	John Page	290 A; £60. Adj.: James Nobles. Wit.: Nathan Mayo
234	3-22-1777	John Hardee	Anthony Mills (CRAV)	300 A; £60. Wit.: John Williams
236	1-29-1777	Edward Travis	William Joiner	142 A; £77+. Wit.: John Joyner, Isreal Joyner
238	9-27-1775	Benjamin Allen	John Simpson	½ A. lott #137; £5. Wit.: Isaac Hardee, Martin Nelson
240	11-25-1776	David Williams (Pat. 1756)	William Hancock	80 A; £5. Wit.: Stewart Gordon, John Williams
242	2-23-1776	John Pope	Geo. Falkner	½ A. lott #101; £10. Wit.: Thos. Williamson
244	1-14-1775	William Travis (Pat. 1767)	Daniel Wilson, Sen.	250 A; £13+. Adj.: Henry Jerrell. Wit.: John Brooks, Wm. Hancock
246	4-23-1777	Ann Dixon	Jeremiah Dixon, son	½ A. lott #79; love & aff. Wit.: William English, George Evans
247	1-29-1777	Coll. John Hardee	William Hellen	150 A; £25. Wit.: James Lanier
249	9-19-1776	James Lockhart	George Evans	280 A; £133. Adj.: Abraham Barrow. Former owner: Richard Barrow (Pat. 1755)
251	7-15-1776	Benjamin Buck	Joseph Boyd	200 A; £7. Adj.: Rolen Dixon. Former owner: Isaac Buck (Pat. 1757). Wit.: William Buck, Walter Dixon
253	7-23-1776	Comm. of Martinborough	Ann Dixon	3 (½A.) lotts #70, 17, 27; £6.

DEED BOOK F (1774-1801)

Page	Date	Grantor	Grantee	Additional Information
255	10-16-1776	Moses Hart	Watkins Hart	50 A; £16. Wit.: Robert Hart. Former owner: William Stafford
257	11- 4-1776	William Hancock (Pat. 1767)	William Wilson	160 A; £50. Wit.: William Burney, William Hardee
259	1-28-1777	George Evans	Thomas Goff	90 A; — 2A; £150. Wit.: Edmund Williams, Richard Moye
261	7-30-1776	Jacob Blount (Pat. 1775)	Mary Jackson	81 A; £10. Wit.: John Sirman, John Wilson, Jr.
263	12-24-1776	William Slaughter, shoe maker	Sampson Slaughter	50 A; £20. Former owners: John Slaughter (D-1763) Larrance Kirvin (Pat. 1762). Adj.: David Williams. Wit.: James Hancock
265	1-28-1777	William Hancock (Pat. 1775)	William Wilson	132 A; £20.
267	2-16-1776	Sarah Stancell, widow	John Stancell and Godfrey Stancell, sons	Former owner: John Stancell, dec. husband of Sarah. Wit.: Matthew Little, George Cockburn, Charles Waldrom
268	2-22-1777	Jacob Atkinson	Britain Edwards	120 A; £100. Wit.: James Gardner
270	10-30-1777	William Baldwin, shoe maker	Robert Salter	100 A; £20. Former owners: Thomas Giddens (Pat. 1743), Lazarus Pearce
272	1-30-1776	Joshua Proctor and William Proctor	William Baldwin, shoe maker	100 A; £13+. Men.: William Proctor, Sen., father of Joshua and William, grantors. Wit.: Major Harris, Shadrich Cobb
274	10- 4-1776	George Moye (Pat) and Elizabeth Moye, wife	John Barber	100 A; £—.
276	10-30-1777	George Moye (Pat. 1775)	Francis Rountree	— A; £100.
278	10- 7-1777	John Sirman(D)	Francis Rountree	50 A; £10. Former owners: Daniel Oquin (Pat. 1750), William Travis
280	3-20-1775	John Fulford	John Braxton	20 A; £5. Former owner: Col. John Simpson (Pat. 1762). Wit.: James Braxton
281	4-24-1775	John Braxton	James Braxton	100 A; £20. Former owner: John Willson (Pat. 1764). Wit.: Geo. Granbery
283	1-25-1775	Shadrick Pope	John Pope	125 A; £50. Former owners: Joseph Barrow, John Charlcraft. Wit.: Henry Ellis, John Ellis, Christian Ellis, Priscilla Pope
284	4-25-1775	John Smith (Pat. 1762) and Mary Smith, wife	David Williams	200 A; £100. Wit.: Stewart Gordon
286	2-14-1775	John Willson	George Willson	530 A; £80. Wit.: Joseph Henly, Jonas Williams
287	4- 1-1775	John Griffin	Solomon Shepard	1 A; £1. Wit.: Ann Shepard

DEED BOOK F (1774-1801)

Page	Date	Grantor	Grantee	Additional Information
289	3-15-1775	Hillery Cason (1758)	Lemuel James	200 A; £100. Former owner: William Cason (1740), who made D of G to Hillery Cason. Wit.: John Jordan
290	———1771	Alex. Stewart, exr. for Benjamin Hull, dec.	James Latham	170 A; £50. Wit.: Anne Stewart
292	2-15-1775	John Simpson, merchant (D-1771)	Joshua Putnell	100 A; £30.. Former owners: James Avery (Pat. 1761), John Avery (D of G 1764). Wit.: Mary Hardee, John Hardee
293	4-11-1774	Andrew Hardee (Pat. 1772), William Williams and Ann Williams, wife	David Mills	100 A; £27. Men.: Ann Fergerson, now Ann Williams. Wit.: Pearson Tuten, William Hardee
294	10- 1-1772	Comm. of Martinborough	Shadrick Wooten	½ A. lott #9; 40 sh.
295	11- 1-1774	George McGowns	William McGowns	50 A; £10. Wit.: Robt. Hardee, Josias Hardee
297	7-21-1777	John Cannon	Thomas Cannon	271 A; £40. Former owner: Abraham Duncan (Pat. 1752). Wit.: Samuel Granger, Henry Cannon
298	7-22-1777	John Cannon	Thomas Granger	54 A; £15. Former owner: Joseph Hardee, dec. (Pat. 1755)
299	10-26-1777	William Bryant (DOB)	William Turnage	200 A; £200. Former owner: George Turnage (Pat. 1738). Wit.: Richard Moye, John Moye
300	10-26-1777	William Turnage	Richard Moye	200 A; £200. Adj.: Benjamin Mathews
301	2 ———1776	Noah Robson	Larance Anderson	— A; £30. Former owner: Solomon Robson, father of Noah, grantor. Wit.: William Robson, Sovereign Robson
302	7-30-1777	Samuel Truss	Gideon Pettit	½ A. lott #124; £5.
303	3 ———1777	John Williams and Dorcas Williams	Lemuel Bullock	71 A; £45. Former owner: Edward Williams (Pat. 1760). Wit.: Catherine Williams
304	9- 2-1776	James Robson	Larrance Anderson	57 A; £26. Former owner: Solomon Robson. Wit.: William Robson, Henry Anderson
306	10- 3———	George Moye, Sen.	Francis Roundtree	100 A; £20. Former owner: Daniel Oquin (Pat. 1755). Wit.: John Sirman
307	10-27-1777	James Lanier	Isom Lanier, son	100 A; love & aff. Wit.: Jacob Allen
308	10- 1-1777	John Cook, Sen.	Edward Gatling (MART)	200 A; £115. Adj.: Thomas Cook. Wit.: Ephraim Bullock, Edmund Andrews
309	—————	Luke Mounts	Samuel Erby	300 A & furn; good will. Men.: Amos and Rachel Erby, parents of Samuel, grantee. Former owner: Richard Evans. Wit.: Leah Brown, Matthias Johnson
310	10- 8-1777	Francis Rountree	John Sirman	100 A; £10. Former owners: Geo. Moye, Sen., Daniel Oquin

DEED BOOK F (1774-1801)

Page	Date	Grantor	Grantee	Additional Information
311	——-1777	Joseph Jackson, Jr.	Ephraim Herrington	100 A; £20. Former owners: John Simpson, Paul Herrington. Wit.: Paul Herrington
312	2-20——	James May, Jr.	John Whitehurst	160 A; £72. Former owner: William Archdeacon. Wit.: John Hines
313	2-22-1777	Thomas Gwaltney (CRAV) (Pat.)	Parker Lacey	200 A; £40.
314	10——-1777	David Powers	Ephraim Powers	150 A; 10 sh. Former owner: Caleb Wallace (1761)
315	12- 6-1774	Samuel Stokes and Sarah Stokes	George Moye, Jr.	200 A; £105. Men.: Samuel Stokes, dec., father of Samuel Stokes, grantor, (Pat. 1756 and 1762). Wit.: John Tison and Jacob Dixon
316	7-25-1777	William Smith (Pat. 1763)	Moab Rountree	200 A; £15.
318	11-12-1776	Benjamin Cooper	John Wooten	200 A; £60. Wit.: John Williams, Dorkis Williams, Drury Stokes
319	7-26-1777	Thomas Hodges and Sarah Hodges, wife	Luke Mounts, ship carpenter	110 A; £60. Wit.: Phillip Holland, Matthias Johnson
320	10-28-1777	John Moye, jr.	Ann Dixon	½ A. lott #68; £3. Wit.: Agnus Dixon
321	9——-1777	Matthew Parrimore (DOB)	John Jones	170 A; £75. Former owner: Wm. Speir (Pat. 1761). Wit.: John Brinkley, James Wainwright
322	10- 1-1772	Comm. of Martinborough	John Jones	½ A. lott #67; 40 sh.
323	10-15-1777	Nesby Mills, Jr. (D-1773)	John Simpson (Pat. 1764)	150 A; £154. Former owner: James Brooks (1765). Wit.: John Albritton, Samuel Simpson
324	9-10-1777	Edward Cannon (CRAV)	John Simpson	500 A; £45. Former owner: David Cannon (Pat. 1745), father of Edward Cannon, grantor. Wit.: Nathaniel Cannon, Hannah White
325	10- 6-1777	Dennis Cannon Sen.	Dennis Cannon, Jr.	150 A in Craven; £10. Wit.: Elizabeth Cannon
328	1-24-1778	Andrew Hardee (1774)	Simon Burney, Sen.	140 A; £50.
329	1-24-1778	John Tison, Jr. and Elizabeth Tison, wife	David Hines, Sen. (EDG)	200 A; £230. Wit.: Sterling Dupree, Benjamin Dupree
331	1-26-1778	Joshua Putnell	Benjamin Sutton	100 A; £100. Wit.: Nathaniel Pettit
332	8-10-1775	John Tison (D-1767)	John Tison, son	200 A; love & aff. Former owners: Thomas Tison (Pat. 1745), Major Tison (D-1752), William Edwards (D-1758). Wit.: Job Tison, Sabra Tison
332	12-10-1773	John Willaims (Pat. 1762)	Henry Williamson	51 A; £6. Wit.: Elizabeth Williams
334	1-22-1778	Joshua Taylor (MART)	Thomas Whitley	640 A; £600. Wit.: Fran Crisp, Samuel Wheatly

F 311-334

DEED BOOK F (1774-1801)

Page	Date	Grantor	Grantee	Additional Information
335	5-28-1774	Daniel Rogers	Robert Sanders	100 A; £30. Wit.: Absolum Rogers, Josiah Gremmer, Jacob Gremmer
337	----1777	Archibald Adams, Sen., Cordevainer	Peter Adams, son	143 A; love. Former owner: Wm. Baldwin (1757). Wit.: Colson Adams, George Williams
338	10-27-1777	Timothy Harris	William Bell, blacksmith	180 A; £35. Former owner: William Stafford (Pat. 1756). Wit.: James Harris, Burrel Bell
340	4-27-1774	Comm. of Martinborough	Henry Williamson	½ A. lott #51; 40 sh.
341	----1777	Kely Tucker	Matthias Moor	100 A; £72. Former owner: Capt. George Moye. Men.: Samuel Moor, Sen. Wit.: Richard Moy
342	2-16-1777	George Moye, Jr.	Portlock Hodges, shoemaker	50 A; £49. Former owner: Samuel Stokes. Wit.: Joseph Culpepper, William Hart, Bethany Mayo
344	8-23-1777	William Stancel	John Dowdee	200 A; £65. Former owner: John Becton
345	5- 9-1777	Abel Dail, Jr.	John Deel	100 A; £40. Wit.: Abel Dail, Sen.
346	9-16-1771	William Lewis	James Smith	75 A; £35. Adj.: James Glisson. Wit.: William Knox, Josiah Knox
348	11-26-1777	John Ward (DOB)	Solomon Ward, son	160 A; love & aff. Former owner: Thomas Ward
349	3- 2-1776	John Herrinton (Pat. 1773)	Benjamin Blount	138 A; £5. Wit.: Isaac Blount
351	2- 6-1771	Walter Session	Josiah Knox	15 A; £7. Wit.: William Knox, Davis Vance
352	1-27-1778	Peter Moss	James Quatermus	140 A-10 A; £50. Former owner: John Stocks
353	7- 5-1773	John Newton (D-1767)	Walter Newton	100 A; £35. Former owner: Wm. Speir (1758)
355	1- 9-1778	Thomas Travis	Jacob Wale	142 A; £75. Former owner: Thomas Travis, Sen. (1761)
356	11- 1-1777	William Nichols	Drury Bullock	50 A; £52. Wit.: Amos Atkinson
358	1- 1-1769	George Moye, Sheriff	James May	Goods, plantation inc. 240 A; £100. Men.: Abraham Tison, dec., former sheriff. Former owners: Caleb Wallace, Joseph Howell, William Brantley (EDG). Wit.: Timothy Herrington
362	1- 3-1778	John Hardee	John Cannon	640 A; £100. Wit.: John Enloe, Elizabeth Enloe
363	1-28-1778	Edward Salter and Robert Salter	Levi Noble	100 A; £20. Former owners: Seth Pilkington (Pat. 1738), Walter Dixon, dec. Wit.: John Hatton
365	12-12-1778	Paul Allen	Elizabeth Allen, daughter	Negro; love & aff. Men.: Capt. Henry Ellis. Wit.: James Lanier, Jr, William Ellis
366	10-20-1775	James Buck	Rolin Dixson and Frances Dixson, wife	100 A; £50. Former owner: Isaac Buck

No.	Grantor	Grantee	Date	Description
367	Robert Salter	Apsley Lesslie	2-17-1777	Negro; love & aff. Men.: John and Nancy Lesslie, parents of Apsley Lesslie, grantee
368	Harry Smith	Henry Smith	1-26-1778	100 A; £100.
370	Fitch Harris	John Fleming	11-16-1777	111 A; £35. Wit.: Robert Flake, David Fleming
372	Comm. of Martinborough	Mary Johnston	1-27-1773	½ A. lott #150; 40 sh. Wit.: Peter Hines, Jr.
374	Jacob Blount	Mary Blount, cousin, and Jacob Sutton, cousin, and Isaac Hardee Coward, and Isaac Turnage	1-26-1778	Slaves; love & aff. Men.: Benj. Blount and Pheneliphas Blount, parents of Mary Blount; Solomon and Mary Sutton, parents of Jacob Sutton; Needom and Phoebe Coward, parents of Isaac Coward; Selah Turnage, mother of Isaac Turnage. Wit.: Joshua Moye
376	Nathaniel Lanier and Mary Lanier, wife	Watkins Hart	1-26-1778	31 A; £31. Former owner: Robert Flake (Pat. 1751). Wit.: Robert Hart
378	Henry Jarrel (CRAV)	Daniel Wilson	1-16-1778	50 A; £20. Wit.: Shadrich Sutton.
379	George Dikes	Rebecca Dikes, daughter, and William Dikes, son	5——1775	Cows, hog, household goods, 100 A; love & aff. Wit.: Daniel Macklain, William Johnston
380	James Nobles (DOB)	John Page	11-17-1777	100 A; £80.
382	Nathan Johnston (Pat. 1763)	George Evans	———1778	40 A; £4. Adj.: Matthew Sturdivant
383	William Hardee	Simon Burney, Sen.	1-26-1778	80 A; £50. Former owner: Cornelius Tyson (1738)
385	William Baldwin	Mary Hart, daughter	1- 5-1778	100 A; 10 sh. and love & aff. Men.: Watkins Hart, husband of Mary Hart, grantee. Former owner: John Forbes (Pat. 1745)
386	Felix Kenan (DUPL)	Edward Flannekin	11- 2-1776	114 A; £30. Men.: Robert Stewart, dec. (DUPL)
387	Benjamin Buck	Walter Dixson	7-15-1776	200 A; £15. Former owner: Isaac Buck (Pat. 1757). Wit.: Joseph Boyd, William Buck
388	Comm. of Martinborough	Jacob Johnston	1-27-1773	3 (½A.) lotts, #56, 111, 129; £6. Wit.: Peter Hines, Jr., Nathaniel Moore
390	William Denmark (CRAV) (1774)	Jeremiah Cox	4-21-1778	150 A; £3. Wit.: Edward Salter, Ann Salter
391	John Hodges	John Jordan (HYDE)	2- 9-1778	150 A; £200. Former owners: William Cannon (Pat. 1740), Henry Cooper. Wit.: James Gorham, Joshua James
393	Benjamin Sutton	John Pettit	1-26-1778	45 A; £100. Former owner: John Pane
395	Wm. Whitfield (Pat. 1774), taylor, and Jemima Whitfield, wife	Caleb Tripp	12-29-1776	394 A; £36. Wit.: John Frizzle, Jacob Waller, James Herrington
397	Sampson Powel (Pat. 1775)	Wm. Whitfield, taylor	3-22-1776	50 A; £10.

DEED BOOK F (1774-1801)

Page	Date	Grantor	Grantee	Additional Information
399	12- 6-1777	Joseph Culpepper	Samuel Stokes	20 A; £35. Former owner: Samuel Stokes, Sr. (Pat. 1756). Wit.: Samuel Stafford, Robert Williams
400	1-24-1778	John Tyson, Sen. and Betheny Tyson, wife	David Hines, Sr. (EDG)	100 A; £125. Wit.: Sterling Dupree, Benjamin Dupree
403	12-10-1778	George Evans	Henry Williamson	40 A; £4. Former owner: Nathan Johnson (Pat. 1763)
404	10- 1-1772	Comm. of Martinborough	Joel Sugg	½ A. lott #63; 40 sh.
405	12- 5-1777	Nathaniel Lanier	William Ellis	140 A; £70.
406	12-24-1777	John Herrington (Pat. 1773)	Thomas Ringgold (HYDE)	100 A; £50. Wit.: Samuel Grainger
408	3-15-1775	Samuel James	Hillery Cason	128 A; £100. Former owner: William Stafford (Pat. 1740)
410	4-26-1778	Isaac Stocks (D-1769)	John Stocks, Jr.	100 A; £40. Former owners: John Williams, Sr, John Williams, Jr, Thos. Hardy, Jno. Simpson, Shadrich Allen. Wit.: Samuel Powell, John Powell
412	3-14-1778	Sampson Powell (NASH) (Pat. 1775)	Moses Granbery	2 A; £40.
414	11-16-1773	Robert Grimmer	George Evans	100 A; £35. Adj.: Thomas Ivey. Wit.: Benjamin Bowers, John Lewis
415	———1778	Levi Adams	Agustine Spain	½ A. lott #30; 40 sh.
416	10- 1-1772	Comm. of Martinborough	Edward Flannakin	½ A. lott #60; 40 sh.
418	10- 1-1772	Comm. of Martinborough	Isaac Stocks	84 A; £80. Former owners: William Willson, Jno. Felingim
419	2-28-1777	William Hays	James Latham	240 A; £—. Former owner: Simon Jones (Pat. 1752)
420	3-10-1778	Henry Jones	Thomas Tuten	100 A; £—.
422	———1768	Jesse Kennedy	Alex Stewart	250 A; £30. Wit.: Sampson Sikes
423	11-21-1771	Francis Hobson	Simon Gray (EDG)	½ A. lott —; 40 sh.
425		Comm. of Martinborough	Robert Grimmer	
426	1-16-1778	Richard Caswell (DOBB) (1761)	Robert Washington (DOBB)	140 A; £100.
428	3- 4-1778	John Cook (ONSL)	Thos. Cook	120 A; £5.
429	2- 2-1778	John Edwards	Matthew Cartwright	125 A; £—.
430	4- 1-1778	Thomas English	Lemuel Cherry	81 A; £40. Former owner: Larance Kirvin (1761)
432	8- 8-1762	John Eastwood	Mary Eastwood, wife	All possessions; love & aff.
433	11-24-1777	Jacob Waller (Pat. 1772) and Sarah Waller	Thomas Ringold (HYDE)	100 A; £50.
435	8- 7-1771	James CharlesCraft	Michael Coutanche Evans	1 A; £5. Wit.: Edmund Perkins
437	11-29-1777	Frederick Gibble	James Gorham	435 A - 100 A; £—. Men.: Isaac Buck (1738)
438	4-28-1778	Parker Lacy	Levis Adams	100 A; £35. Wit.: John Lewis, Benjamin Bowers

DEED BOOK F (1774-1801)

Page	Date	Grantor	Grantee	Additional Information
440	2- 8-1778	John Hearn	John Edwards	100 A; £110. Former owners: Richard Cheek (Pat.), James Hearn, father of John Hearn, grantor
441	10- 1-1772	Comm. of Martinborough	Thos. Wallace	½A. lott #40; 40 sh.
443	11- 7-1771	Earl Granville	Nehemiah Wrotten	82 A; 10 sh.
447	6-26-1762	Earl Granville	John Mooring	77 A; 10 sh.
450	6-30-1778	John Simpson and Robert Salter (Pat. 1770)	Edward Salter	640 A; £100.
451	6-30-1778	Edward Salter	Robert Salter	320 A; £—.
453	4-30-1778	John Hardy	Robert Salter	— A; £—.
454	6-30-1778	Robert Salter and Clare Salter, wife	John Salter, son	150 A + 420 A + 623 A + 323 A; love & aff.
456	7- 9-1778	Jacob Blount (Pat. 1775)	Needom Coward, hatter (DOBB)	144 A; £5.
458	5-11-1778	Pearson Tuten	Nathaniel Cannon	150 A; £100.
460	3-28-1778	Paul Allen	Thos. Wallis, Jr.	150 A; £55. Former owner: Robert Land (Pat. 1761)
462	3- 4-1778	James Cason	William Everit	310 A; £90+. Wit.: David Averett
463	2- 7-1778	Watkins Hart	Robert Hart	150 A; £80.
464	5-11-1778	Pearson Tuten	Nathaniel Cannon	100 A; £100. Former owner: Anthony Mills (1760)
467	11- 3-1777	Nichols Bynum	Benjamin Bynum	100 A; £5. Wit.: James Bynum
468	5- 6-1778	Benjamin May, saddler (1772)	William Corbet	180 A; £70. Wit.: Nathaniel Moore, Moses Owen
469	4- 8-1778	George Falconer	Speir Holland	½A. lott #97; £18.
471	5- 2-177–	George Moy, Sheriff	James May	350 A; £30. Former owner: Caleb Wallace. Wit.: Robert Williams, Benjamin May
474	2-21-1778	Benjamin Blount and Penellope Blount, wife	Jessee Rountree	1 A; £2. Wit.: Roundtree, Francis Buck
476	4- 4-1778	Thomas Downs and Deborah Downs, wife	Azaniah Langley (BEAU)	100 A; £85. Adj.: John May. Wit.: John Price, Thomas Walston
478	3——1778	Francis Roundtree	Joshua Hardinson	240 A; £180. Men.: George Moye Sr. (1775). Wit.: John Roundtree, Moab Roundtree
479	12-16-1777	Thos. Wallis, Jr.	Hillary Hodges	412 A; £150. Wit.: Thomas Wallas, Robt. Williams, Mary Stokes
481	2- 1-1775	John Brady and Silvia Brady, wife	James Brady, Sen.	100 A; £45. Adj.: John Pollard. Wit.: Mary Brady, Ann Brady, Wm. Brady, Sen.

F 440-481

DEED BOOK F (1774-1801)

Page	Date	Grantor	Grantee	Additional Information
483	10- 1-1772	Comm. of Martinborough	Wm. Averitt	½ A. lott #39, 40 sh.
484	3- 4 1778	Francis Roundtree (D-1777)	Joshua Hardinson	100 A; £40. Former owner: Daniel Oquin
486	8- 6-1771	John Dowdney	Matthias Crandell	100 A; £120. Former owner: Thomas Williams (Pat. 1743)
487	1-31-1778	William Mayo (EDG)	Amos Mayo, brother	77 A; love & aff. Wit.: Samuel Warren, Matthew Luter, Amos Atkinson
489	12-20-1777	William Bell, blacksmith	Burrell Bell	90 A; £20. Former owner: William Stafford (1756). Wit.: Nathaniel Lanier, John Ellis
491	3-16-1778	Robert Williams, Sen. (1738)	Matthew Sturdivant	220 A; £200. Adj.: Joel Sugg. Wit.: John Williams, Susanna Stokes, Sarah Stokes
492	3- 7-1778	Samuel Smith (CRAV) (1761 and 1772)	Paul Allen	370 A; £60.
495	6- 4-1778	Mary Jackson	Needom Coward (DOBB), hatter	81 A; £64. Wit.: Jacob Blount, John Sirman. Former owner: Jacob Blount (Pat. 1775)
496	———1777	Betty Hare	James Edwards (CRAV)	150 A in Pitt & Beau.; £30. Former owner: William Judkins, dec, father of Betty Hare, grantor. Men.: Thomas Judkins, son of Wm. Judkins
498	9- 7-1778	David Mills	Nathaniel Cannon	100 A; £80. Former owner: Andrew Hardy (1772)
499	1-20-1779	Elisha Gray and Lucy Gray, wife	Joshua Barnes	145 A; £260. Former owner: John Washington (Pat. 1758). Wit.: Isaac Cason
501	11-21-1778	William Smith (DOBB) (Pat. 1760)	Joseph Smith	100 A; £20. Wit.: Eli Sirman
503	9- 1-1778	William Crisp	Francis Crisp	100 A. Wit.: Jesse Crisp, Samuel Crisp
504	6-24-1777	Winifred Wilson	Thomas Hodges	272 A; £55. Wit.: Moses Hodges
506	1———1779	George Moore (MART) (D-1761)	Matthias Moore	150 A; £300. Former owner: Ebenezer Folsom. Wit.: Samuel Moore, James Cooper
507	2- 5-1778	William Elot	John Frizzle	150 A; £220. Former owner: John Lamberson (Pat. 1750)
509	10- 3-1778	Thos. Judkins and Hannah Judkins, wife	Francis Hatteway	150 A; £100. Former owner: William Judkins, father of Thomas Judkins, grantor. Wit.: George Pearce, George Palmer
510	4-12-1775	Brittain King (CRAV)	William King	200 A; £100. Wit.: Eliphalet King, John Slayden King. Former owners: William Williams, father of David Williams
512	2-25-1778	Obed Rountree and Feril Rountree, wife	John Vinson	— A; £130. Wit.: Josiah Vinson, Wm. Whitfield

DEED BOOK F (1774-1801)

Page	Date	Grantor	Grantee	Additional Information
514	1-19-1779	Joell Whitfield	Jessee Jolley	— A; £60. Wit.: Elizabeth Andrews
515	11-30-1778	Solomon Whichard	John Jones	— A; £300. Former owner: Ebenezer Folsom (1761). Wit.: Cornelius Mundin, Isaac Mundin
517	3-16-1777	Samuel Davis (1770)	Lewis Davis	240 A; £50. Wit.: James Gay
519	1-15-1779	James Smith and William Smith	William Clements	50 A; £500. Wit.: Jonah Collins, John Ward
521	1-25-1779	Joell Whitfield	Peter Mayo (EDG)	123 A; £—.
522	6-17-1775	Richard Smith (BLAD) (D-1769)	Daniel Williams	150 A; £58. Former owner: John Johnston (Pat. 1740), Solomon James, Sen, Solomon James, Jr. Wit.: Daniel Clark
524	11-18-1778	Thomas Cook	Peter Martin	120 A; £150. Wit.: Edmund Andrews, Josiah Bullock
525	11-17-1778	Daniel Williams (DUPL)	Solomon Jolley	150 A; £200. Wit.: Samuel Ward, David Cannon, Samuel Williamson
527	9- 9-1778	Stephen Swain	William Clements	276 A; £356. Wit.: David Perkins, Peter Jolley
529	9-18-1772	Benjamin Wombwell	Henry Anderson	— A; £20. Wit.: Wm. Robson, John Robson
532	7-29-1778	Benjamin Bowers, Sheriff	John Cason	100 A; £160. Former owner: John Herrington
533	11- 5-1778	Mason Hearn	John Hearn (DOBB)	100 A; trade
535	7-29-1779	Thomas Wilson	James Spiller (Wilmington)	Interests; £5. Wit.: Daniel Seabrook
536	2-19-1780	George Evans	David Donnan	— A; £4500.
537	2-16-1780	George Evans	David Donnan	½ A. lott #45; £2. Wit.: Michael Evans, Richard Evans
537	5-22-1779	John Hodges (WASH)	Howell Hodges, brother	Power of attorney for 150 A.
538	4-25-1779	Stephen Mundin	Charles Cason	50 A; £50.
540	12-20-1779	Southey Cobb	Anthony Whichard	35 A; £50. Former owner: Wm. Judkins (1762)
541	8- 5-1780	James Gorham, exr. and Edward Salter, exr. for Robert Salter, dec.	William Harris	100 A; £800. Men.: William Harris, father of William Harris, grantee. Former owners: William Proctor, Joshua Proctor. Wit.: John Salter, Wm. Baldwyn
542	3- 9-1780	Samuel Cannon	John Cannon	125 A; £1000. Wit.: John Deal, Abel Deal
543	7-24-1779	Thomas H. Hall (FRAN)	Geo. Falconer	½ A. lot #115; £200. Wit.: John Holland
543	8- 7-1778	Samuel Charlcraft	James Johnson	173 A; £300. Former owner: Joseph Hardee (Pat. 1758). Wit.: Roderick Williams, Jeremiah Luter
544	10-23-1779	James Johnson	Thomas Crawson	173 A; £350. Wit.: James Bynum
546	10-27-1780	John Jordan	John Jones	150 A; £10,000. Former owner: William Cannon (D-1740). Wit.: William Jordan

DEED BOOK F (1774-1801)

Page	Date	Grantor	Grantee	Additional Information
547	8-20-1766	Abraham Tyson, Sheriff	Moses Tison	640 A; £40. Former owner: Theophilus Pew. Wit.: Matthias Tison
548	1-25-1768	Moses Tison	Abraham Tison	640 A; £40. Wit.: Timothy Harris
549	5- 1-1780	Azariah Tison	Cornelius Tison	320 A; £4000. Former owners: John Baptist Tison, father of Azariah; also grandfather Cornelius Tison, father of John Baptist Tison. Men.: Abraham Tison, father of Cornelius Tison, grantee. Wit.: Lucy Tison, Joel Tison
550	9-17-1778	Watkins Hart		200 A; £300.
551	6-17-1779	Nathaniel Lanier and Mary Lanier, wife Sarah Tucker, widow	Tally Tucker, daughter; Celia Tucker, daughter; Reddick Tucker, son; Wright Tucker, son; Joshua Tucker, son; John Tucker, son.	Household goods, animals; love & aff.
552	8-14-1780	John Jones, blacksmith	Solomon Whichard	150 A; negro man. Men.: John Whichard, son of Solomon Whichard
553	7-23-1779	James Barrow	John Jones	100 A; £10. Former owner: Geo. Moye (Pat. 1738)
554	1-25-1780	Howell Hodges	Isaac Carrell	150 A; £1300. Former owner: John Hodges. Wit.: Drury Stokes
555	4-24-1780	Stephen Mundin	Silvanus Pomphrey	50 A; £30. Wit.: Lazarus Pomphrey
556	9- 7-1780	Thomas Curtis	Thomas Goff	1 A; £4. Former owner: Ednund Tison, dec.
556	10-29-1779	Joel Sugg	Thomas Goff	1 A; £50. Former owner: George Sugg, dec. Wit.: Geo. Wolfenden
557	10-27-1779	Thomas Crowson	Geo. Falconer	8 A; £40. Wit.: James Stockdale
558	10-12-1780	John Jones, blacksmith	John Jordan	170 A; £10,000. Former owner: Wm. Speir (Pat. 1761)
559	7-22-1780	William Moreing	Peter Diggins	½ A. lott #85; £180. Wit.: Jesse Moye, Richard Moye
560	5- 8-1801	Wm. Eastwood, Sheriff	Henry Smith	100 A; £6+. Men.: David Smith, father of Henry Smith, grantee. Former owner: John Conner, dec. Wit.: Geo. Green
562	4-22-1801	Elizabeth Pugh, widow	Lewis Cox Bryan, in trust	640 A. Elizabeth Pugh, widow of Hugh Pugh, Jr., to marry Jonathan Fellows, blacksmith, of CRAV. Former owner: Hugh Pugh, Jr.
566	10-17-1801	Parker Lacey	John Jones	—. Wit.: Ben Tison, Joseph Fulford

F 547-566

DEED BOOK F (1774-1801)

Page	Date	Grantor	Grantee	Additional Information
567	4-16-1801	Charles Judkins	John Noble	100 A; £90. Wit.: Thomas Bryan
568	2-19-1801	James Powell	William Broome	41 A; £25. Men.: John Haven (Pat. 1773). Wit.: Aaron Atkinson, John Jackson
571	1-25-1801	Solomon Cherry	John Maning	150 A; £50. Wit.: William Cherry
572	4-26-1801	Simon Keel and William Keel	Solomon Jolly	— A; $200. Wit.: Thos. Daniel, Watkinson Wynn
573	3-28-1801	John Gilbert	Silas Gilbert	— A; £35. Wit.: Jesse Barnhill
574		Sarah Session	Thomas Chance	25 A; £50.
577	10-16-1800	John Mooring	Wm. Mooring, son	Negroes; love & aff. Wit.: Josiah Carney, Pleasant Little
578	1- 3-1801	Samuel Vines (BEAU)	Benjamin May, Jr.	158½ A; $435. Men.: Wm. Vines, father of Samuel Vines. Wit.: Stephen Rogers, Thomas Hall
579	12-23-1800	James Baker	John B. Baker	Goods; — Former owner: Jesse Baker. Wit.: Elias Carr
580	12- 1-1800	Charles Tripp	Solomon Richards	100 A; $150. Wit.: Joshua Tucker, Wm. Braxton
581	5-16-1795	Thomas Person (GRANV)	Sharpe Blount	525 A in Guilford Co.; £5.

GRANT BOOK G (1779-1784)

Page	Date	Grantee	Grant for	Additional Information (CB denotes chain bearers.)
1	7- 1-1779	Thomas Albritton	300 A.	CB: Richard Albritton, John Albritton
2	7- 1-1779	Archibalt Adams, Jr.	600 A.	——
3	7- 1-1779	Wm. Eastwood	100 A.	CB: Peter Moye, Archibald Adams
4	7- 1-1779	Sampson Slater	400 A.	CB: Benjamin King, David Williams
5	7- 1-1779	Sampson Slater	50 A.	Men.: John May
6	7- 1-1779	Henry Moore	300 A.	——
7	7- 1-1779	Peter Moss	250 A.	——
8	7- 1-1779	John Moy	640 A.	——
9	7- 1-1779	Benjamin May	500 A.	Men.: George Wilson
10	7- 1-1779	Richard Williams	350 A.	CB: James May, Robert Williams. Men.: Dempsy Allen
11	7- 1-1779	John Braxton	200 A.	CB: Thos. Braxton, Paul Deal
12	7- 1-1779	John Fulford	200 A.	CB: James Braxton, John Braxton
13	7- 1-1779	Thomas Braxton	100 A.	CB: Adam Langham, Paul Herrington
14	7- 1-1779	Thomas Hardee	300 A.	CB: Fedrick Mills, James Hancock
15	7- 1-1779	James Brooks	100 A.	CB: William Hattock, Admiral Hattock
16	7- 1-1779	James Brooks	100 A.	——
17	7- 1-1779	Joseph Boyd	400 A.	CB: Theo. Arnold, Rolin Dixon
18	7- 1-1779	William Slauter	200 A.	CB: George McGowns, Sampson Slater
19	7- 1-1779	John Price	100 A.	CB: Wm. Moore, Jordan Moore
20	7- 1-1779	Samuel Simmons	150 A.	CB: Sampson Slater, William Hellen
21	7- 1-1779	William Moore	640 A.	CB: William Brantly, Jordan Moore
22	7- 1-1779	Richard Gay	300 A.	CB: Samuel Davis, Wm. Moore, Jr.
23	7- 1-1779	Samuel Stokes	350 A.	CB: George Moye, James Speir
24	7- 1-1779	John Williams	79½ A.	CB: John Corbit, Merday Corbitt
25	7- 1-1779	Abraham Adams	400 A.	——
26	7- 1-1779	Jacob Blount	200 A.	CB: John Barber, John Sirman
27	7- 1-1779	Isaac Stocks	100 A.	CB: William Hardee, Isaac Stocks, Jr.
28	7-17——	Frederick Mills	300 A.	CB: Thos. Hardee, Jr., Jas. Hancock
29	7- 1-1779	Samuel Stafford	450 A.	CB: Henry Ellis, John Ellis
30	7- 1-1779	George McGowns	100 A.	CB: Wm. McGowns, John McGowns
31	7- 1-1779	Samuel Davis	300 A.	CB: William Brantley, Jordan Moore
32	7- 1-1779	James Jones	200 A.	CB: Thomas Arnold, Joseph Boyde
33	7- 1-1779	John Hardee, Jr.	200 A.	CB: Archibald Adams, Robert Hardee
34	7- 1-1779	John Watkins	520 A.	CB: Robert Boyde, John Salter

GRANT BOOK G (1779-1784)

Page	Date	Grantee	Grant for	Additional Information (CB denotes chain bearers.)
35	7- 1-1779	Wm. Corbett	450 A.	Men.: John Corbett, Marday Corbett. CB: James Handberry, Joseph Mathews
36	7- 1-1779	Marday Corbitt	321 A.	CB: John Williams, John Corbitt
37	7- 1-1779	James Armstrong	208 A.	CB: Thos. Arnold, Joseph Boyde
38	7- 1-1779	Robert Salter	134 A.	CB: Jacob Millison, Major Harris
39	7- 1-1779	Joseph Forbes	150 A.	CB: Zachariah Allen, Benj. Smith
40	7- 1-1779	Phillip Pippin	150 A.	CB: Daniel Pipkin, John Moye
41	7- 1-1779	David Williams	400 A.	CB: John Williams, Sampson Slauter
42	7- 1-1779	Benj. Blount	45 A.	CB: Thos. Ringold, John Dowdee
43	7- 1-1779	Joseph Walls	100 A.	CB: Joseph Walls, Jr., Thos. Godley
44	7- 1-1779	Ephraim Herrington	100 A.	CB: Thomas Braxton, Adam Langham
45	7- 1-1779	Paul Deale	200 A.	CB: John Cannon, John Braxton
46	7- 1-1779	Sterling Dupree	426 A.	CB: Henry Sturdivant, Marday Corbitt. Men.: James Dupree, Benjamin Dupree, Mathew Owen
47	7- 1-1779	Reading Blount	640 A.	CB: Ralph Richards, James Knox
48	7- 1-1779	John Grist	100 A.	CB: Benjamin Grist, Joseph Walls
49	10-21-1782	James Latham	140 A.	CB: Obediah Moore, Isaac Boyde
50	10-21-1782	James Latham	200 A.	CB: John Ball, Ephraim Brown
51	10-21-1782	James Latham	640 A.	CB: Obediah Moore, Isaac Boyde
52	10-21-1782	John Salter	200 A.	CB: Obediah Moore, Isaac Boyde
53	10-21-1782	David Perkins	400 A.	CB: Richard Wallace, James Griffin
54	10-21-1782	David Perkins	50 A.	CB: Joshua Oliver, Joseph Harvey
55	10-21-1782	Joel Sugg	100 A.	CB: James Lanier, River Jordan
56	10-21-1782	Richard Moye	40 A.	CB: John Moye, Jonathan Jolley
57	10-21-1782	Richard Moye	150 A.	CB: William Moye, Joel Moye
58	10-21-1782	Richard Moye	70 A.	CB: Jonathan Jolley, John Moye
59	10-21-1782	Martin Nelson	115 A.	CB: James Nelson, Samuel Nelson
60	10-21-1782	Jacob Blount	50 A.	CB: Will Moye, William Joyner
61	10-21-1782	Matthew Randolph	16 A.	CB: Benjamin Dupree, Joel Lockhart. Men.: Matthew Sturdivant
62	10-21-1782	James Blackston	200 A.	CB: John Braxton, James Braxton, Jr.
63	10-21-1782	Arthur Forbes	200 A.	CB: Arthur Dean, Joseph Forbes
64	10-21-1782	Shadrach Wooten	100 A.	CB: John Wooten, Charles Edwards
65	10-21-1782	John Powers	200 A.	CB: John Williams, Jr, Joseph Page, Jr.
66	10-21-1782	Benjamin Barrow	100 A.	CB: Shadrach Moore, Elisha Moore

GRANT BOOK G (1779-1784)

Page	Date	Grantee	Grant for	Additional Information (CB denotes chain bearers.)
67	10-21-1782	Israel Joyner	100 A.	CB: Joseph Barber, John Barber
68	10-21-1782	James Griffin	150 A.	CB: David Perkins, Richard Wallace
69	10-21-1782	John Gray Blount	640 A.	CB: Joseph Boyde, Samuel Elks
70	10-21-1782	John Gray Blount	100 A.	CB: John Kennedy, James Bonner (Col.)
71	10-21-1782	John Gray Blount	169 A.	CB: Bryan Blount, Stephen Harding
72	10-21-1782	John Gray Blount	60 A.	CB: John Kennedy, James Bonner
73	10-21-1782	John Gray Blount	192 A.	CB: Thos. Godley, Benj. Godley
74	10-21-1782	John Gray Blount	400 A.	CB: Joseph Boyde, Samuel Elks
75	10-21-1782	Nathan Godley, Jr.	187 A.	CB: Benjamin Grist, Thos. Godley
76	10-21-1782	Nathan Godley	115 A.	Men: Thomas Lattinghouse. CB: Thomas Godley, Nathan Godley, Jr.
77	10-21-1782	Nathan Godley	124 A.	CB: Thomas Godley, Benjamin Godley
78	10-21-1782	Nathan Godley	182 A.	
79	10-21-1782	Lewis Blount	150 A.	CB: Geo. Hill Pearce, John Godley
80	10-21-1782	Mathew Hodges	640 A.	
80	10-21-1782	Henry Hodges	640 A.	CB: Jesse Proctor, William Warren, William Hodges
81	10-21-1782	Mathew Hodges	200 A.	CB: Floyd Hodges, William Hodges
82	10-21-1782	Mathew Hodges	300 A.	CB: John Dowden, Samuel Williams
83	10-21-1782	Mathew Hodges	100 A.	Men.: William Martin
84	10-21-1782	Mathew Hodges	274 A.	CB: John Hodges, Charles Whitehead
85	10-21-1782	Mathew Hodges	100 A.	
86	10-21-1782	Mathew Hodges	100 A.	CB: William Stewart
87	10-21-1782	Samuel Nelson	100 A.	CB: Martin Nelson, James Nelson
88	10-21-1782	Levi Nobles	100 A.	CB: John Buck, Thomas Smith
89	10-21-1782	Levi Nobles	100 A.	CB: Charles Tillesby, John Nelson
90	10-21-1782	Jeremiah Lester	200 A.	CB: Samuel Bullock, Nathaniel Bullock
91	10-21-1782	Jeremiah Lester	30 A.	
92	10-21-1782	James Johnson, Sr.	640 A.	CB: Abraham Joiner, Benjamin Jordan. Men.: James May
93	10-21-1782	Jessee Proctor	200 A.	CB: Benjamin Dupree, Gabriel Allen
94	10-21-1782	Joseph Page, Jr.	150 A.	CB: William Page, John Powers. Men.: Benjamin May, William Page
95	10-21-1782	James Cottenhead	400 A.	CB: Samuel Wheatly, Joel Whitfield
96	10-21-1782	George Falconer	15 A.	CB: Bradbury Teel, William Teel
97	10-21-1782	George Falconer	10 A.	
98	10-21-1782	George Falconer	15 A.	
99	10-21-1782	Lazarus Pearce	150 A.	CB: Joseph Slade, Andrew Willebee, Jr.

GRANT BOOK G (1779-1784)

Page	Date	Grantee	Grant for	Additional Information (CB denotes chain bearers.)
100	10-21-1782	Daniel Demcy Moss	200 A.	CB: William Rountree, John Dew. Men.: James Spivey
101	10-21-1782	George Pearce	289 A.	CB: James Edwards, Charles Hattaway
102	10-21-1782	John Salter	300 A.	CB: Edward Salter, John Watkins
103	10-21-1782	Isaac Balderee	100 A.	CB: Moses Tison, John Low
104	10-21-1782	Lemuel Cherry	100 A.	CB: William Moreing, Thomas English
105	10-21-1782	Lemuel Cherry	100 A.	CB: Henry Hodges, Samson Slater. Men.: William Slaughter
106	10-21-1782	Starling Dupree	50 A.	CB: Benjamin Dupree, Burd Dupree. Men.: Gabriel Allen
107	10-21-1782	William Brierly	42 A.	CB: Abner Proctor, James Robson
108	10-21-1782	Samuel Nelson	200 A.	CB: Martin Nelson, Daniel Nelson
109	10-21-1782	John Hardee	150 A.	CB: Isaac Hardee, Abraham Hardee
110	10-21-1782	Godfrey Stancil	104 A.	CB: Mathew Luter, Joel Nicholson
111	10-21-1782	Godfrey Stancil	126 A.	CB: Luke Osborn, James Cottenhead. Men.: William Stansel Crisp, Mary May
112	10-21-1782	Godfrey Stancil	100 A.	CB: Joel Nicholson, Wm. Nicholson. Men.: Benj. Nicholson
113	10-21-1782	Gabriel Allen	160 A.	CB: Thos. Belcher, Nathan Lewis. Men.: Richard Proctor, Sterling Dupree
114	10-21-1782	Davis Vance	250 A.	CB: John Brinkley
115	10-21-1782	Joseph Wall	150 A.	CB: Nathan Godley, Joseph Wall, Jr.
116	10-21-1782	Joseph Wall	40 A.	CB: John Wall
117	10-21-1782	Joseph Wall, Sr.	80 A.	CB: John Grist
118	10-21-1782	John Jordan	640 A.	CB: John Cherry, Solomon Whichard
119	10-21-1782	John Jordan	469 A.	CB: Samuel Barrow, Wm. Jordan. Men.: Thomas James
120	10-21-1782	Thomas Braxton	100 A.	CB: Thomas Garrett, Ephraim Herrington
121	10-21-1782	Isaac Hardee	250 A.	CB: William King, Thomas Corey
122	10-21-1782	Richard Grist	200 A.	CB: Joseph Slade, Andrew Willebeigh. Men.: Stephen Harding
123	10-21-1782	Richard Grist	500 A.	CB: Benj. Grist, Isaac Nobles. Men.: Lewis Blount
124	10-21-1782	Edward Sirman	105 A.	CB: Michael Coutanche Evans, William Dixon, Josiah Gorman
125	10-21-1782	Joseph Boyde	200 A.	CB: Isaac Boyde, Solomon Ward
126	10-21-1782	Joseph Boyde	100 A.	
127	10-21-1782	Richard Grist	150 A.	CB: Stephen Harding, Willis Whitehead. Men.: Thomas Worsley, Joshua Hill
128	10-21-1782	James Spivey	100 A.	CB: Daniel Morlain, Eli Sirman
129	10-21-1782	Lemuel James	100 A.	CB: John James, Mathew James
130	10-21-1782	Lemuel James	80 A.	

GRANT BOOK G (1779-1784)

Page	Date	Grantee	Grant for	Additional Information (CB denotes chain bearers.)
131	10-21-1782	John James	50 A.	CB: Joshua James, Enoch Daniel
132	10-21-1782	Isaac Little	14 A.	CB: Samuel Clarke, Christopher Moreing. Men.: John Moreing
133	10-21-1782	Thomas Chance	150 A.	CB: William Knox, Josiah Knox
134	10-21-1782	Thomas Chance	200 A.	Men.: Edmund Andrews
135	10-21-1782	Edmund Andrews	320 A.	CB: Thomas Chance, John Ward. Men.: Benjamin Blount
136	10-21-1782	Edmund Andrews	640 A.	Men.: Walter Session, Joseph Bullock
137	10-21-1782	John Hatton	200 A.	CB: John Hatton, Jr., John Barber, Jr. Men.: Kelly Tucker, Peter Ambrose
138	10-21-1782	John Hatton	60 A.	
139	10-21-1782	Major Harriss	100 A.	CB: John Barber, Jr., Wm. Harris, Jr. Men.: John Hatton, William Barber
140	10-21-1782	Levi Andrews	100 A.	CB: Josiah Bullock, Thos. Cason. Men.: Reuben Manning, Benj. Wilkerson
141	10-21-1782	Richard Allen	20 A.	CB: Paul Allen, Benjamin Keeps
142	10-21-1782	Martin Nelson	200 A.	CB: Thomas Arnol, Joseph Stevens. Men.: John Watkins
143	10-27-1782	Daniel Buntin	125 A.	CB: James Edmundson, Stephen Blann. Men.: John Holland
144	10-21-1782	Francis Hataway	60 A.	CB: Geo. Hill Pearce, John Nobles. Men.: Jacob Palmer
145	10-21-1782	Batson Whitehouse	200 A.	CB: Daniel Bullock, Levi Andrews. Men.: Isaac Rogers, Peter Martin
146	10-21-1782	Thomas Lathinghouse	100 A.	CB: Andrew Lathinghouse, Young Lathinghouse. Men.: Elias Hodge
147	10-21-1782	Batson Whitehouse	200 A.	
148	10-21-1782	Batson Whitehouse	400 A.	
149	10-21-1782	Aaron Tison	320 A.	CB: Isaac Baldree, Spier Holland. Men.: Richard Evans, Edmund Tyson, Michael Evans
150	10-21-1782	Henry Tantor	150 A.	CB: John Williams, Jr.
151	10-21-1782	Frederick Tison	82 A.	CB: Job Tison, Jacob Tison. Men.: Jesse Jordan, John Tison
152	10-21-1782	Benj. Wilkerson	400 A.	CB: James Nicholson, Wm. Wilkerson
153	10-21-1782	Benj. Wilkerson	200 A.	
154	10-21-1782	Solomon Ward	320 A.	CB: Abner Eason, Samuel Davis
155	10-21-1782	John Ward	500 A.	CB: Ephraim Bullock, William Sessions. Men.: Josiah Bullock, Archibald Knox, Joseph Page
156	10-21-1782	Samuel Warren	100 A.	CB: Samuel Browen, Arthur Browen
157	10-21-1782	Edward Williams, Sr.	640 A.	CB: Richard Williams, Henry Stokes. Men.: Shadrack Williams
158	10-21-1782	John Kennedy	150 A.	CB: James Bonner, Jr., Joseph Walls. Men.: William Grist
159	10-21-1782	Simeon Jones	600 A.	CB: John Salter, Stephen Ward
160	10-21-1782	Thomas Tison	400 A.	CB: John Ellis, Burrell Bell. Men.: Wm. Baldwyn, John Tison
161	10-21-1782	William Hart	157 A.	CB: Wm. Peoples, Benj. Smith

GRANT BOOK G (1779-1784)

Page	Date	Grantee	Grant for	Additional Information (CB denotes chain bearers.)
162	10-21-1782	Edmund Hatterway	100 A.	CB: Robert Meeks, John Windham. Men.: William Perry, John Meeks, Joseph Little
163	10-21-1782	Thos. Hattaway, Sr.	50 A.	CB: Thomas Hatteway, Jr., Enos Norvill. Men.: David Hatterway
164	10-21-1782	Jesse Jolley	420 A.	CB: Frederick Bryan, Reuben Manning
165	10-21-1782	William Knox	80 A.	CB: Thomas Chance, Joseph Knox
166	10-21-1782	Isaac Eason	100 A.	CB: Abner Eason, Stephen Eason. Men.: Wm. Moore, Sr.
167	10-21-1782	Thomas Gwaltney	56 A.	CB: William Brady, Ephraim Evans
168	1-14-1783	John Hardee	580 A.	CB: Abraham Hardee, William Hellen. Men.: Lemuel Cherry
169	10-21-1782	Simon Taylor	400 A.	CB: Sam Elks, William Elks. Men.: Jacob Taylor, Joseph Boyd
170	10-21-1782	Nathaniel Lanier	50 A.	CB: Watkins Hart, Charles Allen. Men.: Samuel Stafford
171	10-21-1782	Nathaniel Lanier	300 A.	CB: Watkins Hart, Charles Allen. Men.: Wm. Baldwyn, Samuel Stafford
172	10-21-1782	James Lanier	242 A.	CB: Williami Bell, Benjamin Smith
173	10-21-1782	Moses Moore	100 A.	CB: Nathan Nobles, Caleb Moore. Men.: John Page
174	10-21-1782	Isaac Nobles	100 A.	CB: Francis Hattaway, James Edwards
175	10-21-1782	Jacob Palmer	123 A.	CB: George Palmer, Isaac Nobles. Men.: Richard Grist, Edward Salter
176	10-21-1782	John Bowers	83 A.	Men.: Jonathan Taylor
177	10-21-1782	Roland Dixon	193 A.	CB: Ralph Richards, John Buck. Men.: Edward Salter, Joseph Boyd, Reading Blount
178	10-21-1782	Francis Crisp	100 A.	CB: Joel Whitfield, Samuel Whitley. Men.: Aleaxnder Whitley, Robert Williams, William Pulle
179	10-21-1782	John Cason	550 A.	CB: William James, Emanuel Daniel. Men.: Lemuel James, Henry Cason, Joseph James, Robert Daniel, John Jordan
180	10-21-1782	Solomon Cherry	95 A.	CB: James Edmundson, Stephen Blann
181	10-21-1782	Solomon Cherry	100 A.	Men.: William Osborn
182	10-21-1782	John Bowers	135 A.	CB: William House, Joshua Taylor
183	10-21-1782	John Braxton	250 A.	CB: James Braxton, James Braxton, Jr. Men.: John Simpson William Joiner
184	10-21-1782	James Brown	150 A.	CB: Samuel Warren, Arthur Brown. Men.: Samuel May
185	10-21-1782	William Baldwin	97 A.	CB: John Ellis, Burrell Bell. Men.: John Tison
186	10-21-1782	Wm. Balderee	97 A.	CB: Corse Adams, Kelly Tucker. Men.: John Jones
187	10-21-1782	Wm. Speir	250 A.	CB: Floyd Hodges, Robert Hodges
188	10-21-1782	Nathan Nelson	300 A.	CB: Job Smith, Thomas Smith
189	10-21-1782	Jesse Jordan	22 A.	CB: Jacob Tison, Job Tison. Men.: Frederick Tison
190	10-21-1782	John Mayo	200 A.	CB: James Jones, Edward Salter. Men.: Thomas Arnold

GRANT BOOK G (1779-1784)

Page	Date	Grantee	Grant for	Additional Information (CB denotes chain bearers.)
191	10-21-1782	John Fleming	240 A.	CB: Robert Flake, David Flemming. Men.: William Mitchel, Wm. Robson, Abner Proctor, John Little
192	10-21-1782	Henry Cason	160 A.	CB: John James, Mathew James. Men.: Lemuel James
193	10-21-1782	Joshua James	640 A.	CB: Henry James, William James. Men.: John Wallis, Robert Lanier Daniel, John Cason, Lemuel James
194	10-21-1782	Simon Taylor	52 A.	CB: Pollas Avery, Samuel Elks
195	10-21-1782	Simon Taylor	5 A.	CB: Apollas Avery. Men.: Col. John Simpson, William Dixon
196	10-21-1782	George Walston	190 A.	CB: William Corbett, Ezekiel Coats. Men.: Benjamin May
197	10-21-1782	Nathaniel Moore	640 A.	CB: Thomas Duffil, acob Tison. Men.: John May, John Tison
198	10-21-1782	George Evans	150 A.	CB: William Dixon, Michael Evans. Men.: Thomas Armstrong, James English
199	10-21-1782	John Fry	300 A.	CB: Edward Sirman, Men.: William Moore
200	10-21-1782	George Falconer	10 A.	CB: Bradbury Teal, William Teal. Men.: Wm. Harris, Sr.
201	10-21-1782	Jesse Moye	45 A.	CB: Abraham Barber, John Barber. Men.: George Moye, Israel Joiner, John Willson
202	10-21-1782	Phillip Knowis	200 A.	CB: James Crandell, William Little
203	10-21-1782	John Ball	200 A.	CB: Jesse Swanner, John Ball, Jr. Men.: James Bonner
204	10-21-1782	Mary Winkle	550 A.	Men.: Edward Flanagan, George Willson
205	10-21-1782	Joseph Breely	100 A.	Men.: Jonas Shivers, Robert Flake
206	10-21-1782	Thomas Davis	45 A.	Men.: Robert Flake
207	10-21-1782	Hillery Cason	200 A.	Men.: John Jones
208	10-21-1782	Henry Hodges	500 A.	CB: Michael Moses, Henry Smith. Men.: Col. Wm. Speir, Mathew Hodges
209	10-21-1782	Benjamin Hodges	73 A.	Men.: Edward Salter, Robert Hodges
210	10-21-1782	Abraham Adams	300 A.	CB: Michael Moses. Men.: Shade Allen
211	10-21-1782	William Averett	100 A.	Men.: Thomas Sumerling, David Averett
212	10-21-1782	John Church	244 A.	CB: Thos. S. Summerlin, Thos. Summerlin, Jr. Men.: Isaac Church
213	10-21-1782	Robert Hodges	49 A.	Men.: Edward Salter, Mathew Hodges
214	10-21-1782	Robert Hodges	337 A.	Men.: Benj. Hodges
215	10-21-1782	Parker Lacey	8 A.	CB: Caleb Ewell, Isaac Little
216	10-21-1782	Thomas Downs	400 A.	CB: William Corbitt, Joseph Martin. Men.: Henry Tant, Shadrach Wooten, John Powers
217	10-21-1782	William Peoples	250 A.	CB: Benj. Smith, Averett Pope
218	10-21-1782	James Sampson Clarke	8 A.	CB: Ephraim Evans
219	10-21-1782	William Robson	100 A.	CB: Soverin Robson, Parker Lacey

GRANT BOOK G (1779-1784)

Page	Date	Grantee	Grant for	Additional Information (CB denotes chain bearers.)
220	10-21-1782	William Robson	100 A.	CB: Parker Lacey, Lawrence Anderson
221	10-21-1782	William Robson	300 A.	
222	10-21-1782	William Robson	20 A.	
223	10-21-1782	William Robson	30 A.	James Sampson Clark, Nehemiah Wooten. Men.: John Herrinton
224	10-21-1782	Peter Rives	200 A.	CB: Robert Rives, Joseph Gremmer. Men.: Benj. Womble, Nicholas Bynum
225	10-21-1782	Soveron Roberson	75 A.	CB: John Roberson, Nathan May. Men.: William Roberson
226	10-21-1782	John Roberson	16 A.	CB: Thomas Jordan, Edmund Reeks
227	10-21-1782	John Roberson	20 A.	CB: William Roberson. Men.: Jonas Shivers
228	10-21-1782	John Roberson	100 A.	
229	10-21-1782	John Roberson	640 A.	CB: Drury Spain, Bradbury Teel. Men.: William Teal, Thos. Gwaltney
230	10-21-1782	Robt. Hardee	100 A.	CB: Josiah Hardee, Isaac Hardee. Men.: Anna Dixon
231	10-21-1782	Dempsey Right Allen	46 A.	CB: Samuel Stokes, James Evans. Men.: Reading Stokes
232	10-21-1782	James Avery	100 A.	CB: Robert Meeks, Green Windham. Men.: Edmund Hattaway
233	10-21-1782	Peter Adams	150 A.	CB: John Hatton, John Barber. Men.: Kelly Tucker, Wm. Barber, Robert Salter, Wm. Baldwyn
234	10-21-1782	James Barrow	400 A.	CB: Wm. James, Enoch Dixon. Men.: Nathan Cherry
235	10-21-1782	Samuel Barrow	150 A.	CB: John Jordan, John Cherry. Men.: James Barrow
236	10-21-1782	Edward Gatlin	640 A.	CB: John Ward, John Catto. Men.: Benj. Blount, Edmund Andrews, Batson Whitehouse
237	10-21-1782	Samuel Joiner	150 A.	CB: John Barber, Levi Sirman. Men.: Jacob Blount
238	10-21-1782	Henry James	100 A.	CB: Joshua James, William James
239	10-21-1782	Archibald Knox	200 A.	CB: William Sessions, Ephraim Bullock. Men.: John Ward, Know Page, Josiah Bullock
240	10-21-1782	George Little	50 A.	CB: James Cremain, William Little
241	10-21-1782	William Little	240 A.	CB: Samuel Dudley, John Dowden. Men.: Mathew Hodges
242	10-21-1782	Thomas Summerling	100 A.	CB: John Church. Timothy Cello. Men.: David Averet, William Averet
243	10-21-1782	Joseph Page	85 A.	CB: Ephraim Bullock, Wm. Sessions
244	10-21-1782	Thomas Walston	640 A.	CB: Joseph Page, John Powers. Men.: Benjamin May, James Moor
245	10-21-1782	Benjamin Womble	9 A.	CB: Elisha Womble, James Brady. Men.: Peter Reeves
246	10-21-1782	Solomon Shepard	200 A.	CB: Charles Whitehead, Wm. Stewart. Men.: Mathew Hodges, Stewart Oliphant
247	10-21-1782	Solomon Shepard	60 A.	Men.: William Warren
248	10-21-1782	Lewis Smith	120 A.	CB: Benjamin May, John May
249	10-21-1782	John Tison	150 A.	CB: Geo. Moye, Jr., Samuel Husey. Men.: John Joiner

GRANT BOOK G (1779-1784)

Page	Date	Grantee	Grant for	Additional Information (CB denotes chain bearers.)
250	10-21-1782	John Moye	420 A.	CB: William Winkles, Edward Flannagan. Men.: John May
251	10-21-1782	George Moye	200 A.	CB: Barrain Hart, Joab Tison. Men.: John Joiner
252	10-21-1782	Arthur Moore	640 A.	CB: Shadrach Moore, Elisha Moore. Men.: Wm. Johnston, William Joiner
253	10-21-1782	Arthur Moore	200 A.	CB: Benj. Barrow
254	10-21-1782	Simon Meeks	100 A.	CB: Robert Meeks, William Mosely. Men.: Thomas Hattaway
255	10-21-1782	William Mosely	100 A.	CB: Robert Meeks, Able Thomas. Men.: Thomas Hatterway
256	10-21-1782	Benjamin May	150 A.	CB: Moses Tison, Abraham Tison. Men.: Benjamin Barrow, Frederick Becton, Cornelius Tison
257	10-21-1782	Benjamin May	100 A.	CB: Moses Tison, John May
258	10-21-1782	Benjamin May	200 A.	CB: Thomas Walston, William Page. Men.: John May
259	10-21-1782	Benjamin May	160 A.	CB: William Fatheree, John May. Men.: Nathaniel Moore
260	10-21-1782	Dempsey Grimes	75 A.	CB: John Buck, John Homes. Men.: John Hackburne
261	10-21-1782	Jonas Shivers	640 A.	CB: Wm. Teel, Abram Briley. Men.: Levi Adams, Joseph Briley, Parker Lacey
262	10-21-1782	Dennis Cannon	400 A.	CB: Dennis Cannon, Jr., Lewis Cannon. Men.: Reading Blount, John Cannon
263	10-21-1782	Robert Hart	200 A.	CB: Benjamin Smith, Abraham Tison
264	10-21-1782	Robert Hart	100 A.	Men.: Moses Tison
265	10-21-1782	Edward Dixon	200 A.	CB: Lemuel Golding, John Dixson. Men.: Peter Albritton, Richard Powell
266	10-21-1782	Isaac Rogers	400 A.	CB: Batson Whitehouse, Peter Martin. Men.: Thomas Cason
267	10-21-1782	Anthony Whichard	100 A.	CB: John Moore, John Vainwright. Men.: Anna Pinket
268	10-21-1782	Anna Pinket	100 A.	Men.: William Cousall
269	10-21-1782	Wm. Lanier, Jr.	300 A.	CB: Seth Lanier, Randal McDaniel. Men.: Thos. Williams
270	10-21-1782	Seth Lanier	640 A.	CB: William Lanier. Men.: Thos. Williams
271	10-21-1782	Abraham Tison	130 A.	CB: Moses Tison, Jacob Tison
272	10-21-1782	James Crandell	100 A.	CB: John Baull, Josiah Little. Men.: James Bonner
273	10-21-1782	James Crandell	300 A.	CB: Josiah Little, Philip Knowis
274	10-21-1782	James Crandell	200 A.	CB: Henry Hodges, James Hodges
275	10-21-1782	Daniel Maclain	100 A.	Men.: Daniel Oqwin, John Braxton
276	10-21-1782	James Cobb, Sr.	400 A.	CB: Edward Cobb, Thomas Lewis. Men.: John Hearn, Jacob Summerlin, Jacob Atkinson
277	10-21-1782	James Cobb, Sr.	170 A.	———
278	10-21-1782	James Cobb, Jr.	100 A.	CB: Edward Cobb. Men.: Jacob Atkinson
279	10-21-1782	James English	640 A.	CB: Noah Tison, Wm. Mooreing. Men.: George Evans, Thomas Armstrong

GRANT BOOK G (1779-1784)

Page	Date	Grantee	Grant for	Additional Information (CB denotes chain bearers.)
280	10-21-1782	Henry Ellis for Simon Pope, orphan	77 A.	CB: Sadrach Ellis, John Ellis. Men.: Simon Pope, dec.
281	10-21-1782	George Daniel	535 A.	CB: Thomas James. Men.: John Cason, Robert Daniel
282	10-21-1782	Robert Lanier Daniel	560 A.	CB: Thomas James, George Daniel
283	10-21-1782	Robert Lanier Daniel	500 A.	CB: George Daniel, Enoch Daniel
284	10-21-1782	Mealus Browne	200 A.	CB: Phillip Pipkin, John Bently. Men.: Judith Bently, John Moye
285	10-21-1782	Josiah Little	150 A.	CB: James Crandell, Philip Knowis
286	10-21-1782	William Johnston	500 A.	CB: Israel Joiner
287	10-21-1782	Samuel May	140 A.	CB: Peter May, William May
288	10-21-1782	John Watkins	125 A.	CB: Edward Salter, James Gorham. Men.: Thomas Arnold
289	10-21-1782	John Wallace	500 A.	CB: Richard Wallace, Wm. Smith
290	10-21-1782	John Wallis	139 A.	CB: Richard Wallis, James Congleton
291	10-21-1782	Samuel Ellkes	200 A.	CB: Obediah Moore, Wm. Ellkes. Men.: Reading Blount
292	10-21-1782	Samuel Ellkes	400 A.	Men.: John Haddock
293	10-21-1782	Samuel Ellks	200 A.	—
294	10-21-1782	Ralph Richards	203 A.	CB: Thomas Richards, John Horne
295	10-21-1782	Benj. Paxton	100 A.	CB: John Buck, Walter Dixon. Men.: James Buck, Edward Salter, Henry Moore
296	10-21-1782	Frederick Mills	250 A.	CB: Thomas Hardee, James Hancock. Men.: James Brooks, Able Deale
297	10-21-1782	Thomas Pollard	150 A.	CB: Anthony Mills
298	10-21-1782	Thomas Pollard	300 A.	—
299	10-21-1782	Hardee Stevens	162 A.	CB: Anthony Mills, Frederick Pollard. Men.: Samuel Smith
300	10-21-1782	John Cannon	300 A.	CB: Thomas Granger, Caleb Cannon. Men.: Dennis Cannon, Solomon Sutton
301	10-21-1782	Howell Hodges	200 A.	Men.: James Dudley, Samuel Dudley
302	10-21-1782	Thomas Hardee	150 A.	—
303	10-21-1782	Benj. Corey	100 A.	Men.: Anna Dixon
304	10-21-1782	Josiah Bullouck	140 A.	—
305	10-21-1782	Joseph Page, Jr.	100 A.	Men.: William Page
306	10-21-1782	Shadrach Moore	500 A.	Men.: Elijah Moore, Benj. Barrow, Arthur Moore
307	10-21-1782	Job Smith	80 A.	Men.: Nathan Nelson
308	10-21-1782	Lawrence Anderson	183 A.	CB: John Anderson, Henry Anderson. Men.: Benj. Bowers
309	10-21-1782	Lawrence Anderson	50 A.	—
310	10-21-1782	Lawrence Anderson	95 A.	CB: Benj. Bowers, Jr., Will Bowers

GRANT BOOK G (1779-1784)

Page	Date	Grantee	Grant for	Additional Information (CB denotes chain bearers.)
311	10-21-1782	Parker Lacey	43 A.	
312	10-21-1782	Thomas James	400 A.	CB: James Griffith, Abraham Congleton. Men.: John Jordan
313	10-21-1782	Thomas James	400 A.	CB: Robert Daniel, Geo. Daniel
314	10-21-1782	Parker Lacey	50 A.	CB: David Green, John Lacey
315	10-21-1782	Parker Lacey	50 A.	
316	10-21-1782	Benjamin Smith	198 A.	CB: Benj. Buck, Job Smith
317	10-21-1782	Jesse Swanner	50 A.	CB: John Ball, Josiah Little
318	10-21-1782	Flowers Summerlin	54 A.	CB: Green Windham, Enos Norvall. Men.: Benj. Windham, Thos. Hattaway
319	10-21-1782	Geo. Wolfenden	55 A.	CB: James Swanner, Joshua Freeman. Men.: James Lanier
320	10-21-1782	William Joiner	100 A.	CB: Arthur Moore, Shadrach Moore
321	10-21-1782	James May	400 A.	CB: Samuel Truss, Demsie Allen. Men.: Richard Williams, James Williams
322	10-21-1782	James May	640 A.	CB: John Williams, Jr., Abraham Williams. Men.: John Williams, Thomas Wallace
323	10-21-1782	Henry Jones	84 A.	CB: Benj. Bynum, Rubin Bynum. Men.: Nicholas Bynum
324	10-21-1782	Thomas Arnal	175 A.	CB: Edward Salter, James Gorham. Men.: John Watkins, James Jones
325	10-21-1782	Henry Harris	300 A.	CB: David Hines, James Harris. Men.: John Joiner, Samuel Hussy
326	10-21-1782	Henry Harris	300 A.	Men.: Timothy Harris, Samuel Stokes
327	10-21-1782	James Harris	100 A.	CB: David Hines, Jr., Henry Harris. Men.: William Hart
328	10-21-1782	Timothy Harris	300 A.	
329	10-21-1782	Benj. Nicholson	640 A.	CB: Wm. Nicholson, James Nicholson
330	10-21-1782	Joel Nicholson	171 A.	CB: Godfrey Stancil. Men.: Benj. Wilkerson
331	10-21-1782	Peter May	32 A.	CB: Samuel May, Wm. May
332	10-21-1782	Joel Sugg, trust for Ambrose Jones and William Jones	200 A.	CB: Jiles Sute, Wm. Arnal. Men.: Walter Newton
333	10-21-1782	William Perry	100 A.	
334	10-21-1782	Israel Joiner	400 A.	CB: John Barber, Levi Sirman. Men.: George Moy
335	10-21-1782	Israel Joiner	200 A.	CB: Wm. Joiner, John Joiner
336	10-21-1782	Nathaniel Nobles	100 A.	CB: Moses Moor, Caleb Moor. Men.: Edward Moor
337	10-13-1783	Peter Albritain	150 A.	CB: Nehemiah Tuten, Jacob Moore
338	10-13-1783	John May, Sr.	375 A.	CB: Edward Cobb, James Cobb
339	10-13-1783	Moses Tison, Jr.	270 A.	CB: Jacob Tison, George Bland

GRANT BOOK G (1779-1784)

Page	Date	Grantee	Grant for	Additional Information (CB denotes chain bearers.)
340	10-13-1783	Moses Tison	169 A.	CB: James Tison, Henry Tison. Men.: Aron Tison, Aron Tison
341	10-13-1783	Amos Atkinson	103 A.	
342	10-13-1783	Amos Atkinson	76 A.	CB: Daniel Rogers, Jacob Atkinson. Men.: John Lee
343	10-13-1783	Thomas Grainger	145 A.	CB: Furney Cannon, Jas. Hancock
344	10-13-1783	Simon Taylor	100 A.	CB: Samuel Kite, Levi Noble
345	10-13-1783	James Lanier	222 A.	CB: Geo. Wolfenden, John Gardner. Men.: Thomas Tison
346	10-13-1783	Nathaniel Lanier	100 A.	CB: James Lanier, Richard Williams
347	10-13-1783	John Slaughter	300 A.	CB: William Furner, Samuel Slaughter
348	10-13-1783	Benjamin Brown	29 A.	CB: John Little, Samuel Brown. Men.: Joel Williams
349	10-13-1783	Isaac Eason, Sr.	350 A.	CB: Shadrach Eason, Stephen Eason. Men.: William Moore, William Stuckey
350	10-13-1783	Lazarus Pearce	175 A.	CB: James Knox, Reading Gaust. Men.: Nathan Godley
351	10-21-1782	Robert Boyd	150 A.	CB: Nathan Nelson, Simon Jones. Men.: John Salter
352	10-13-1783	Benjamin Blount	31 A.	CB: Thos. Ringold, Reading Blount
353	10-13-1783	William Edwards	300 A.	CB: Nehemiah Tuten, David Avery
354	10-21-1782	William Mosley	100 A.	CB: Robert Meeks, Abel Thomas
355	10-13-1783	John Simpson	250 A.	CB: William King, John Dreeding. Men.: John Hardee, Isaac Hardee
356	10-13-1783	Azariah Mobley	300 A.	CB: Joseph Collins. Men.: Joseph Gray, David Knox, Peter Jolly
357	10-13-1783	Thos. English	120 A.	CB: Leml. Cherry, Benj. McDonald
358	10-13-1783	Thomas English	300 A.	Men.: Lemuel Cherry
359	10-13-1783	Thos. Surmon	500 A.	CB: Wm. Turner, Thos. Hardee. Men.: Samuel Sermon
360	10-13-1783	Joseph Gainer	380 A.	CB: Chas. Whitehead, Jos. Gainer, Jr. Men.: Wm. Crafford
361	10-13-1783	David Perkins	100 A.	CB: John Jurdon, John Harvey. Men.: John Wallace, Thomas James
362	10-21-1782	David Hines, Jr.	150 A.	CB: John Tison, Henry Harris. Men.: David Hines, Sr., James Harris, Will Hart
363	10-13-1783	Samuel Kight, Sr.	100 A.	CB: William Edwards, Nehemiah Tuten, David Averet
364	10-13-1783	Benjamin May	90 A.	CB: David Askey, John May. Men.: George Walston, Lemuel DuBerry, Jurel May, Nathaniel Moore
365	10-13-1783	Joshua Thigpen	50 A.	CB: James Hanly, Solomon Smith. Men.: Mary Winkle, George Willson
366	10-13-1783	James Edmondson	85 A.	CB: Daniel Buntin, Stephen Barns. Men.: Solomon Cherry
367	10-13-1783	Daniel Buntin	70 A.	CB: James Worsley, John Taylor
368	10-13-1783	James Avery	400 A.	CB: Jonathan Nicholson
369	10-13-1783	John Taylor	50 A.	CB: John Brian. Men.: Jeremiah Taylor
370	10-13-1783	John Taylor	100 A.	CB: William Taylor. Men.: James Avery, Frederick Bryan

GRANT BOOK G (1779-1784)

Page	Date	Grantee	Grant for	Additional Information (CB denotes chain bearers.)
371	10-13-1783	William Hodges	400 A.	CB: William Warren, John Tucker. Men.: John Bawl, John Lanier
372	10-13-1783	William Davis	200 A.	CB: John Lanier, Seth Lanier. Men.: James Latham
373	10-21-1782	Benjamin Bowers	225 A.	CB: Frederick Bryan, Henry Barnhill. Men.: Jesse Jolley
374	10-13-1783	William Hopkins	100 A.	CB: William May, Charles Waldron
375	10-13-1783	John Kennedy	300 A.	CB: John Cherry, Charles Cherry
376	10-13-1783	John Cherry	375 A.	CB: Robert Warren
377	10-13-1783	John Cherry	300 A.	
378	10-13-1783	Aaron Tison	640 A.	CB: James Tison, Ichabod Tison
379	10-13-1783	Aaron Tison	320 A.	CB: Aaron Tison, Jr. Men.: George Tison
380	10-13-1783	David Knox	500 A.	CB: Joshua Harvey, Joseph Collins. Men.: Azariah Mobile, Joseph Oliver, David Perkins
381	10-13-1783	Joseph Hickman	105 A.	CB: Thomas Hattaway, Jesse Hickman. Men.: William Perry, Marcus Stookes
382	10-13-1783	Moses Dean	200 A.	CB: Anthony Dean, John Bowin. Men.: Wm. Crawford, Seth Lanier
383	10-13-1783	John Worsley	78 A.	CB: James Worsley, Pilmore Worsley
384	10-13-1783	Mathew Cartwright	30 A.	CB: Laurence Anderson, William Taylor. Men.: Robert Saunders, Benjamin Hern
385	10-13-1783	George Youbanks	200 A.	CB: John Youbank, Moses Moore. Men.: James Gorham, William Speir
386	10-13-1783	James Brown	9 A.	CB: Isaac Brown, Auter Brown. Men.: Samuel Warren
387	10-13-1783	William May	70 A.	CB: William Hopkins, Chas. Waldron
388	10-13-1783	William Clemons	100 A.	CB: Peter Jolley, David Gurganus. Men.: John Ward
389	10-13-1783	James Oliver	277 A.	CB: Robert Knox, Josiah Collings. Men.: David Knox, David Perkins
390	10-13-1783	James Gorham	178 A.	CB: Richard Wallace, John McDearman
391	10-13-1783	James Gorham	150 A.	CB: John Buck, Robert Dixon
392	10-13-1783	James Gorham	50 A.	CB: Isaac Carrell, Wm. Consol. Men.: John Harrell, Robert Daniels
393	10-13-1783	James Gorham	80 A.	
394	10-13-1783	James Gorham	48 A.	Men.: Edward Salter
395	10-13-1783	James Gorham	300 A.	Men.: John Simpson, James Speir
396	10-13-1783	James Gorham	150 A.	
397	10-13-1783	James Gorham	200 A.	
398	10-13-1783	Willis Wilson	100 A.	CB: Samuel Kite, William Willson. Men.: Andrew Hardee
399	10-13-1783	Henry Tison	200 A.	CB: Wm. Peoples, Ichabod Tison. Men.: James Tison, Aaron Tison
400	10-13-1783	James Tison	200 A.	CB: William Peoples, Ichabod Tison
401	10-13-1783	Thomas Moore	50 A.	CB: John Moore, Gabriel Cason

GRANT BOOK G (1779-1784)

Page	Date	Grantee	Grant for	Additional Information (CB denotes chain bearers.)
402	10-13-1783	John Hatton	190 A.	CB: John Hatten, Jr., William Barber
403	10-13-1783	William Robson	170 A.	CB: Wm. Nicholson. Men.: Amos Atkinson, Mathew Luter
404	10-13-1783	George Cannon	150 A.	CB: Shade Cannon, Jonathan Herrington
405	10-13-1783	George Cannon	150 A.	CB: Shadrach Cannon
406	10-13-1783	Abel Thomas	50 A.	CB: Wm. Nicholson, Solomon Windham. Men.: Thomas Hattaway
407	10-13-1783	Anne Robson	100 A.	CB: Jacob Palmer, James Palmer
408	10-13-1783	Henry Mills	300 A.	CB: Charles Smith, Nesby Mills. Men.: William Travis, Pearson Tuten
409	10-13-1783	Nesby Mills	300 A.	CB: John Brooks, Frederick Mills. Men.: David Mills, Isaac Mills
410	10-13-1783	George Sugg	150 A.	CB: Benjamin Cooper, Henry Harris
411	10-21-1782	James Bonner and John Cowper	640 A.	CB: James Bonner, Jr., Joseph Wall. Men.: Simon Grist
312	10-21-1782	John Bonner	52 A.	Men.: Col. James Bonner
413	10-21-1782	James Bonner	200 A.	CB: John Ball, Sr., John Ball, Jr.
414	10-13-1783	Benjamin Smith	200 A.	CB: John Buck, Levi Noble. Men.: Henry Moore, Benjamin Paxton, Martin Nelson, Edward Salter, Simon Taylor
415	10-13-1783	Thomas Goff	318 A.	CB: Henry Goff, Geo. Falconer. Men.: Richard Evans, Cornelius Tison, Pitt Allen, Jonathan Tison
416	10-21-1782	William Ozburn	69 A.	CB: Matthew Lewis, Luke Ozburn. Men.: Ephraim Jones
417	10-21-1782	Reading Blount	211 A.	CB: Thos. Richards, John Homes. Men.: Roland Dixon, Ralph Richards
418	10-21-1782	Reading Blount	250 A.	CB: Benjamin Grist
419	10-13-1783	Thomas Tildesley	100 A.	CB: Charles Tildesley, George Fleming. Men.: Priscilla Dixon, James Gorham, John Simpson
420	10-13-1783	Anna Pinkett	71 A.	CB: Wm. Consall, Geo. Culpepper
421	10-13-1783	Benjamin Blount	150 A.	CB: Thomas Chance, William Knox
422	10-21-1783	Jacob Brown	300 A.	CB: John Floyd, Moses Hodges
423	10-13-1783	Nicholas Bynum	16 A.	CB: Benjamin Bynum, Reuben Bynum. Men.: Richard Reeves, Thomas Jordan, Henry Jones
424	10-13-1783	Thomas Wallace	300 A.	CB: Williams, Caleb Wallace. Men.: John Butts
425	10-13-1783	Thomas Wallace	150 A.	Men.: Menjamin May
426	10-13-1783	George Bland	150 A.	CB: Moses Tison, John Bland
427	10-13-1783	Ralph Richards	300 A	CB: Thomas Richards, John Homes
428	10-13-1783	Benjamin Bowers	100 .A	CB: David Barnhill, Wm. Bowers
429	10-13-1783	Wm. Nicholson, Sr.	640 A.	CB: James Nicholson, Timothy Kelley
430	10-13-1783	John Williams	100 A.	CB: Thomas Duffil, Caleb Wallace. Men.: Henry Taunton, Thomas Dowen

GRANT BOOK G (1779-1784)

Page	Date	Grantee	Grant for	Additional Information (CB denotes chain bearers.)
431	10-13-1783	Benjamin Nicholson	50 A.	
432	10-13-1783	Wm. Moore	60 A.	CB: Wm. Moner, Abel Moner. Men.: James Moore
433	10-21-1782	Thomas House	240 A.	CB: Reuben Manning, Frederick Bryan. Men.: John Bowers
434	10-13-1783	David Hines, Jr.	150 A.	CB: Charles Allen, James Hines. Men.: Thomas Wallace, James Harris
435	10-13-1783	David Hines, Jr.	640 A.	CB: Roger Allen, Pitt Allen. Men.: James Tison, Aaron Tison, Arthur Forbes, Samuel Stafford
436	10-13-1783	Isaac Stocks	400 A.	CB: Simon Burney, Isaac Stocks, Jr. Men.: Shadric Allen
437	10-13-1783	John Jolley	300 A.	CB: John Knox, David Gurganus. Men.: John Butler, Stephen Gurganus, James Crandell
438	10-13-1783	John Harrell	20 A.	CB: Cannady Moore, Isaac Carrell. Men.: George Moye
439	10-13-1783	John Bawl	200 A.	CB: John Cherry, William Warren
440	10-13-1783	Randal McDaniel	500 A.	CB: John Lanier, Wm. Lanier
441	10-13-1783	John Nelson	47 A.	CB: Shade Tuten, James Nelson. Men.: Levi Nobles, Samuel Nelson
442	10-13-1783	Pearson Tuttle	30 A.	CB: William Willson, Isaac Hardee. Men.: Simon Burney
443	10-13-1783	Godfrey Stancil	100 A.	CB: Jonathan Nicholson, Reuben Nicholson. Men.: Benj. Nicholson
444	10-13-1783	Stewart Gordon	100 A.	CB: William Hellen, Joel Moye
445	10-13-1783	John Lanier	240 A.	CB: William Lanier, Randal McDaniel. Men.: William Davis, James Latham
446	10-13-1783	John Lanier	600 A.	CB: Seth Lanier, Randolph McDonald
447	10-13-1783	Seth Lanier	300 A.	Men.: Thomas Williams
448	10-13-1783	William Lanier	640 A.	Men.: Wm. Lanier, Jr.
449	10-13-1783	Alexander Williams	200 A.	CB: Benjamin May, Solomon Smith. Men.: George Willson
450	10-21-1782	John Brinkley	200 A.	CB: Samuel Barrow, Wm. Jordan. Men.: John Jordan, Mathew Hodges, Wm. Smith
451	10-13-1783	Samuel English	200 A.	CB: Samuel Simmons, Thos. Hardee. Men.: Margaret Nobles, Thomas Sermon
452	10-13-1783	James English, in trust for Sarah Marioner	200 A.	CB: Samuel Slaughter, Wm. Turner. Men.: Samuel English
453	10-13-1783	Samuel Simons	200 A.	CB: Wm. Mooreing, Wm. Turner. Men.: Thomas Sirmans
454	10-13-1783	Wm. Turner	340 A.	CB: Abraham Turner
455	10-13-1783	Wm. Turner	60 A.	
456	10-13-1783	Edward Moore	100 A.	CB: Edmund Moore, Reading Moore
457	10-13-1783	Edward Moore	200 A.	———
458	10-13-1783	Edward Moore	100 A.	———

G 431-458

GRANT BOOK G (1779-1784)

Page	Date	Grantee	Grant for	Additional Information (CB denotes chain bearers.)
459	10-13-1783	Shadrach Alen	100 A.	CB: Leavin Ross, Simon Burney
460	10-13-1783	John Jordan	240 A.	CB: Joshua James, William James. Men.: Henry Cason, Lemuel James
461	10-13-1783	Solomon Sheppard	100 A.	CB: Jordan Sheppard, James Sheppard
462	10-13-1783	James English, in trust for William Nobles	100 A.	CB: Samuel Simmons. Men.: Samuel English
463	10-13-1783	William Rogers	200 A.	CB: William Wiggs, William Bland
464	10-13-1783	Stephen Ewell	100 A.	CB: Thos. Richards, James Creemore. Men.: Reading Blount
465	10-13-1783	Levi Adams	383½ A.	Men.: Parker Lacey, Joseph Brierly, William Teal
466	11- 6-1784	John Fulford	200 A.	CB: Caleb Tripp, Wm. Braxton
467	11- 6-1784	Obediah Moore	70 A.	CB: Kennedy Moore. Men.: Samuel Moore, Colson Adams, Keley Tucker, Sarah Tucker. CB: Rite Tucker
468	11- 6-1784	Bryan Blount	250 A.	CB: Israel Harding, Jesse Blount
469	11- 6-1784	Shadrach Wooten	80 A.	CB: Lemuel Bullock, Nathaniel Bullock. Men.: Wm. Corbett
470	11- 6-1784	Shadrach Wooten	200 A.	CB: Charles Edwards, John Wooten, Sr. Men.: John Wooten, Hillery Hodges, dec.
471	11- 6-1784	Shadrach Wooten	160 A.	CB: Kinchen Edwards, John Wooten. Men.: James May, James Johnston
472	10-21-1782	John Gray Blount	37 A.	CB: Richard Blackledge, Augustus Harvey
473	10-21-1782	Wm. Nicholson	100 A.	CB: Joel Nicholson, Willis Nicholson
474	11- 6-1784	Cornelius Tison	100 A.	CB: Richard Moye, Wm. Bentley
475	10-13-1783	Stephen Gurganus	150 A.	CB: Joseph Oliver, Rubin Gurganus. Men.: Joseph Gainer
476	10-13-1783	Stephen Gurganus	150 A.	Men.: John Jolley

DEED BOOK H (1778-1782)

Page	Date	Grantor	Grantee	Additional Information
*7	10-15-1778	Paul Allen	Charles Allen	220 A; £350. Adj.: Thomas Wallace. Wit.: Henry Ellis, Samuel Stafford, Nathaniel Lanier
8	10-21-1778	Thomas Wallis	Joel Sugg, merchant	— A; £100. Former owner: Robert Land (1761). Wit.: Henry Ellis, Richard Allen, Paul Allen
9	10- 3-1778	George Albritton and Lydia Albritton	Edward Dixon	200 A; £400. Former owners: Simon Burney (Pat.), Wm. Taylor, Sr. Wit.: Peter Albritton, Abraham Dixon
10	5- 4-1778	John Church	John Lewis	100 A; £40. Adj.: Thos. Drake, James Little, Jos. Little, Frances Meeks, Walter Meeks. Wit.: Cornelius Church, Jessee Church
10	9-25-1778	James Lanier	Nathaniel Lanier, son	Negro; love & aff. Wit.: James Lanier, Jr., Thomas Hardie
11	2-14-1769	James Cobb, Sen.	James Cobb, Jr.	230 A; £10. Adj.: Thomas Little, Wit.: Edward Cobb, Amos Atkinson
11	10-22-1778	John Griffin	James Griffin, son	300 A+; love & aff.
12	10-13-1778	Thomas Willis	Seth Lanier	200 A; £20. Former owner: William Willis (1761)
12	4——1778	Benjamin Corie, Robert Hardee, and Isaac Hardee	John Simpson, merchant	Trees on 400 A; —.
13	1-30-1773	Edward Salter (D-1774)	John Simpson, merchant	320 A; £50. Former owner: Robert Salter (1770). Wit.: John Carson
14	12-29-1770	Robert Washington	Benjamin Jourdan, Jr.	205 A; £200. Wit.: Benjamin May, Jessee Jordan
15	2-27-1779	Thomas Whitmill (BERT) (Pat. 1740)	Walter Sessions (TYRR)	320 A in Tyrr; £25. Wit.: Thomas Worsley
16	9- 9-1771	Thomas Wallis	John Butt	460 A; £25.
16	2- 5-1779	Willaim Avorrett	David Avorrett, Jr.	310 A; £90+. Wit.: Cornelius Church, David Avorreth
17	2-22-1779	Nathan Cherry, cooper (1773)	William Kinsaul, waterman	100 A; £107. Adj.: Matthias Moore. Former owners: Solomon Whichard (D-1759); Ebenezer Folsom (Pat. 1741). Wit.: John Cason, Thomas Pinkett
18	2- 3-1779	John Williams and Mary Williams	John Little	200 A; £100. Wit.: Jacob Little, Jacob Williams, Bradbury Teel
18	3-22-1779	Thomas Wilson (Pat. 1756) and Sabra Wilson, wife	Thomas Tyson	200 A; £300. Wit.: John Fleming, Tabitha Allen, Henry Ellis
19	1-18-1778	William Denmark (CRAV) (Pat. 1773)	Pearson Tuten	280 A; $120.

* Book H starts with page 7.

DEED BOOK H (1778-1782)

Page	Date	Grantor	Grantee	Additional Information
20	7-30-1777	Simon Neusome (EDG)	Thomas Wallace	460 A; £75. Wit.: James Hill, Benjamin Griffin, Don Sutherland
20	3- 1-1779	David Avourett (Pat. 1761)	Wm. Avourett	160 A; £25. Adj.: Benj. Evans, Isaac Church, Thomas Sumerill
21	3-20-1779	Benjamin Smith (1761) and Sarah Smith, wife	Arthur Forbes	100 A+ 4 A; £350. Former owners: Sarah Allen, (Pat. 1752), Thomas Allen. Men.: John Fulford. Wit.: Thomas Allen, Sarah Allen
22	3-11-1779	James Brooks (1765)	Azariah McCaffie	150 A; £300. Former owner and wit.: John Simpson (Pat. 1764)
22	2-10-1779	Joshua Hardison	Jethro Kittrel	100 A; £200. Former owner: Daniel Oquin (Pat.). Wit.: Jacob Rountree, Thomas Ringgold
23	4-27-1779	Moses Tison, Sen. (Pat.)	Moses Tison, Jr.	— A; £10.
24	3-24-1779	Edmund Williams	William Mooring, taylor	½ A. lott #85; £100. Wit.: John Speir, Jacob Little
24	11-18-1778	Daniel O'Quin, Jr. (NORTH)	James Spivey (CRAV)	320 A; £200. Former owner: Daniel Oquin, Sen. Wit.: Wm. Whitfield, John Sirman
25	4-15-1779	Francis Rountree (CRAV)	Jethro Kittrel	100 A. in Pitt and Craven; £300. Wit.: Thomas Ringgold, Moab Rountree
26	2-10-1779	Joshua Hardison	Jethro Kittrel	240 A; £600.
26	3- 6-1779	John Hodges	Nathan Cherry, cooper	200 A; £600. Former owner: Ebenezer Folsom (1761)
27	3-31-1779	Joel Sugg	William Hart	50 A; £200. Former owner: Robert Land (1761). Wit.: George Sugg, Abigail Jones
28	12-29-1776	William Whitfield (Pat. 1774), taylor and Jemima Whitfield, wife	Willis Williams	122 A; £20. Adj.: Widow Oquin
29	4-29-1779	William Prescott	Thomas Davis	50 A; £35. Wit.: John Fleming, Jr., Robert Flake
29	12-31-1778	John Wooten	Jeremiah Lester	200 A; £200. Wit.: Henry Hines, Thos. Williams
30	3- 1-1779	David Averrett, Jr.	David Averrett, Sr. (1771)	120 A; £50. Wit.: William Nichols, James Averritt
31	9-30-1776	Obed Rountree (BERT) (Pat. 1775)	William Whitfield	300 A; £20. Wit.: Moab Rountree, Reuben Rountree, Isaac Blount
32	5-22-1779	Edward Williams, saddler	Thomas Downs, bricklayer	80 A; £80. Wit.: John Williams, Samuel Stokes
33	10- 4-1773	John Rogers	Absalom Rogers	125 A; £84. Wit.: Joseph Rogers, Henry Rogers
33	9-26-1775	Joseph Jolley, Sen.	William Whiteacker	150 A; £35. Former owner: Absalom James (1761). Wit.: Alexander Brown

DEED BOOK H (1778-1782)

Page	Date	Grantor	Grantee	Additional Information
34	6-12-1778	Matthias Johnson	Daniel Johnson, son	All lands and possessions; love & aff. Wit.: Moses Hodges, Griffin Floyd
35	4-18-1775	Hardee Keel (D-1775)	Solomon Sheppard	25 A; £5. Former owner: Robert Hodges. Wit.: Aaron Dudley
36	3-10-1772	James Lanier	Henry Jones and John Salter	553 A; £100. Wit.: William Jones, Allen Sugg, Richard Kenedy
37	10- 5-1779	Thomas Moore (Pat. 1761)	George Cannon	68 A; £50. Wit.: Joshua Porter, William Porter, Shadrick Porter
38	3-18-1779	Edmund Williams, wheelright (1761 and 1764)	Peter Diggins	165 A; £1126. Wit.: John Brinkley, James Gorham. Former owners: Ebenezer Folsom (1760), John Moye
39	7-18-1779	Richard Allen (1761)	George Sugg	174 A; £75.
39		John Salter	Henry Jones	553 A; £50.
40	1-23-1781	James Shivers	Jessee Shivers, son	—; love & aff. Wit.: John Pope
40	2-12-1781	James Johnston, Sr.	James Johnston, Jr.	100 A; £100. Wit.: Nathaniel Moore, Richard Jordan
41	10-26-1779	Martin Nelson, tradesman	John Nelson	30 A; 10 sh. Former owner: Martin Nelson, father of grantor (Pat. 1745)
42	1- 8-1780	Thomas Albritton, saddler (Grant # 38-1779)	John Albritton	300 A; £100. Adj.: Isaac Brooks
43	2-23-1782	Joshua Hill (Pat. 1764) and Charity Hill	Wm. Denning (BEAU)	100 A; £80. Wit.: Lewis Blount, Isaac Clarke, James Blount
44	10-26-1779	Meredith Corbett	James Dupree	39 A; £10. Adj.: John Williams. Wit.: William Corbett, Benjamin Dupree
45	10-27-1779	William Wilson (G-1779)	Emanuel Teel, Jr.	250 A; £500. Wit.: William Robson, Matt Moore
47	10—-1779	Daniel Wilson, Sen., and Elisabeth Wilson, wife	Willis Wilson, son	300 A; love & aff. Men.: Daniel Wilson, Jr. Wit.: William Wilson
47	10-26-1779	John Brooks (Pat. 1757)	John Morse	260 A; £10.
48	1-29-1779	Benjamin Jordan and Eliza Jordan, wife	Thomas Jordan	200 A; $350. Wit.: Edmund Reeks, Benjamin Bynum, James Bynum
49	3-30-1779	John Corbitt (EDG)	John Corbitt, son	100 A; love & aff. Wit.: Maredith Corbitt
50	10- 4-1779	John Simpson (1764-1777)	Nesby Mills, Jr.	150 A; $154. Former owner: James Brooks (1765)
52	7-18-1778	William Denmark (CRAV) (1766)	Pearson Tuten	100 A; $250. Wit.: John Eavey. Former owner: Jacob Blount (Pat. 1759)

DEED BOOK H (1778-1782)

Page	Date	Grantor	Grantee	Additional Information
53	3-10-1781	John Simpson	Edward Sirman	300 A; £65. Former owner: Ichabod Simpson, father of John Simpson, grantor; George Duncan. Wit.: Amos Travers
54	10-25-1779	John Frizell and Mary Frizell	William Rountree	50 A; £250. Wit.: John Vinson, Joshua Hardison
55	10-25-1779	John Frizel and Mary Frizel, wife	William Rountree	290 A; £250. Former owner: Absalom Kitteral (Pat. 1770)
56	1-24-1780	Henry Moore (1779)	Edward Salter	30 A; £30. Wit.: John Mayo, Dennis Grimes
57	2- 5-1780	Robert Hart	Everitt Pope	150 A; £2500. Wit.: Benjamin May, Henry Ellis, Moses Tison
58	1-24-1780	George Wilson	Joseph Thigpen (DOBB)	200 A; £30.
60	9-10-1779	Michael Becton (JOHN)	Frederick Edwin Becton	— A; £20. Former owner: Richard Becton, uncle of Michael Becton, grantor. Wit.: John Becton
61	7-26-1779	Woodey Belcher (DOBB)	John Pipkin	5 A; £5. Former owner: Luke White. Wit.: Daniel Pipkin, William Mathis
61	12-10-1779	James Cobb, Sen.	Daniel Walker	16-yr. lease
62	1-24-1780	Henry Moore	Dempsie Grimes	270 A; £1970
63	1- 3-1780	James Lanier and Mary Lanier, wife	Richard Foreman	300 A; £6000. Former owner: John Hurley (Pat. 1742). Wit.: John Foreman, Joshua Foreman
64	10-24-1780	Sarah Newton, widow	Giles Shute	150 A; £300. Former owners: William Speir (Pat. 1758); John Newton, dec., former husband of Sarah Newton, grantor. Wit.: Thomas Angel, Anney Smith, Jacob Shute
65	10-29-1778	John Permento (EDG) and Sarah Permento, wife	Mathee Randolph	260 A; £260. Former owner: Barwill Evans, (Pat. 1738), father of Sarah Permento, grantor. Adj.: Benjamin Dupree. Wti.: Amos Johnson, James Johnson, Henry Williams
67	8-18-1779	John Simpson, merchant (Pat. 1767, 1771, 1778)	Henry Cannon (CRAV)	100A+ 100A+ 100 A; £100. Former owners: Nesby Mills (Pat. 1738), John Benson, John Price (1751). Wit.: Dennis Cannon, Lewis Cannon
68	————	Comm. of Martinborough	John Pollard	½A. lot #36; 40 sh. Wit.: Peter Hines, Jr.
69	12-30-1779	James Lanier	James Lanier, Jr, son	150 A; love & aff. Wit.: Nathaniel Lanier
70	1-28-1779	Jacob Blount (G-1779)	John Barber	100 A; £20. Wit.: William Butler
71	————1779	Hugh Ross (MART)	William Ross	230 A; good causes. Wit.: Edmund Andrews, Etheldred Andrews

DEED BOOK H (1778-1782)

Page	Date	Grantor	Grantee	Additional Information
73	——1780	George Wilson	Benjamin May	330 A; £900. Adj.: John Wilson, Joseph Thigpen. Former owner: William Wilson, father of John Wilson. Wit.: John May
74	1-20-1780	William Corbitt	Benjamin May	180 A; £12000. Former owner: John May, dec.; Celia May, daughter of John May. Wit.: John Jefferson, Abraham Moore
75	10- 3-1780	Frederick Mills (1774)	David Mills	100 A; £40. Former owner: James Buck. Wit.: Simon Burney, Jr., Nathaniel Pettit
76	9-12-1781	William Fatheree	Benjamin May, saddler	125 A; £20. Adj.: John White. Wit.: Joseph Askew, Lewis Smith
77	7-23-1782	Rives Jordan (1761)	Benjamin May, saddler	200 A; £60.
78	12-18-1779	William Dixson	James Gorham	100 A; £1200. Adj.: Walter Dixson, Jr. Former owner: Walter Dixson; John Dixson, son of Walter Dixson. Wit.: James Armstrong, James Buck
79	7-26-1780	Isaac Carrel, bricklayer	James Gorham	160 A; £300. Former owners: Wm. Cason (Pat. 1740), Stephen Mundin (1761), Wm. Judkins (1762). Wit.: Jesse Moye
80	8-14-1780	Gabriel Allen (EDG)	Jesse Proctor	5 A; £100. Former owners: Samuel Swearingham (Pat. 1738), Thos. Swearingham, Daniel Johnson. Wit.: Robert Williams, Frederick Little
81	11-10-1779	John Price (Wilkes, Ga.)	James Moore	100 A; £57+. Adj.: Benjamin May. Wit.: Nathaniel Moore, Thomas Weston
82	7- 3-1779	John Brown	Joel Whitfield	200 A; £800. Adj.: Charles Finnecan. Wit.: Mark Mayo, James Brown
83	11-10-1779	John Doudna and Sarah Doudna	Joshua Hardison	200 A; £3000. Wit.: William Rountree, Thos. Ringgold
83	11-15-1762	William Pollard	John Polard, carpenter	65 A; £14. Wit.: Peter Rives, Benjamin Pollard. Former owner: James Mayo
85	9——1779	John Lewis	Joseph Little	100 A; £500.
85	11-14-1780	Thomas Albritton, saddler (Pat. 1763)	Henry Albritton	200 A; £100.
86	——1779	George Falconer, inholder (1771, 1777, 1776)	Thomas Curtis, taylor	Former owners: Samuel Charlcraft, George Williams, John Pope

DEED BOOK H (1778-1782)

Page	Date	Grantor	Grantee	Additional Information
88	4-17-1780	Aaron Tyson and William Tyson	Jonathan Tison	60 A; £2000. Adj.: Thomas Goff. Former owner: Edmund Tison, father of William Tyson, grantor. Wit.: Hezekiah Tyson, Roger Allen
89	11- 1-1779	Peter Nelson	Shadrack Tuten (CRAV)	200 A; £32. Former owner: Seth Pilkington (Pat. 1741)
90		Archibald Adams, Jr. and Asaha Adams	George Williams	334 A; £10.
92	——1780	Benjamin Buck	Capt. Roland Dixon	20 A; £10. Wit.: Richard Moye
92	2- 1-1780	Everitt Pope	William Sherrod	250 A; £2500. Adj.: Shadrich Ellis
94	1- 1-1780	Isom Lanier and James Lanier	John Foreman	100 A; £1000. Wit.: Geo. Moye, Jr.
95	2- 9-1780	Moses Hart	Robert Hart	300 A; £2000. Wit.: Benjamin May, Moses Tison
96	——1780	John Brinkley	John Whitehead	100 A; £200. Wit.: Henry Hennington
97	4- 1-1780	Edward Salter (G-1779)	Capt. Simon Jones	100 A; —. Wit.: Giles Shute
98	8-13-1779	James Mayo, Jr.	William Wallace	330 A; £200. Adj.: Peter May. Wit.: William May, Stephen Lee, John Bowers, William Hopkins
99	4-10-1780	Joel Sugg	William Osborne	320 A; £260. Men.: Abraham Tison, guardian of Joel Sugg. Wit.: William Wallace, James Brown
100	——1780	John Moy	James Quartermus (Pat. 1760)	147 A; £7. Wit.: Thomas Curtis
101	11-30-1778	Thos. Gwaltney (CRAV)	Drury Spain	120 A; £40. Adj.: Thomas Ivey. Wit.: Moses Chance, William Gwaltney
102	4——1780	Sterling Dupree (G-1779)	Benjamin Dupree	140 A; £1050. Adj.: James Dupree, Richard Proctor. Wit.: James Bynum
103	3-30-1780	Jacob Mercer	Jacob Mercer, son	100 A; love & aff. Adj.: Thomas Mercer. Wit.: John Vines, John Mercer
104		James Cremean (D-1761)	James Crandell	30 A; £200. Former owner: Seth Pilkington. Wit.: Josiah Little, Sr., George Littel, Wm. Littel
105	4-20-1780	Sterling Dupree	James Dupree	120 A; £100. Adj.: Benjamin Dupree, Richard Proctor. Wit.: James Bynum
106	11- 1-1779	Comm. of Martinborough	John Knowis, Jr.	½ A. lot #156; 40 sh.
107		Francis Hattaway	John Milburn	100 A; £100. Wit.: Abell Thomas, William Hattaway
109	5- 4-1775	Elizabeth Williams	Robert Flake, son, and Arthur Flake, son	All household goods; £1400. Wit.: John Fleming

DEED BOOK H (1778-1782)

Page	Date	Grantor	Grantee	Additional Information
109	9-29-1779	Howell Hodges	John Doudna	100 A; £1400. Former owners: Seth Pilkington (Pat. 1739), Elias Hodges (1740), Samuel Hargroves, Jno. Hodges. Wit.: Thos. Sheppard, Henry Hodges, Jordan Shepherd
110	——1779	Thos Williams	John Knowis	50 A; £10.
111	11-24-1779	David Perkins	Solomon Shepherd	100 A; £15. Former owners: Joseph Jolley, Jesse Kenedy, Col. Alex Stewart, dec.
112	11- 2-1779	Eliz. Shepherd, extrx. and William Speir, exr. and Reading Blount, exr. and Dempsie Grimes, exr.	David Perkins	100 A; £15. Former owner: Col. Alex Stewart, dec.
113	1-30-1782	Robert Grimmer	Thomas Crowson	½ A. lot #25; £12.
114	10- 1-1772	Comm. of Martinborough	Simon Jones	½ A. lot #133; 40 sh.
116		William Teal	Bradbury Teal	50 A; £1000. Wit.: Wm. Robson
117	5-15-1779	Nathaniel Cannon	Pearson Tuten	100 A; £100. Former owners: Anthony Mills, (Pat.), Samuel Smith (D). Wit.: Caleb Cannon
118	1- 5-1780	Benjamin Warner	William Rountree	200 A; 1 cow & 1 calf. Wit.: Wm. Whitfield
119	5-25-1780	John Cason	John Moore	100 A; £1500. Wit.: Colson Adams
120	5-15-1779	Nathaniel Cannon	Pearson Tuten	150 A; £400.
121	5-25-1780	John Moore	Colson Adams, wheelwright	100 A; £2000. Former owner: Samuel Moore
123	3-20-1780	Samuel Cannon (Pat. 1771)	Charles Hardee, Sen.	175 A; £800. Wit.: Paul Dail
124	10-29-1772	James Brooks (Pat. 1770)	George Falconer	100 A; £50. Wit.: Abraham Adams
125	10- 2-1780	John Simpson (D-1771)	Sarah Taylor, widow	100 A; —. Men.: Charles Taylor, dec, former husband of Sarah Taylor, grantee; Emanuel Taylor, minor son of Charles and Sarah Taylor. Former owners: James Appolis Averit (Pat. 1764)
126	8-15-1780	Edward Salter, exr. and James Gorham, exr.	Mayor Slade	200 A; 100 bbl. tar. Edward Salter and James Gorham, exr. for Col. Robert Salter, dec. Former owner: Edward Salter (Pat. 1740). Wit.: John Godley
127	5-29-1780	John Nelson	Giles Nelson	150 A; £20. Former owners: Benjamin King, Isaac Buck (Pat. 1743). Wit.: James Nelson
128	8-30-1780	Lazarus Pumphrey	Mayor Harriss	Wit.: John Presson, Hood Harris
129	10-19-1780	George McGowans	Thomas Judkins	50 A; £20.
130	9- 8-1780	James May	Edmond Reeks	80 A; £24. Former owner: Caleb Wallace. Wit.: Henry Williams

DEED BOOK H (1778-1782)

Page	Date	Grantor	Grantee	Additional Information
131	12-21-1780	John Williams, Sen.	Joel Williams, son	All goods, 280 A; love & aff. Former owner: Wm. Hamm
132	10- 9-1780	Robert Hart	Samuel Vines	350 A; £200. Former owners: William Stafford, Moses Hart, Wit.: Azaniah Langley, Wm. Tuten
133	10- 2-1779	Charles Hardee	Hannah Hall	Negro girl; —. Wit.: Nortley Tripp, Caleb Tripp
134	11-17-1780	John Williams (Pat. 1760)	Joel Williams	215 A; £5. Wit.: Caleb Ewell
135	12-21-1779	Jeremiah Cox	Pearson Tuten	150 A; £40. Former owner: William Denmark (Pat. 1774). Wit.: Abraham Cox
136	2-22-1781	John Mayo	Hardy Mayo	150 A; £50. Wit.: John Hines, Chas. Waldrom, Jr. Thos Hattaway, Jr.
137	——1780	John Doudna	Philip Knowis (D-1771)	50 A; £40. Former owners: Patrick Maule (Pat. 1723) Joseph and Sarah Bryan, John Knowis (1752).
138	——1781	William Hardee	Pearson Tuten	— A; £50. Former owner: Cornelius Tyson (Pat. 1728). Wit.: William Tuten, James Handcock
139	4-21-1781	Thomas Allen	Pitt Allen	100 A; £2000. Former owners: Thomas and Sarah Allen, parents of grantor. Wit.: Henre Harris
140	4-20-1781	Henry Albritton	Joshua Martin	62 A; £25. Former owner: James Albritton (Pat.), father of Henry Albritton, grantor. Wit.: Will Buck, Richard Albritton
141	5-30-1782	Isaac Mundin	John Harrell	55 A; £30.
142	4-21-1781	John Frizzle and Mary Frizzle, wife	Daniel Dimps Mors	50 A; £15. Former owner: John Lambert (Pat. 1750)
143	2-21-1781	Jeremiah Lester	Patrick Peaden	150 A; £25,000. Former owner: John Wooten
144	6-19-1781	John Cannon	John Curlie, watter	125 A; £40. Wit.: John Barber, Paul Herrington
145	2-24-1781	James Crandell	Robert Knox	100 A; £10. Wit.: James Cremean
146	1-25-1773	Nathaniel Cannon	Pearson Tuten	100 A; £20. Former owners: Andrew Hardee, Ann Ferger-son, William Williams and Anne Williams, David Mills. Wit.: Henry Smyth
147	3-21-1781	Walter Meeks	Nathan Meeks	50 A; £15. Wit.: Francis Meeks, Israel Edwards
148	4-20-1781	Thomas Williams	Philip Knowis	50 A; £10. Wit.: Erwin J. Boyd
149	5-15-1779	Edward Gatling and Ann Gatling	Charles Kelly	100 A; £500. Adj.: Peter Martin. Wit.: Edmund Andrews, Tulley Kelley
150	2- 7-1781	Elizabeth Alberson (1764)	John Warner	40 A. except grave; animals. Former owner: Solomon Alberson (D-1764)
151	2-11-1780	Henry Anderson	James Bynum	— A; £125. Wit.: Thomas Jordan

DEED BOOK H (1778-1782)

Page	Date	Grantor	Grantee	Additional Information
152	7-25-1781	Simon Burney, Sen.	Simon Burney, Jr.	150 A; £30. Former owner: J. Williams, sen.
153	10-23-1781	Simon Jones	Wm. Roberson	½ A, lot #133; £7+. Wit.: Wm. Moreing
155	8-22-1781	Jesse Moye	Thomas Wallis	150 A; £10000. Former owner: Robert Land (1761). Wit.: George Moye, Jr., Samuel Stafford
156	10-17-1781	Parker Lacy	John May	150 A; £100+.
157	10-20-1781	Parker Lacy	John Lacy	100 A; £20000. Former owner: Thomas Gwaltney
158	8-29-1768	George Moye	James Ward and Swain Ward and John Ward and Nancy Ward	Household goods; favour & esteem. Wit.: Edmond Williams Lemuel Barrow
159	1-28-1780	Dorcas Taunt and Elizabeth Taunt	Benj. Grice (BEAU)	100 A; £150 & mare. Former owner: John Taunt. Wit.: Edward Dixon, Sally Dixon, Joseph Wall
160	4-12-1780	Israel Edwards and Simon Edwards	William Averitt	— A; £30. Former owner: Samuel Edwards. Wit.: David Averitt, Timothy Riley
161	8- 8-1781	Dempsey Rite Allen (1764 & 1779)	John Edwards	106 A; £50. Former owners: Samuel Stokes, Richard Williams (D-1763 & G-1779). Wit.: Jesse Proctor, James Spier, Betsey Allen
163	1- 3-1781	David Hines	Crissey Dupree, granddaughter	Negro girl; love & aff. Wit.: Benjamin Dupree, Robert Williams
163	7-16-1781	Edward Williams	Abraham Williams, son	183 A; love & aff. Wit.: Richard Allen, Edward Williams, Edmond Ricks
164	4-30-1781	John Joyner (Pat. 1762)	Jeremiah Messer	200 A; 1 yr. service. Wit.: James Humber, John Vines
166	4-14-1781	Jeremiah Mounts	Samuel Erby	55 A; trade. Adj.: Phillip Holland. Wit.: Edward Cole, Elexander Hay
167	7-17-1781	John Brooks, Sen., (1763)	William Morse	170 A; £20. Former owners: Peter Morse, Michael Morse, Thos. Albritton. Wit.: George Williams, Jacob Taylor
168	1-10-1782	John Worsley	James Worsley	112 A; £25.
169	12-29-1781	James Crandell, mill wright (1763)	Christopher Crandell	250 A; £30.
170	11-14-1781	Henry Albritton	Thomas Albritton	100 A; £30.
171	12-31-1781	Moses Evans	Ephraim Evans	25 A; £100.
172	12-30-1781	Arthur Flake	John Flake, son	150 A; love & aff.
173	4- 2-1782	Thomas Curtis	Anna Pettit	50 A; £30.
174	——-1782	John Moye	Gardner Moye, son	180 A; love & aff.
175	——	John Moy	John Moy, son	180 A; love & aff.

DEED BOOK H (1778-1782)

Page	Date	Grantor	Grantee	Additional Information
177	——1781	William Corbitt (Pat.)	Charles Edwards	150 A; £100.
178	9-17-1781	George Palmer	Nathaniel Keel (BEAU)	50 A; £10.
179	11-12-1781	Meredith Corbitt (G-1779)	John Corbitt, Jr.	80 A; £5. Wit.: Thomas Downs
181	3-28-1782	Joseph Slade (CRAV)	Richard Moy	200 A; £140.
183	1-11-1782	Joshua Putnall	John Hattock	100 A; £30.
184	4-17-1782	William Harris	John Moreing	70 A; £55. Men.: Timothy Harris, father of William Harris. Wit.: Jacob Little, Jr., Pleasant Little
185	3-12-1782	John Tison (1754)	Joel Tison	198 A; £80.
186	2- 7-1782	John Lacy	Joseph Brierly	100 A; £25.
187	11-15-1781	William Averritt, blacksmith	Arthur Bryan (EDG)	166 A; £60.
189	——1782	Henry ——	Pearson Tuten	200 A; £50.
191	4-23-1782	Samuel Simmons	Joshua Putnall	— A; £43.

INDEX
TO
DEEDS

INDEX TO DEED BOOKS B, C, D, E, F, G, H
PITT COUNTY, NORTH CAROLINA

A

ADAMS, ABRAHAM—(ee)G-25; (ee)G-210

ADAMS, ARCHABALD—(A)B-484; (ee)C-48; (W)C-69; (F)C-319

ADAMS, ARCHIBALD—(or)B-95; (or)B-96; (ee)B-96; (W)C-169; (or) C-203; (F)C-203; (or)C-489; (ee)E-4; (or)F-337; (ee)G-2; (CB)G-3; (CB)G-33; (or)H-90

ADAMS, ASAHA—(or)H-90

ADAMS, COLSON—(W)F-337; (M)G-467; (W)H-119; (ee)H-121

ADAMS, CORSE—(CB)G-186

ADAMS, LEVI—(ee)B-95; (W)C-50; (ee)C-247; (W)C-270; (or)F-415; (ee)F-438; (M)G-261; (ee)G-465

ADAMS, PETER—(ee)F-337; (ee)G-233

ADAMS, WILLIAM—(F)C-241

ADDAMS, ABRAHAM—(W)H-124

ADKINSON, AMOS—(ee)B-19; (W)F-24

ALBERSON, ELIZABETH—(ee)E-254; (or)H-150

ALBERSON, SOLOMON—(or)E-254; (F)H-150

ALBERTON, MATHEW—(W)E-73

ALBERTSON, SAMUEL—(W)B-294

ALBRITAIN, JAMES—(ee)C-148

ALBRITAIN, PETER—(ee)G-337

ALBRITON, JAMES—(F)C-278

ALBRITON, MATHEW—(ee)B-425

ALBRITON, MATTHEW—(or)B-450; (or)D-65

ALBRITTAIN, AMI—(M)F-140

ALBRITTAIN, GEORGE—(ee)F-140

ALBRITTAIN, HENRY—(ee)F-140

ALBRITTAIN, JAMES—(or)D-67; (ee)D-68; (ee)D-71; (F)F-140

ALBRITTAIN, PETER—(ee)D-31

ALBRITTON, GEORGE—(W)D-67; (ee)F-75; (or)F-87; (or)H-9

ALBRITTON, HENRY—(ee)H-85; (or)H-140; (or)H-170

ALBRITTON, JAMES—(or)C-187; (or)F-75; (F)F-75; (F)H-140

ALBRITTON, JOHN—(W)F-323; (CB)G-1; (ee)H-42

ALBRITTON, LYDIA—(or)H-9

ALBRITTON, MATHEW—(ee)C-464; (or)F-73

ALBRITTON, MATTHEW—(W)E-269; (or)F-75

ALBRITTON, PETER—(ee)C-134; (or)F-75; (W)F-208; (M)G-265; (W)H-9

ALBRITTON, RICHARD—(W)F-75; (or)F-208; (CB)G-1; (W)H-140

ALBRITTON, THOMAS—(or)B-441; (ee)B-457; (or)F-75; (ee)G-1; (or)H-42; (or)H-85; (F)H-167; (ee)H-170

ALDERSON, THOMAS—(W)E-2; (M)F-111

ALLEN, BENJAMIN—(or)F-238

ALLEN, BETSEY—(W)H-161

ALLEN, CHARLES—(ee)E-49; (CB)G-170; (CB)G-171; (CB)G-434; (ee)H-7

ALLEN, DEMCY—(ee)C-157

ALLEN, DEMPSEY RIGHT—(ee)G-231

ALLEN, DEMPSEY RITE—(or)H-161

ALLEN, DEMPSEY WRIGHT—(ee)E-116

ALLEN, DEMPSY—(M)G-10

ALLEN, DEMSIE—(CB)G-321

ALLEN, ELIZABETH—(ee)F-365

ALLEN, EPHRAIM—(or)C-47

ALLEN, GABRIEL—(ee)E-49; (CB)G-93; (M)G-106; (ee)G-113; (or)H-80

ALLEN, JACOB—(W)F-307

ALLEN, JOHN—(W)F-104

ALLEN, JOSEPH—(W)C-474

ALLEN, MARTHA—(or)E-229; (or)E-318

ALLEN, MERIMAN—(or)E-116

ALLEN, MERYMAN—(W)B-480

ALLEN, MERRYMAN—(ee)C-123; (ee)E-49

ALLEN, PAUL—(or)F-365; (or)F-460; (ee)F-492; (CB)G-141; (or)H-7; (W)H-8

ALLEN, PITT—(W)E-139; (M)G-415; (CB)G-435; (ee)H-139

ALLEN, POLL—(W)D-97

ALLEN, RICHARD—(A)B-289; (or)B-300; (or)B-307; (W)D-16; (or)E-229; (or)E-318; (ee)G-141; (W)H-8; (or)H-39; (W)H-163

ALLEN, ROGER—(ee)C-28; (W)C-523; (CB)G-435; (W)H-89

ALLEN, SARAH—(F)D-97; (F)E-139;
(F)E-213; (F)E-83; (W & F) H-21;
(F)H-139
ALLEN, SARY—(M)C-389
ALLEN, SHAD—(F)C-531
ALLEN, SHADE—(M)G-210
ALLEN, SHADRACH—(F)B-473;
(or)C-471; (ee)G-459
ALLEN, SHADRIC—(M)G-436
ALLEN, SHADRICH—(F)F-410
ALLEN, SHADRICK—(F)D-51
ALLEN, TABITHA—(W)H-18
ALLEN, THOMAS—(ee)C-16;
(F)C-521; (or)C-542; (or)D-97;
(ee)E-5; (or)E-83; (or)E-139;
(or)E-150; (W & F)H-21; (or)H-139;
(F)H-139
ALLEN, TIMOTHY—(F)C-47
ALLEN, ZACHARIAH—(W)D-97;
(CB)G-39
ALLEN, ZACRIAH—(ee)E-139
AMBROSE, PETER—(M)G-137
ANDERSON, HENRY—(ee)C-20;
(W)E-11; (ee)E-125; (or)F-63;
(W)F-304; (ee)F-529; (CB)G-308;
(or)H-151
ANDERSON, JACOB—(ee)C-8;
(or)C-398
ANDERSON, JAMES—(ee)E-324
ANDERSON, JOHN—(CB)G-308
ANDERSON, LARANCE—(ee)F-301;
(ee)F-304
ANDERSON, LAURENCE—(ee)G-309;
(CB)G-384
ANDERSON, LAWRENCE—
(CB)G-220;(ee)G-308; (ee)G-310
ANDREWS, EDMON—(ee)E-12
ANDREWS, EDMUN—(ee)E-232;
(W)E-250; (W)F-67
ANDREWS, EDMUND—(W)D-95;
(W)F-189; (W)F-308; (W)F-524;
(M)G-134; (ee)G-135; (ee)G-136;
(M)G-236; (W)H-71; (W)H-149
ANDREWS, ELIZABETH—(W)F-514
ANDREWS, ETHELDRED—(W)C-76;
(W)C-478; (W)H-71
ANDREWS, JAMES—(W)E-13
ANDREWS, LEVI—(ee)C-477;
(ee)G-140; (CB)G-145
ANDREWS, LEVY—(W)C-76;
(ee)E-306
ANDREWS, WARREN—(ee)C-75;
(ee)C-269; (or)C-477; (MA)E-232
ANGEL, THOMAS—(ee)F-92; (W)H-64
ARCHDEACON, WILLIAM—(or)B-113;
(W)C-31; (or)C-147; (or) C-266;
(or)C-295; (or)C-324; (or)C-510
(ee)C-519; (or)G-536; (or)D-25;
(or)E-56
ARCHDEACAN, WM.—(F)F-312

ARMSTRONG, JAMES—(ee)D-30;
(W)E-67; (ee)G-37; (W)H-78
ARMSTRONG, THOMAS—(M)G-198;
(M)G-279
ARNAL, THOMAS—(ee)G-234
ARNAL, WM.—(CB)G-332
ARNOL, THOMAS—(CB)G-142
ARNOLD, THEO—(CB)G-17
ARNOLD, THOMAS—(M)G-288;
(CB)G-32; (M)G-190
ARNOLD, THOS.—(CB)G-37
ASHMAID, JOSEPH—(M)F-126
ASKEW, JOSEPH—(W)H-76
ASKEW, JOSIAH—(ee)D-151;
(W)E-254; (W)F-147
ASKEY, DAVID—(CB)G-364
ATCHISON, SAMUEL—(ee)D-79;
(ee)D-70; (W)D-94
ATFORD, JACOB—(W)D-100
ATKINSON, AARON—(W)F-568
ATKINSON, AMOS—(or)B-63;
(or)B-104; (W)B-232; (ee)B-398;
(or)C-176; (or)C-402; (W)C-486;
(W)D-21; (F)D-125; (W)D-159;
(W)E-18; (or)E-91; (F)E-220;
(W)E-241; (F)F-181; (W)F-487;
(ee)G-341; (ee)G-342; (M)G-403;
(W)H-11
ATKINSON, JACOB—(W)B-226;
(W)C-486; (ee)D-21; (W)E-203;
(ee)E-241; (W)E-264; (W)F-94;
(W)F-157; (M)G-276; (M)G-278;
(CB)G-342
ATKINSON, MARY—(W)F-94
ATKISON, AMOS—(W)F-357
ATKISOI, JACOB—(or)F-268
AUTREY, WILLIAM—(ee)B-533;
(F)C-383
AUTRY, ALEXANDER—(W)B-252
AUTRY, ANN—(or)F-29
AUTRY, ELICKSANDER—(ee)E-13
AUTRY, JOHN—(ee)B-432; (ee)E-23;
(or)F-29; (or)F-56
AUTRY, WILLIAM—(or)B-392;
(or)B-423; (or)B-432; (F)F-56
AVERET, DAVID—(M)G-242;
(CB)G-363
AVERET, WILLIAM—(M)G-242
AVERETT, DAVID—(ee)B-501;
(or)C-255; (or)C-263; (or)C-376;
(ee)D-92; (or)F-20; (ee)F-20;
(W)F-462; (M)G-211
AVERETT, JAMES—(or)C-141
AVERETT, JAMES APPOLAS—
(or)E-72
AVERETT, JOHN—(or)B-279;
(or)C-362
AVERETT, WILLIAM—(W)C-540;
(W)D-92; (W)F-20; (ee)G-211
AVERIT, DAVID—(F)E-49
AVERIT, JAMES APPOLIS—(F)H-125

AVERITT, DAVID—(W)D-79;
  (W)H-160
AVERITT, JAMES—(W)D-91;
  (or)E-323; (W)H-30
AVERITT, JOHN—(or)E-322
AVERITT, MATHEW—(F)E-324
AVERITT, WILLIAM—(ee)F-483;
  (ee)H-160
AVERRETT, DAVID—(or)B-283;
  ·(W)C-140; (or)C-341; (or)C-539;
  (W)E-31; (W)E-38; (W)E-55;
  (or)H-30; (ee) (F)H-30
AVERRETT, SUSANNA—(W)C-140
AVERRETT, WILLIAM—(W)E-31
AVERRETTE, DAVID—(W)E-38
AVERRITH, JOHN—(W)C-224
AVERY, APOLLAS—(CB)G-195
AVERY, DAVID—(CB)G-353
AVERY, JAMES—(F)F-292;
  (ee)G-232; (ee)G-368; (M)G-370
AVERY, JOHN—(F)E-282; (F)F-292
AVERY, POLLAS—(CB)G-194
AVOREY, GEORGE—(or)C-155
AVORRETH, DAVID—(ee)H-16;
  (W)H-16
AVORRETH, WILLIAM—(or)H-16
AVOURETT, DAVID—(or)H-20
AVOURETT, WILLIAM—(ee)H-20
AVRITT, WILLIAM—(or)H-187

B

BAGGETT, JAMES—(or)C-240
BAGGETT, JESSE—(W)B-252;
  (W)C-74
BAKER, JAMES—(or)F-579
BAKER, JESSE—(F)F-579
BAKER, JOHN B.—(ee)F-579
BALDENA, ISAAC—(ee)G-103
BALDEREE, WM.—(ee)G-186
BALDERY, WILLIAM—(or)D-5; E-169
BALDREE, GEORGE—(W)D-33
BALDREE, ISAAC—(CB)G-149
BALDRY, WILLIAM—(ee)B-312
BALDWIN, MARY—(M)F-385
BALDWIN, WILLIAM—(ee)C-200;
  (W)E-3; (or)E-20; (ee)E-66;
  (W)E-192; (or)F-270; (ee)F-272;
  (F)F-337; (or)F-385; (ee)G-185
BALDWYN, WILLIAM—(F)B-95;
  (W)B-394; (or)B-484; (ee)B-484
  (W)C-6; (or) C-48; (W)C-120;
  (ee)C-203; (F)C-318; (W)D-5;
  (ee)D-141; (F)E-4; (or)E-19;
  (W)E-33; (W)F-541
BALDWYN, WM.—(M)G-160;
  (M)G-171; (M)G-233
BALL, JOHN—(or)C-36; (F)D-72;
  (CB)G-50; (ee)G-203; (CB)G-203;
  (CB)G-317; (CB)G-413
BALLARD, JOHN—(W)B-82

BALLARD, JOSEPH—((W)B-82
BALLARD, ROBERT—(ee)B-82;
  (W)B-115
BARBER, ABRAHAM—(CB)G-201
BARBER, DINAH—(or)B-244
BARBER, JOHN—(ee)B-275;
  (or)C-278; (ee)E-46; (ee)F-217;
  (ee)F-274; (CB)G-26; (CB)G-67;
  (CB)G-137; (CB)G-139; (CB)G-201;
  (CB)G-233; (CB)G-237; (CB)G-334;
  (ee)H-70; (W)H-144
BARBER, JOSEPH—(ee)B-224;
  (W)G-67; (W)D-45
BARBER, WILLIAM—(or)B-244;
  (W)F-217; (M)G-139; (CB)G-402;
  (M)G-233
BARBEREE, JESEY—(ee)E-32
BARBRE, JESSE—(W)C-102
BARBRE, JESSY—(or)F-27
BARBRE, PETER—(W)F-58
BARENHILL, JOHN—(or)E-9
BARNES, JOSHUA—(ee)F-34;
  (ee)F-124; (ee)F-499
BARNET, JAMES—(or)C-108
BARNETT, WILLIAM—(or)C-496
BARNEY, BENJAMIN—(ee)D-41;
  (ee)D-43; (or)E-265; (or)E-266
BARNHILL, ALEXANDER—(W)B-93
BARNHILL, DAVID—(CB)G-428
BARNHILL, HENRY—(ee)B-268;
  (ee)F-113; (CB)G-373
BARNHILL, JAMES—(W)E-315
BARNHILL, JESSE—(W)F-573
BARNHILL, JOHN—(W)B-268;
  (ee)B-303; (W)F-121
BARNHILL, MARGARET—(or)F-170
BARNS, STEPHEN—(CB)G-366
BARR, JAMES—(ee)D-29; (ee)D-47;
  (or)D-61; (W)D-87
BARROW, ABRAHAM—(W)B-254;
  (ee)B-292; (or)C-208; (A)F-249
BARROW, BENJ.—(CB)G-253;
  (M)G-306
BARROW, BENJAMIN—(M)B-447;
  (ee)C-500; (or)E-37; (ee)E-45;
  (ee)G-66; (M)G-256
BARROW, ELIZABETH—(ee)B-292;
  (or)E-37
BARROW, JAMES—(W)B-376;
  (or)C-193; (W)C-256; (W)C-264;
  (W)C-332; (or)D-106; (W)E-11;
  (or)E-51; (W)F-34; (W)F-125;
  (or)F-553; (ee)G-234; (ee)G-235
BARROW, JOHN—(ee)C-255;
  (or)E-51
BARROW, JOSEPH—(F)B-551;
  (F)C-193; (ee)C-332; (ee)C-370;
  (W)C-500; (or)D-42; (or)D-97;
  (F)D-106; (F)E-29; (F)F-228;
  (F)R-283
BARROW, LEMUEL—(W)H-158

BARROW, MARY—(W)D-121;
(or)E-210; (or)F-32
BARROW, REUBEN—(ee)D-97;
(or)D-115
BARROW, RICHARD—(ee)B-75;
(or)C-331; (ee)D-90; (W)D-97;
(or)D-115; (W)D-121; (W)E-55;
(or)E-209; (or)F-32; (F)F-249
BARROW, SAMUEL—(W)C-26;
(W)E-234; (W)F-199; (CB)G-119;
(ee)G-235; (CB)G-450
BARROWS, JOHN—(or)E-190
BARROWS, RICHARD—(F)E-187
BARRY, JAMES—(W)C-468
BARTLET, THOMAS—(W)F-118
BARTLETT, JOHN—(or)D-1
BASS, ALEXANDER—(W)E-227
BATE, LUKE—(W)F-32
BATES, DANIEL—(W)D-45;
(W)E-209
BAUL, JOHN—(CB)G-272
BAULL,JOHN— (CB)G-272
BAWL, JOHN—(M)G-371;
(ee)G-440
BAXTER, DAVID—(ee)B-368;
(ee)C-24
BAXTER, ISRAEL—(or)B-368;
(or)C-24
BAXTER, REBECCA—(ee)B-368
BAXTER, SARAH—(ee)B-368;
(ee)C-24
BAXTER, STEPHEN—(ee)B-368;
(ee)C-24
BAXTER, THEOPHILUS—(ee)B-368;
(ee)C-24
BEAMAN, WILLIAM—(W)B-418
BECK, GEORGE—(A)C-262
BECTON, EDMUND—(M)C-347
BECTON, ELIZABETH—(M)B-447
BECTON, FREDERICK—(or)B-245;
(ee)B-447; (ee)C-347;
(or)D-89; (M)G-256
BECTON, FREDERICK EDWIN—
(ee)H-60
BECTON, GEORGE—(or)C-347
BECTON, JOHN—(F)B-447;
(F)C-347; (F)C-529; (W)H-60
BECTON, MICHAEL—(M)C-347;
(or)H-60
BECTON, RICHARD—(F)B-245;
(F)B-447; (F)C-347; (F)D-89;
(M)E-24; (F)H-60
BELCHER, THOS.—(CB)G-113
BELCHER, WOODDE—(or)H-61
BELCHER, WOODEY—(ee)F-202
BELL, BURREL—(W)F-338
BELL, BURRELL—(ee)F-489;
(CB)G-160; (CB)G-185
BELL, STARKEY—(ee)E-169
BELL, WILLIAM—(W)D-49;
(ee)F-338; (or)F-489; (CB)G-172
BENSON, JOHN—(F)C-329; (or)C-539;

(F)C-533; (F)H-67
BENTLEY, WM.—(CB)G-474
BENTLY, JOHN—(CB)G-284
BENTLY, JUDITH—(M)G-284
BERGENUM, ELIAS—(ee)B-537
BERGERON, ELIAS—(W)-123;
(W)B-256; (W)B-296; (W)B-378;
(W)B-550; (W)C-116; (W)C-138;
(W)C-154; (W)C-178; (W)C-182;
(W)C-276; (W)E-143; (W)F-125
BERSTON, BENJ.—(W)D-79
BETTON, JAMES—(W)E-105
BLACKLEDGE, RICHARD—(CB)G-472
BLACKSTON, JAMES—(ee)G-42
BLACKSTON, JOHN—(or)D-85
BLACKSTONE, JOHN—(ee)D-59;
(ee)D-154
BLAND, GEORGE—(or)B-436;
(CB)G-339; (ee)G-426
BLAND, JOHN—(CB)G-426
BLAND, WILLIAM—(CB)G-463
BLANN, STEPHEN—(CB)G-143;
(CB)G-180
BLOUNT, ALLIS—(ee)C-159
BLOUNT, ANNE—(W)C-474
BLOUNT, BENJ.—(ee)G-42; (M)G-236
BLOUNT, BENJAMIN—(M)C-159;
(ee)E-315; (or)F-152; (ee)F-349;
(M)F-374; (or)F-474; (M)G-135;
(ee)G-352; (ee)G-421
BLOUNT, BRYAN—(CB)G-71;
(ee)G-468
BLOUNT, FRANCIS—(F)E-96
BLOUNT, ISAAC—(W)F-222;
(W)F-349; (W)H-31
BLOUNT, JACOB—(ee)B-490;
(or)C-473; (F)E-315; (F)F-152;
(or)F-261; (or)F-374; (or)F-456;
(W)(F)F-495: (ee)G-26; (ee)G-60;
(M)G-237; (F)H-52; (or)H-70
BLOUNT, JAMES—(or)C-79; (F)C-79;
(ee)C-155; (or)C-159; (M)C-217;
(or)E-185: (W)H-43
BLOUNT, JESSE—(CB)G-468
BLOUNT, JOHN GRAY—(ee)G-69;
(ee)G-70; (ee)G-71; (ee)G-72;
(ee)G-73; (ee)G-74; (ee)G-472
BLOUNT,—JOSEPH—(W)C-111
BLOUNT, LEWIS—(ee)G-79;
(M)G-123; (W)H-43
BLOUNT, MARY—(ee)F-374
BLOUNT, NATHANIEL—(W)C-111
BLOUNT, PENELLOPE—(or)F-474
BLOUNT, PHENELIPHAS—(M)F-374
BLOUNT, READING—(ee)C-110;
(W)C-111; (ee)C-216; (e)C-225;
(ee)G-47; (M)G-177; (M)G-262;
(M)G-291; (CB)G-352; (ee)G-417;
(ee)G-418; (M)G-464; (or)H-112
BLOUNT, SHARPE—(ee)F-581
BLOUNT, THOMAS—(F)C-66;
(F)F-131

BLUNT, BENJAMIN—(or)D-12;
(ee)B-91; (ee)B-108; (W)F-71;
(A)F-194
BLUNT, JACOB—(W)B-91; (or)D-45;
(or)F-186
BLUNT, JAMES—(or)B-91; (or)B-108;
(F)B-402
BLUNT, KATHERINE—(or)B-108
BOND, JOHN—(W)B-115
BOND, THOMAS—(ee)B-115; (or)E-32
BONDFIELD, CHARLES—(ee)D-76;
(ee)E-320
BONNER, ANNE—(F)E-286
BONNER, HENRY—(ee)B-236;
(ee)B-237; (or)C-491
BONNER, JAMES—(ee)B-10; (A)C-8;
(or)C-75; (or)C-114; (F)D-22;
(W)D-54; (F)E-222; (CB)G-70;
(CB)G-72; (CB)G-158; (M)G-203;
(M)G-272; (ee)G-411; (CB)G-411;
(M)G-412; (ee)G-413
BONNER, JOHN—(W)C-118;
(or)E-286; (ee)G-412
BONNER, SARAH—(or)E-93
BONNER, THOMAS—(or)B-236;
(or)B-237; (W)B-237; (F)C-491;
(A)D-23; (or)E-93
BOTTEN, RICHARD—(W)C-224;
(W)D-169
BOWERS, BENJ.—(M)G-308;
(CB)G-310
BOWERS, BENJAMIN—(W)B-97;
(or)B-268; (W)C-270; (ee)D-5;
(W)F-88; (W)F-226; (W)F-415;
(W)F-438; (or)F-529; (ee)G-373;
(ee)G-428
BOWERS, JOHN—(W)D-5; (W)D-7;
(W)F-187; (W)F-226; (ee)G-176;
(ee)G-182; (M)G-433; (W)H-98
BOWERS, WILL—(CB)G-310
BOWERS, WILLIAM—(W)H-137
BOWERS, WM.—(CB)G-428
BOWIN, JOHN—(CB)G-382
BOYD, ELIZABETH—(W)E-325
BOYD, ERWIN J.—(W)H-148
BOYD, JOSEPH—(ee)C-422; (or)D-30;
(W)E-148; (W)E-325; (W)F-26;
(ee)F-251; (W)F-387; (ee)G-17;
(M)G-169; (M)G-177
BOYD, ROBERT—(W)C-164;
(or)C-366; (ee)C-366; (or)C-422;
(E)D-30; (W)F-26; (ee)G-351
BOYDE, ISAAC—(CB)G-49; (CB)G-51;
(CB)G-52; (CB)G-125
BOYDE, JOSEPH—(CB)G-32;
(CB)G-37; (CB)G-69; (CB)G-74;
(ee)G-125; (ee)G-126
BOYDE, ROBERT—(CB)G-34
BRACKSTONE, JOHN—(W)D-64
BRACKSTONE, THOMAS—(ee)D-64
BRADDY, JAMES—(W)B-430
BRADDY, WILLIAM—(A)B-88;
(W)B-430

BRADLEY, HENRY—(F)C-529;
(F)C-533
BRADY, ANN—(W)F-481
BRADY, JAMES—(ee)C-428;
(W)D-99; (M)F-52; (W)F-178;
(ee)F-481; (CB)G-245
BRADY, JOHN—(ee)D-99;
(or)F-481
BRADY, MARY—(W)F-481
BRADY, REUBEN—(ee)D-166
BRADY, SILVIA—(or)F-481
BRADY, WILLIAM—(or)C-428;
(or)D-99; (or)D-166; (ee)F-52;
(or)F-52; (W)F-481
BRANTLEY, WILLIAM—(F)E-112;
(F)F-358; (CB)G-31
BRANTLY, WILLIAM—(F)B-480;
(W)F-165; (CB)G-21
BRAXTON, JAMES—(W)F-280;
(ee)F-281; (CB)G-12; (CB)G-62;
(CB)G-183
BRAXTON, JOHN—(or)D-85;
(ee)F-280; (or)F-281; (ee)G-11;
(CB)G-12; (CB)G-45; (CB)G-62;
(CB)G-183; (M)G-275
BRAXTON, THOMAS—(ee)G-13;
(CB)G-44; (ee)G-120
BRAXTON, THOS.—(CB)G-11
BRAXTON, WILLIAM—(W)F-580
BRAXTON, WM.—(CB)G-466
BRAXSTONE, JOHN—(ee)E-26;
(or)E-35
BRAXSTONE, MARY—(or)E-35
BREELER, ABRAHAM—(ee)B-300;
(or)D-23
BREELER, JAMES—(W)D-23
BREELY, JOSEPH—(ee)G-205
BRIAN, JOHN—(CB)G-369
BRIERLY, JOSEPH—(ee)C-360;
(M)G-465; (ee)H-186
BRIERLY, WILLIAM—(ee)C-360;
(or)E-153; (or)F-68; (ee)F-68;
(ee)G-107
BRILEY, ABRAM—(C)G-261
BRILEY, JOSEPH—(ee)D-8; (M)G-261
BRINKLEY, JOHN—(W)F-321;
(C)G-114; (ee)G-450; (W)H-38;
(or) H-96
BRINSON, JOHN—(ee)C-14; (or)C-537
BRITTEN, BENNET—(or)B-404
BRITTON, BENNETT—(A)B-165
BRODY, WILLIAM—(CB)G-167
BROOKS, ISSAC—(A)H-42
BROOKS, JAMES—(ee)B-234;
(ee)B-394; (or)C-58; (or)C-179;
(ee)C-222; (ee)C-229; (ee)C-316;
(F)C-329; (or)D-17; (or)D-59;
(ee)D-155; (ee)E-135; (or)E-284;
(or)F-37; (F)F-323; (ee)G-15;
(ee)G-16; (M)G-296; (or)H-22;
(F)H-50; (F)H-67; (or)H-124
BROOKS, JOHN—(ee)B-238;

(CB)G-423; (W)H-48
BYNUM, DREWRY—(W)E-209;
  (W)F-32
BYNUM, JAMES—(W)F-467;
  (W)F-544; (W)H-48; (W)H-102;
  (W)H-105; (ee)H-151
BYNUM, NICHOLAS—(M)G-224;
  (M)G-323; (ee)G-423
BYNUM, NICHOLS—(ee)E-209;
  (ee)E-210; (ee)F-32; (or)F-467
BYNUM, REUBEN—(CB)G-423
BYNUM, RUBIN—(CB)G-323

C

CALEF, JAMES—(or)C-445;
  (ee)C-446; (or)C-449
CALEF, JOHN—(ee)C-449
CALEF, MARGARET—(M)C-449
CALEF, ROBERT—(ee)C-449
CALHOUN, SAMUEL—(M)F-126
CALLAHAN, ROBERT—(F)B-450
CAMELL, ELISABETH—(W)B-379
CAMPBELL, ARCH—(W)E-67
CAMPBELL, JAMES—(W)B-75;
  (W)C-524
CAMPBELL, WILLIAM—(ee)F-137
CANNON, CALEB—(CB)G-300;
  (W)H-117
CANNON, DAVID—(W)B-289;
  (A)B-388; (F)B-450; (F)C-288;
  (F)D-67; (A)E-42; (F)F-324;
  (W)F-525
CANNON, DENNIS—(W)F-191;
  (or)F-325; (ee)F-325; (ee)G-262;
  (CB)G-262; (M)G-300; (W)H-67
CANNON, DENNISS—(ee)C-498
CANNON, EDWARD—(F)B-266;
  (W)B-289; (W)B-402; (F)B-450;
  (or)F-324
CANNON, ELIZABETH—(W)F-325
CANNON, FURNEY—(CB)G-343
CANNON, GEORGE—(ee)B-185;
  (or)C-25; (ee)C-38; (F)F-192;
  (ee)G-404; (ee)G-405; (ee)H-37
CANNON, HENRY—(or)B-254;
  (M)B-289; (or)C-498; (W)D-56;
  (W)F-104; (W)F-297; (ee)H-67
CANNON, JOHN—(ee)C-274; (ee)D-56;
  (ee)E-2; (or)F-297; (or)F-298;
  (ee)F-362; (ee)F-542; (CB)G-45;
  (M)G-262; (ee)G-300; (or)H-144
CANNON, LEWIS—(CB)G-262;
  (W)H-67
CANNON, MARY—(or)B-254;
  (ee)B-289
CANNON, NATHANIEL—(or)F-194;
  (W)F-324; (ee)F-464; (ee)F-458;
  (ee)F-498; (or)H-117; (or)H-120;
  (or)H-146
CANNON, SAMUEL—(or)F-542;
  (or)H-123

CANNON, SHADE—(CB)G-404
CANNON, SHADRACH—(CB)G-405
CANNON, THOMAS—(ee)F-297
CANNON, WILLIAM—(ee)B-263;
  (F)D-139; (F)F-391; (F)F-546
CARBITT, WILLIAM—(CB)G-216
CARDING, BENJAMIN—(F)C-329
CARNEY, JOSIAH—(W)F-577
CARR, ELIAS—(W)F-579
CARR, JONATHAN—(W)E-204
CARREL, ISAAC—(or)H-79
CARRELL, ISAAC—(ee)F-554;
  (CB)G-392; (CB)G-439
CARRIL, ISAAC—(ee)F-50; (or)F-54
CARRUTHERS, JOSEPH—(W)C-524
CARSON, JOHN—(W)H-13
CARSON, THOMAS—(ee)F-187;
  (ee)F-189
CARTER, GEORGE—(W)F-67
CARTER, STEPHEN—(ee)F-67
CARTWRIGHT, MATHEW—(ee)G-384
CARTWRIGHT, MATTHEWS—
  (ee)F-429
CASON, CHARLES—(ee)F-538
CASON, GABRIEL—(CB)G-401
CASON, HENRY—(M)G-179;
  (ee)G-192; (M)G-460
CASON, HILLERY—(W)C-334;
  (or)F-192; (or)F-210; (or)F-289;
  (ee)F-408; (ee)G-207
CASON, ISAAC—(W)F-499
CASON, JAMES—(or)C-148;
  (ee)C-163; (W)C-188; (ee)C-214;
  (F)C-335; (or)C-331; (ee)D-73;
  (W)E-200; (F)F-192; (or)F-462
CASON, JOHN—(W)B-95; (W)C-188;
  (W)D-109; (W)F192; (ee)F-529;
  (M)G-193; (M)G-281; (W)H-17;
  (or)H-119
CASON, THOMAS—(ee)F-184;
  (M)G-266
CASON, THOS.—(CB)G-140
CASON, WILLIAM—(F)F-50;
  (F)F-289; (F)H-79
CASWELL, RICHARD—(or)F-426
CATTO, JOHN—(CB)G-236
CELLO, TIMOTHY—(CB)G-242
CHADWICK, DAVID—(or)E-155
CHALCRAFF, JOHN—(ee)B-14
CHALCRAFFT, JOHN—(W)B-226
CHALCRAFT, JOHN—(or)B-88;
  (or)B-380
CHANCE, MOSES—(W)H-101
CHANCE, THOMAS—(ee)F-574;
  (ee)G-133; (ee)G-134; (CB)G-135;
  (CB)(M)G-165; (CB)G—421
CHAPMAN, WIRKS—(W)E-47
CHARLCRAFT, JAMES—(W)F-59
CHARLCRAFT, JOHN—(F)F-228;
  (F)F-283
CHARLCRAFT, SAMUEL—(or)F-206;
  (or)F-543; (F)H-87
CHARLESCRAFT, JAMES—(ee)D-28;

(or)F-435

CHEEK, RICHARD—(F)F-440

CHERRY, CHARLES—(F)C-112;
(F)B-488; (F)C228; (CB)G-375

CHERRY, ELEAZAR—(ee)F-86;
(ee)F-210

CHERRY, GEORGE—(W)D-109;
(W)D-143; (W)E-37

CHERRY, JOHN—(W)B-494;
(W)C-312; (or)E-7; (W)E-108;
(CB)G-118; (CB)G-235;
(CB)(M)G-375; (ee)G-376; (ee)G-377;
(CB)G-440

CHERRY, LEMUEL—(CB)G-357;
(F)B-488; (F)C-112; (F)E-7;
(ee)F-430; (ee)G-104; (ee)G-105;
(M)G-168; (M)G-358

CHERRY, NATHAN—(ee)E-157;
(M)G-234; (or)H-17; (ee)H-26

CHERRY, SAMUEL—(W)C-414;
(W)E-51; (ee)E-131

CHERRY, SOLOMON—(ee)C-413;
(or)F-571; (ee)G-180; (ee)G-181;
(M)G-366

CHERRY, WILLIAM—(F)E-7;
(W)F-571

CHURCH, CORNELIOUS—(W)B-232

CHURCH, CORNELIUS—(W)B-289;
(ee)C-539; (W)D-90; (W)E-11;
(W)E-125; (W)F-63; (W)H-10;
(W)H-16; (W)H-151

CHURCH, HANNER—(W)D-61

CHURCH, ISAAC—(A)C-139;
(ee)C-876; (W)C-539; (W)D-92;
(M)G-212; (A)H-20

CHURCH, JESSEE—(W)H-10

CHURCH, JOHN—(or)C-139;
(F)C-205; (W)(F)D-92; (A)F-24;
(ee)G-22; (CB)G-242; (or)H-10

CIRVAN, LARANCE—(or)C-70

CIRVIN, LARRANCE—(F)C-56

CLARK, DANIEL—(W)F-523

CLARK, JAMES SAMPSON—(CB)G-223

CLARK, WILLIAM—(ee)B-161;
(or)B-430; (W)C-248; (or)C-354;
(F)D-19

CLARKE, ISIAC—(W)H-43

CLARKE, JAMES SAMPSON—
(ee)G-218

CLARKE, MARGARET—(ee)F-170

CLARKE, SAMUEL—(CB)G-132

CLARKE, WILLIAM—(ee)F-170

CLEMENTS, GEORGE—(ee)D-120;
(W)F-45

CLEMENTS, WILLIAM—(W)E-329;
(ee)F-45; (ee)F-519; (ee)F-527;
(ee)G-388

COATS, WILLIAM WILSON—
(ee)B-252; (or)C-303

COBB, EDWARD—(ee)B-226;
(W)C-52; (W)C-486; (A)D-159;
(W)E-91;(W)E-241; (CB)G-276;

(CB)G-278; (CB)G-338; (W)H-11

COBB, JAMES—(W)B-226; (W)B-264;
(W)C-285; (ee)G-276; (ee)G-277;
(ee)G-278; (CB)G-338; (or)H-11;
(ee)H-11; (or)H-61

COBB, SHADRICH—(W)F-274

COBB, SOTHEY—(ee)F-199

COBB, SOUTHY—(or)F-540

COCKBURN, GEORGE—(W)F-267

COCKS, MOSES—(ee)E-118

COLE, EDWARD—(W)H-166

COLHOON, SAMUEL—(ee)E-292

COLHOUN, SAMUEL—(W)F-113

COLLINGS, JOSIAH—(CB)G-389

COLLINS, GEORGE—(A)E-46

COLLINS, JONAH—(W)F-519

COLLINS, JOSEPH—(CB)G-356;
(CB)G-380

COMMISSIONERS OF MARTIN-
BOROUGH—(or)E-111; (or)E-122;
(or)E-174; (or)E-176; (or) E-178;
(or)E-289; (or)E-292; (or)E-294;
(or)E-296; (or)E-299; (or)E-301;
(or)E-304; (or)E-306; (or)E-308;
(or)E-311; (or)E-313; (or)E-326;
(or)F-6; (or)F-8; (or)F-14; (or)F-41;
(or)F-78; (or)F-80; (or)F-126;
(or)F-137; (or)F-139; (or)F-218;
(or)F-253; (or)F-294; (or)F-322;
(or)F-340; (or)F-372; (or)F-388;
(or)F-404; (or)F-416; (or)F-418;
(or)F-425; (or)F-441; (or)F-483;
(or)H-68; (or)H-106; (or)H-114

CONGELTON, WILLIAM—(A)E-30

CONGLETON, ABRAHAM—(ee)F-3;
(CB)G-312

CONGLETON, JAMES—(CB)G-290

CONGLETON, WILLIAM—(W)B-488;
(W)C-78; (A)C-112; (or)F-3;
(A)F-102

CONNER, ANDREW—(F)D-164

CONNER, JAMES—(F)D-80

CONNER, JOHN—(F)F-560

CONSAL, WM.—(CB)G-392

CONSALL, WM.—(CB)G-420

CONWAY, PETER—(F)C-288; (F)E-71

COOK, JOHN—(ee)B-354; (or)E-12;
(or)F-307; (or)F-428

COOK, THOMAS—(A)F-308;
(ee)F-428; (or)F-524

COOK, WILLIAM—(M)E-12

COOMES, THOMAS—(or)B-234;
(or)B-247; (or)C-292; (ee)C-292;
(F)C-513

COOMS, THOMAS—(W)B-366

COOPER, BEN—(W)F-171

COOPER, BENJAMIN—(ee)E-237;
(W)F-18; (or)F-318; (CB)G-410

COOPER, HENRY—(W)B-441;
(W)C-102; (or)D-138; (F)F-391

COOPER, JAMES—(W)F-506

COOPER, JESSE—(ee)C-251; (or)F-161

COOPER, JOHN—(or)B-264; (or)D-147;
  (or)E-31; (or)E-218; (or)F-18
COOPER, THOMAS—(ee)C-258;
  (ee)C-368; (W)D-79; (ee)D-87;
  (W)D-125; (W)D-140
COOPER, WILLIAM—(W)D-139
COOTS, EZEKIEL—(CB)G-196
CORBET, WILLIAM—(ee)F-468
CORBET, JOHN—(M)G-35
CORBET, MARDAY—(M)G-35
CORBETT, MEREDITH—(or)H-44
CORBET, WILLIAM—(CB)G-196;
  (W)H-44
CORBETT, WM.—(ee)G-35; (M)G-469
CORBIT, JOHN—(CB)G-24
CORBITT, JOHN—(CB)G-36;
  (or)H-49; (ee)H-49; (ee)H-179
CORBITT, MARDAY—(ee)G-36;
  (CB)G-46
CORBITT, MAREDAY—(W)H-49
CORBITT, MAREDITH—(or)H-179
CORBITT, MERDAY—(CB)G-24
CORBITT, WILLIAM—(or)H-74;
  (or)H-177
CORDIN, BENJAMIN—(or)B-394;
CORDING, BENJ.—(F)H-67
COREY, BENJ.—(ee)G-303
COREY, THOMAS—(CB)G-121
CORIE, BENJAMIN—(or)H-12
COSON, WILLIAM—(F)B-266
COTES, WILLIAM—(F)B-402
COTTENHEAD, JAMES—(ee)G-95;
  (CB)G-111
COUNCIL, ARTHLR—(W)B-52
COUPER, HENRY—(ee)C-333;
  (ee)C-335
COUSALL, WILLIAM—(M)G-268
COUTANCHE, MICHAEL—(A)F-206;
COWARD, HEEDOM—(M)F-374
COWARD, ISAAC HARDEE—(ee)F-374
COWARD, NEEDOM—(ee)F-456;
  (ee)F-495
COWARD, PHEBE—(M)F-374
COWPER, JOHN—(ee)G-411
COWPLAND, JAMES—(W)C-4
COX, ABIA—(W)C-136; (ee)C-145;
  (or)D-102
COX, ABRAHAM—(W)H-135
COX, CHARLES—(W)C-136
COX, JEREMIAH—(ee)F-390;
  (or)H-135
CRAFFORD, JAMES—(ee)B-218
CRAFFORD, WM.—(M)G-360
CRAFTON, THEOPHILUS—(W)F-155
CRANDALL, JAMES—(ee)G-274
CRANDELL, CHRISTHOPER—
  (ee)H-169
CRANDELL, JAMES—(or)D-84;
  (ee)D-84; (A)D-184; (ee)D-161;
  (W)D-161; (or)E-6; (W)E-6;
  (W)E-146; (ee)F-201; (W)F-201;
  (CB)G-202; (ee)G-272; (ee)G-273;

(CB)G-285; (M)G-437; (ee)H-104;
  (or)H-145; (or)H-169
CRANDELL, MATTHIAS—(ee)F-485
CRANDELL, SAMUEL—(ee)D-84;
  (or)D-161
CRANDELL, THOMAS—(or)C-228
CRANFORD, JAMES—(W)D-51
CRAVY, HUGH—(ee)E-91
CRAWFORD, CHARLES—(W)E-69
CRAWFORD, WILLIAM—(W)F-116
CRAWFORD, WM.—(M)G-382
CRAWSON, THOMAS—(ee)F-544
CREEMORE, JAMES—(CB)G-464
CREMAIN, JAMES—(CB)G-240
CREMEAN, JAMES—(W)C-345;
  (or)H-104
CREMEN, JAMES—(W)H-145
CRISP, BENJAMIN—(W)F-179
CRISP, BRAY—(W)D-100
CRISP, FRAN—(W)F-334
CRISP, FRANCIS—(ee)F-503;
  (ee)G-178
CRISP, JESSE—(W)F-503
CRISP, SAMUEL—(W)F-179;
  (W)F-503
CRISP, WIILIAM—(A)C-145;
  (or)C-350; (A)D-102; (or)F-503
CRISP, WILLIAM STANSEL—
  (M)G-111
CROSS, HENRY—(W)B-305; (W)D-1
CROSS, THOMAS—(W)B-305
CROWSON, THOMAS—(or)F-557;
  (ee)H-113
CULPEPER, JOSEPH—(ee)F-145
CULPEPPER, GEORGE—(CB)G-420
CULPEPPER, JOSEPH—(W)F-342;
  (or)F-399
CUMMING, WILL—(W)C-447
CURLIE, JOHN—(ee)H-144
CURTIS, THOMAS—(or)F-556;
  (ee)H-86; (W)H-100; (or)H-173

D

DAIL, ABEL—(W)D-3; (or)F-345;
  (W)F-345
DAIL, PAUL—(W)H-122
DANIEL, EMANUEL—(CB)G-179
DANIEL, ENOCH—(CB)G-283
DANIEL, GEO.—(CB)G-313
DANIEL, GEORGE—(ee)G-281;
  (CB)G-282; (CB)G-283
DANIEL, JOHN—(or)F-132
DANIEL, ROBERT—(W)C-144;
  (ee)D-133; (A)D-138; (W)E-201;
  (or)F-90; (M)179; (M)G-281
DANIEL, ROBERT LANIER—
  (M)G-193; (ee)G-282; (ee)G-283
DANIEL, ROBT.—(CB)G-313
DANIEL, RUCHARD—(W)E-258
DANIEL, THOMAS—(W)C-13;
  (ee)C-66; (ee)C-83; (or)C-117;

DUBERRY, LEMUEL—(M)G-364
DUDLEY, AARON—(W)H-35
DUDLEY, JAMES—(ee)E-34
DUDLEY, SAMUEL—(CB)G-241;
  (M)G-301
DUDLY, JAMES—(M)G-301
DUDLY, RICHARD—(W)B-438
DUFFIELD, THOMAS—(W)B-432;
  (ee)C-226; (W)F-29
DUFFIL, THOMAS—(CB)G-197
DUFFILL, THOMAS—(CB)G-430
DUNBAR, SAMUEL—(ee)C-325
DUNCAN, ABRAHAM—(or)B-440;
  (F)B-440; (or)C-274; (F)E-85;
  (or)E-105; (F)F-297
DUNCAN, GEORGE—(or)B-440;
  (or)C-274; (F)E-85; (or)E-105;
  (F)H-53
DUNCAN, JOHN—(W)E-105
DUNKIN, ABRAHAM—(F)E-127
DUNLAP, JAMES—(M)F-358
DUNMARKE, WILLIAM—(ee)C-473;
DUPREE, BENJ.—(M)G-46;
  (CB)G-61; (CB)G-93; (CB)G-106
DUPREE, BENJAMIN—(ee)E-197;
  (ee)E-328; (W)F-239; (W)F-400;
  (W)H-44; (A)H-65; (ee)H-102;
  (A)H-105; (W)H-163
DUPREE, BURD—(CB)G-106
DUPREE, CRISSEY—(ee)H-163
DUPREE, JAMES—(ee)D-167;
  (ee)D-168; (or)E-197; (M)G-46;
  (ee)H-44; (A)H-102; (ee)H-105
DUPREE, STARLING—(ee)G-106
DUPREE, STERLING—(ee)D-165;
  (ee)D-169; (W)E-78; (W)F-329;
  (W)F-400; (ee)G-46; (M)G-113;
  (or)H-102; (or)H-105; (W)E-328
DUVALL, LEWIS—(F)C-219;
  (F)D-32; (F)E-27
DUVALL, MARTHA—(F)D-32
DYKS, GEORGE—(ee)B-271;
  (or)B-294

E

EASON, ABNER—(CB)G-154;
  (CB)G-166
EASON, ISAAC—(ee)B-173; (ee)E-111;
  (ee)G-166; (ee)G-349
EASON, SHADRACH—(CB)G-349
EASON, STEPHEN—(CB)G-166;
  (CB)G-349
EASTWOOD, JOHN—(or)F-432
EASTWOOD, JOSEPH—(ee)B-92;
  (or)B-382; (or)B-391
EASTWOOD, MARY—(ee)F-432
EASTWOOD, WILLIAM—(or)F-560
EASTWOOD, WM.—(ee)G-3
EAVEY, JOHN—(W)H-52
EDMINSON, JAMES—(W)F-58
EDMINSON, JAMES—(W)F-58

EDMONSON, JAMES—(ee)G-366;
  (CB)G-143; (CB)G-180
EDWARD, WILLIAM—(W)C-15
EDWARDS, ANDREW—(M)B-477
EDWARDS, BENJAMIN—(W)C-416
EDWARDS, BRITAIN—(ee)F-268
EDWARDS, CHARLES—(W)B-400;
  (CB)G-64; (CB)G-470; (ee)H-177
EDWARDS, CHRISTOPHER—
  (ee)D-108; (W)E-190; (or)E-203
EDWARDS, CLARY—(or)D-38
EDWARDS, DANIEL—(ee)C-53
EDWARDS, ISAAC—(ee)C-419;
  (F)E-67
EDWARDS, ISRAEL—(W)H-147;
  (or)H-160
EDWARDS, JAMES—(or)C-282;
  (A)D-108; (ee)F-496; (CB)G-101;
  (CB)G-174
EDWARDS, JOHN—(ee)B-279;
  (A)B-441; (A)B-457; (or)B-477;
  (or)C-53; (or)C-88; (F)D-143;
  (F)E-282; (ee)F-94; (or)F-429;
  (ee)F-440; (ee)H-161
EDWARDS, KINCHEN—(CB)G-471
EDWARDS, MARY—(W)C-234
EDWARDS, SAMUEL—(ee)C-96;
  (F)H-160
EDWARDS, SIMON—(or)H-160
EDWARDS, WENEFRET—(ee)B-477
EDWARDS, WILLIAM—(ee)C-141;
  (or)D-38; (or)F-4; (F)F-332;
  (ee)G-353; (CB)G-363
ELDRIDGE, SAMUEL—(A)E-60
ELKS, SAM—(CB)G-169
ELKS, SAMUEL—(CB)G-69;
  (CB)B-74; (CB)G-194
ELKS, WILLIAM—(CB)G-169
ELLIGOOD, HILLARY—(A)F-81
ELLIGOOD, HILLERY—(W)B-416;
  (or)D-51
ELLIGOOD, JACOB—(ee)C-440;
  (or)C-446; (or)C-450
ELLIOTT, WILLIAM—(A)D-114
ELLIS, BENJAMIN—(A)B-14;
  (W)B-551; (or)C-437; (W)D-10;
  (ee)D-148; (ee)E-64; (or)E-210;
  (ee)F-41
ELLIS, CHRISTIAN—(W)F-283
ELLIS, DAVID—(W)D-61
ELLIS, HENRY—(ee)B-40; (W)B-551;
  (W)C-250; (or)C-260; (ee)C-437;
  W)D-148; (or)E-192; (or)E-247;
  (W)E-273; (W)F-53; (W)F-168;
  (W)F-283; (M)F-365; (CB)G-29;
  (ee)G-280; (W)H-7; (W)H-8;
  (W)H-18; (W)H-58
ELLIS, JOHN—(W)F-190; (W)F-283;
  (W)F-489; (CB)G-29; (CB)G-160;
  (CB)G-185; (CB)G-280
ELLIS, LUCY—(W)E-192
ELLIS, RICHARD—(W)D-125

FLANAGAN, EDWARD—(M)G-204
FLANNAGAN, EDWARD—(CB)G-250
FLANNAKIN, EDWARD—(ee)F-416
FLANNEKIN, EDWARD—(ee)F-386
FLANNIKIN, EDWARD—(W)F-176
FLEMING, DAVID—(W)F-370
FLEMING, GEORGE—(ee)E-20;
 (CB)G-419
FLEMING, JOHN—(ee)B-404;
 (ee)F-370; (ee)G-191; (W)H-18;
 (W)H-29; (W)H-109
FLEMMING, DAVID—(CB)G-191
FLOYD, GRIFFIN—(W)H-34
FLOYD, JOHN—(CB)G-422
FLOYD, PETER—(W)E-7
FOLMSOM, WILLIAM—(W)C-294
FOLSOM, EBENEZER—(F)B-228;
 (ee)B-292; (or)B-359; (F)C-68;
 (F)C-119; (F)C-169; (or)C-432;
 (F)E-157; (F)F-506; (F)F-515;
 (F)H-17; (F)H-26; (F)H-38
FORBES, ARTHUR—(W)D-23;
 (or)E-66; (ee)E-83; (ee)E-120;
 (W)F-205; (ee)G-63; (M)G-435;
 (ee)H-21
FORBES, CHARLES—(W)C-4;
 (W)C-186; (W)D-104;
FORBES, JOHN—(F)D-16; (A)D-148;
 (F)D-157; (A)F-96; (F)F-385
FORBES, JOSEPH—(ee)G-39;
 (CB)G-63
FORBES, MARY—(M)D-16
FORBUCK, ARTHUR—(W)E-5
FOREMAN, JOHN—(W)H-63; (ee)H-94
FOREMAN, JOSHUA—(W)H-63
FOREMAN, RICHARD—(ee)H-63
FREEMAN, JOSHUA—(CB)G-319
FRIER, JOHN—(A)C-173
FRIZEL, JOHN—(ee)F-10; (or)H-55
FRIZEL, MARY—(or)H-55
FRIZELL, JOHN—(or)H-54
FRIZELL, MARY—(or)H-54
FRIZZEL, JOHN—(ee)F-119
FRIZZLE, JOHN—(W)F-81; (ee)F-155;
 (ee)F-222; (or)F-224; (W)F-395;
 (ee)F-507; (or)H-142
FRIZZLE, MARY—(or)H-142
FRY, JOHN—(W)E-1; (W)E-224;
 (ee)F-59; (W)F-78; (ee)G-199
FULFORD, JOHN—(or)C-16; (or)C-28;
 (ee)C-389; (W)C-523; (ee)C-542;
 (ee)D-97; (or)E-213; (ee)E-269;
 (or)F-280; (ee)G-12; (ee)G-466;
 (M)H-21
FULFORD, JOSEPH—(W)F-566
FULFORD, SARAH—(or)C-16;
 (or)C-28
FULFORD, SARAH ALLEN—
 (M)D-98; (M)E-213
FULLER, EBENEZER—(W)D-72
FULLINGHAM, JOHN, JR.—(ee)C-297

G

GADD, JOSEPH—(F)C-214
GAINER, JOS.—(CB)G-360
GAINER, JOSEPH—(ee)D-78;
 (ee)F-122; (ee)G-360; (M)G-475
GALLOWAY, WILLIAM—(F)B-270
GARALD, DAVID—(ee)C-469
GARALD, SUSANAH—(or)C-469
GARALD, WILLIAM—(or)C-469
GARDNER, ISAAC—(W)F-197
GARDNER, JAMES—(W)F-270
GARDNER, JOHN—(CB)G-345
GARELD, JAMES—(F)B-402
GARELD, MARY—(or)B-402
GARELD, WILLIAM—(or)B-402
GARRALD, DAVID—(ee)C-477
GARRALD, WILLIAM—(or)C-477
GARRALL, DAVID—(or)D-88;
 (or)D-91
GARRET, THOMAS—(CB)G-120
GARRETT, THOMAS—(ee)D-12
GATHEREE, WILLIAM—(CB)G-259
GATLAND, EDWARD—(ee)G-236
GATLIN, EDWARD—(W)E-113;
 (ee)F-211
GATLING, ANN—(or)H-149
GATLING, EDWARD—(ee)F-307;
 (or)H-149
GAUST, READING—(CB)G-350
GAY, JAMES—(W)F-518
GAY, JOHN—(W)C-400
GAY, RICHARD—(ee)B-445;
 (ee)F-83; (ee)G-22
GAY, SIMON—(or)F-83
GAY, WILLIAM—(ee)E-80; (W)F-83
GERRALD, WILLIAM—(ee)B-247;
 (or)C-513
GIBBLE, FREDERICK—(ee)F-11;
 (or)F-437
GIDDENS, ABRAHAM—(or)B-490
GIDDENS, JACOB—(or)D-63
GIDDENS, MARGREAT—(or)B-490
GIDDENS, THOMAS—(or)E-252;
 (F)F-270
GIDDENS, WILLIAM—(M)D-63
GIDDINGS, ISAAC—(ee)B-506;
 (or)C-137
GIDDINGS, THOMAS—(F)F-147
GIDDINGS, WILLIAM—(or)C-257
GIDDINS, ABRAHAM—(or)B-224
GIDDINS, ISAAC—(W)C-116;
 (or)C-213; (ee)C-213; (or)C-493;
 (W)D-146
GIDDINS, JACOB—(W)B-294;
 (ee)C-181; (A)(W)C-284; (or)D-46;
 (M)D-151
GIDDINS, THOMAS—(ee)D-146;
 (or)E-239
GIDDINS, WILLIAM—(or)B-271;
 (ee)B-294; (M)D-151
GILBERT, JOHN—(or)F-573
GILBERT, SILAS—(ee)F-573

GINDRAW, HENRY—(or)D-106;
(F)E-87
GINDRAW, SELAH—(or)D-106
GLISON, ABRAHAM—(A)D-120;
(or)E-329
GLISON, DENNIS—(A)F-121
GLISON, DINNES—(A)E-9
GLISON, SARAH—(or)E-329
GLISSON, ABRAHAM—(ee)B-466
GLISSON, DENNIS—(or)B-81
GLISSON, DENNIS—(or)B-103;
(F)C-277; (A)D-95
GLISSON, ISAAC—(ee)B-103
GLISSON, JAMES—(A)B-81; (F)C-277;
(A)F-346
GLISSON, JOSEPH—(W)B-81;
(W)B-103
GODLEY, BENJ.—(CB)G-73
GODLEY, BENJAMIN—(CB)G-77
GODLEY, JOHN—(W)F-132; (CB)G-79;
(W)H-126
GODLEY, NATHAN—(ee)C-121;
(or)C-217; (or)C-225; (W)D-20;
(ee)E-265; (ee)E-266; (ee)F-131;
(ee)F-132; (ee)G-75; (ee)G-76;
(CB)G-76; (ee)G-77; (ee)G-78;
(CB)G-115; (M)G-350
GODLEY, THOMAS—(CB)G-76;
(CB)G-77
GODLEY, THOS.—(CB)G-43;
(CB)G-73; (CB)G-75
GODWIN, MARY—(W)D-121
GOFF, HENRY—(W)F-190; (CB)G-415
GOFF, THOMAS—(ee)C-249; (W)D-5;
(A)F-205; (ee)F-259; (ee)F-556;
(ee)G-415; (A)H-88
GOFFORD, ANDREW—(W)B-104;
(ee)B-372; (ee)C-1; (or)C-18
GOFFORD, RACHEL—(W)C-146
GOLDING, LEMUEL—(CB)G-265
GORDON, STEWART—(W)F-240;
(W)F-284; (ee)G-444
GORHAM, JAMES—(W)F-391;
(ee)F-437; (CB)G-288; (CB)G-324;
(M)G-385; (ee)G-390; (ee)G-391;
(ee)G-392; (ee)G-393; (ee)G-394;
(ee)G-395; (ee)G-396; (ee)G-397;
(M)G-419; (W)H-38; (ee)H-78;
(ee)H-79; (or)H-126
GORHAM, JOSIAH—(CB)G-124
GRAINGER, SAMUEL—(W)F-326;
(W)F-406
GRAINGER, THOMAS—(ee)G-343
GRANBERY, GEORGE—(W)F-114;
(ee)F-224; (W)F-282
GRANBERY, MOSES—(W)F-114;
(ee)F-412
GRANGER, CALEB—(F)F-26
GRANGER, MARY—(F)F-26
GRANGER, SAMUEL—(W)F-297
GRANGER, THOMAS—(ee)F-298;
(CB)G-300

GRANVILLE, EARL— (Always the
grantor); B-1; B-5; B-10; B-14; B-19;
B-22; B-28; B-32; B-36; B-40; B-44;
B-48; B-75; B-126; B-129; B-133;
B-137; B-141; B-145; B-149; B-153;
B-157; B-161; B-165; B-169; B-173;
B-177; B-181; B-185; B-189; B-193;
B-197; B-201; B-205; B-210; B-214;
B-312; B-316; B-322; B-326; B-330;
B-335; B-339; B-344; B-349; B-354;
B-361; B-452; B-457; B-462; B-466;
B-497; B-501; B-506; B-510; B-514;
B-519; B-524; B-528; B-533; B-537;
B-542; B-546; C-96; C-189; C-271;
C-315; C-453; C-524; F-443; F-447
GRAY, ELISHA—(or)F-499
GRAY, JOSEPH—(ee)C-340; (ee)C-374;
(M)G-356
GRAY, LUCY—(or)F-499
GRAY, SIMON—(W)F-171; (ee)F-423;
GREEN, DAVID—(or)C-247; (CB)G-314
GREEN, GEORGE—(W)F-560
GREEN, SAMUEL—(or)E-118;
(ee)E-155
GREMMER, JACOB—(W)F-335
GREMMER, JOSEPH—(CB)G-224
GREMMER, JOSIAH—(W)F-335
GREMMER, ROBERT—(ee)B-264;
(W)B-376; (W)B-408; (W)C-256;
(ee)C-263; (W)C-476
GRICE, BENJAMIN—(ee)H-159
GRIFFEN, WILLIAM—(W)F-3
GRIFFIN, BENJAMIN—(W)H-70
GRIFFIN, JAMES—(CB)G-53;
(ee)G-68; (ee)H-11
GRIFFIN, JOHN—(ee)C-112;
(or)F-287; (or)H-11
GRIFFIN, OWEN—(W)D-61
GRIFFITH, JAMES—(CB)G-312
GRIMES, DEMSIE—(ee)E-27
GRIMES, DEMPSIE—(ee)H-62;
(or)H-112
GRIMES, DEMPSEY—(ee)G-260
GRIMES, DENNIS—(W)H-56
GRIMES, WILLIAM—(W)D-161
GRIMMER, MARY—(or)F-414
GRIMMER, ROBERT—(W)C-437;
(W)D-147; (ee)F-18; (or)F-414;
(or)H-113; (ee)F-425
GRISARD, HARDY—(W)C-138;
(ee)E-239; (ee)E-252; (or)F-39
GRISERD, HARDY—(ee)C-115
GRIST, BENJ.—(CB)G-123
GRIST, BENJAMIN—(CB)G-48;
(CB)G-75; (CB)G-418
GRIST, JOHN—(W)C-492; (F)D-51;
(ee)G-48; (M)G-117
GRIST, RICHARD—(ee)D-24; (F)D-51;
(F)F-81; (ee)F-118; (ee)G-122;
(ee)G-123; (ee)G-127; (M)G-175
GRIST, SIMON—(M)G-411
GRIST, WILLIAM—(ee)D-20;

(A)F-118; (M)G-158
GRIZZARD, HARDEE—(or)F-147;
(ee)E-304
GRYMES, SAMUEL—(W)C-436
GUFFORD, ANDREW—(or)F-157
GURGANUS, DAVID—(CB)G-388;
(CB)G-438
GURGANUS, RUBIN—(CB)G-475
GURGANUS, STEPHEN—(M)G-437;
(ee)G-475; (ee)G-476
GWALTNEY, THOMAS—(A)B-14;
(A)B-40; (W)B-88; (A)C-260;
(or)D-10; (A)D-166; (W)D-166;
(ee)E-3; (A)E-248; (or)F-313;
(ee)G-167; (or)H-101; (F)H-157;
(M)G-229
GWALTNEY, WILLIAM—(W)B-73;
(or)B-408; (or)B-482; (W)B-492;
(or)C-243; (or)D-10; (W)H-101

H

HACKBURNE, JOHN—(M)G-260
HADDOCK, JOHN—(or)F-129;
(M)G-292
HADDOCK, WILLIAM—(W)F-129
HADDOCK, ZACHRIAH—(ee)F-129
HALL, HANNAH—(ee)H-133
HALL, THOMAS—(W)F-578
HALL, THOMAS H.—(W)D-19;
(or)F-543
HALLEMAN, ELIZABETH—(or)C-415
HALLEMAN, THOMAS—(or)C-415
HAM, WILLIAM—(F)B-421; (F)C-437
HAMM, WILLIAM—(F)H-131
HANCOCK, JAMES—(W)F-263;
(CB)G-14; (CB)G-296
HANCOCK, JAS.—(CB)G-28;
(CB)G-343
HANCOCK, WILLIAM—(ee)E-77;
(or)F-185; (ee)F-240; (W)F-244;
(or)F-257; (or)F-265
HANDBERRY, JAMES—(CB)G-35
HANDCOCK, JAMES—(W)H-138;
(W)B-240; (W)D-3; (W)E-8; (ee)E-85
HANDCOCK, WILLIAM—(W)D-29
HANDSON, LEWIS—(or)D-5
HANLY, JAMES—(CB)G-365
HARDEE, ABRAHAM—(CB)G-109;
(CB)G-168
HARDEE, ANDREW—(or)E-123
(or)E-159; (or)F-99; (F)F-104;
(or)F-293; (or)F-328; (M)G-398;
(F)H-146.
HARDEE, ANEY RELLA—(W)D-82
HARDEE, CHARLES—(W)D-4;
(W)D-12; (W)D-42; (W)D-124;
(ee)H-123; (or)H-133
HARDEE, ISAAC—(ee)B-374;
(W)B-382; (W)B-425; (or)B-428;
(W)C-80; (W)E-132; (W)F-185;
(W)F-240; (CB)G-109; (ee)G-121;

(CB)B-230; (M)G-355; (CB)G-443;
(or)H-12
HARDEE, JOHN—(or)B-92; (ee)B-223;
(W)B-223; (ee)B-382; (ee)B-391;
(W)B-394; (ee)B-406; (W)B-428;
(W)C-24; (ee)C-56; (or)C-64;
(W)C-80; (or)C-128; (W)C-179;
(ee)C-313; (F)C-417; (F)C-541;
(W)D-5; (or)D-47; (or)D-74;
(or)D-75; (or)D-76; (or)D-78;
(ee)D-82; (or)D-114; (ee)E-127;
(A)E-131; (or)E-201; (ee)F-78;
(or)F-211; (or)F-234; (or)F-247;
(W)F-292; (or)F-362; (ee)G-33;
(ee)G-109; (ee)G-168; (M)G-355
HARDEE, JOSEPH—(F)B-56;
(M)C-338; (F)D-114; (or)E-2;
(A)E-263; (F)F-298; (F)F-543
HARDEE, JOSIAH—(W)D-132;
(CB)G-230
HARDEE, JOSIAS—(ee)C-396;
(W)F-295
HARDEE, MARY—(W)E-42;
(W)E-133; (W)F-292
HARDEE, ROBERT—(or)B-223;
(or)B-249; (W)B-382; (ee)B-428;
(W)C-294; (or)C-396; (or)D-136;
(F)E-48; (W)E-323; (W)F-295;
(CB)G-33; (or)H-12; (ee)G-230
HARDEE, THOMAS—(or)C-337;
(or)C-531; (ee)D-3; (F)D-51;
(W)D-124; (or)E-85; (ee)F-99;
(ee)G-14; (CB)G-296; (ee)G-302;
(W)E-135; (CB)G-28; (CB)G-359;
(CB)G-451
HARDEE, WILLIAM—(W)F-257;
(W)F-293; (or)F-383; (CB)G-27;
(or)H-138
HARDEN, ELIZABETH BECTON—
(or)B-447
HARDEN, MARG—(or)B-447
HARDIE, JOHN—(F)C-372
HARDIE, THOS.—(W)H-10
HARDIN, ELIZABETH—(ee)B-245;
(W)E-85
HARDIN, MARK—(W)B-240;
(W)B-244; (ee)B-245; (W)C-236;
(W)D-29; (W)D-89; (W)E-8;
(W)E-85; (W)E-260
HARDING, ISRAEL—(F)D-72;
(CB)G-468
HARDING, STEPHEN—(or)D-72;
(CB)G-71; (M)G-122; (CB)G-127
HARDINSON, JOSHUA—(ee)F-478;
(ee)F-484
HARDISON, JOSHUA—(or)H-22;
(or)H-26; (W)H-54; (ee)H-83
HARDY, ANDREW—(F)F-498
HARDY, JOHN—(or)F-453
HARDY, THOS.—(F)F-410
HARE, BETTY—(ee)F-196
HARE, BETTY JUDKINS—(F)496

HARE, MOSES—(or)C-392; (or)C-514
HARGET, BARBARA—(or)D-93
HARGET, FREDERICK—(F)D-93
HARGET, PETER—(or)D-93
HARGROVES, SAMUEL—(F)H-109
HARPER, THOMAS—(W)B-121;
  (ee)B-220; (or)C-511
HARREL, JOHN—(ee)D-63; (W)D-146;
  (M)G-392
HARRELL, JOHN—(or)D-151;
  (ee)G-439; (ee)H-141
HARRELL, MOSES—(ee)C-228
HARRINGTON, TIMOTHY—(W)F-173
HARRIS, EDWARD—(or)D-102
HARRIS, ELIJAH—(ee)C-114;
  (or)C-378; (F)D-22; (W)E-7;
  (or)E-222
HARRIS, FITCH—(or)F-370
HARRIS, FITZH—(ee)E-207
HARRIS, HENRE—(W)H-139
HARRIS, HENRY—(ee)G-235;
  (ee)G-326; (CB)G-327; (CB)G-362;
  (CB)G-410
HARRIS, HOOD—(W)F-113; (W)H-12
HARRIS, JAMES—(W)F-338;
  (CB)G-325; (ee)G-327; (M)G-362;
  (M)G-434
HARRIS, LEMUEL—(ee)C-378;
  (or)D-22
HARRIS, MAJOR—(W)B-310;
  (W)C-21; (ee)C-518; (W)F-134;
  (W)F-274; (CB)G-38
HARRIS, RICHARD—(A)C-48
HARRIS, TIMOTHY—(ee)B-205;
  (ee)D-35; (F)D-102; (F)D-140;
  (ee)E-273; (or)F-338; (W)F-548;
  (M)G-326; (ee)G-328; (M)H-184
HARRIS, WILLIAM—(ee)B-189;
  (A)C-119; (or)C-204; (ee)C-204;
  (or)D-140; (A)D-148; (or)F-113;
  (ee)F-541; (or)H-184
HARRIS, WM.—(CB)G-139; (M)G-200
HARRIS, MAJOR—(ee)G-139;
  (ee)H-128
HART, BARRAIN—(CB)G-251
HART, MARY—(ee)F-385
HART. MICAJAH—(W)D-40
HART. MOSES—(ee)E-44; (ee)E-46;
  (or)E-181; (or)F-65; (F)F-174;
  (or)F-255; (or)H-95; (F)H-132
HART, ROBERT—(W)F-65; (W)F-255;
  (W)F-376; (ee)F-463; (ee)G-263;
  (ee)G-364; (or)H-57; (ee)H-95;
  (or)H-132
HART, WATKINS—(ee)F-174;
  (ee)F-255; (ee)F-376; (M)F-385;
  (or)F-463; (ee)F-550; (CB)G-170;
  (CB)G-171
HART, WILL—(M)G-362
HART, WILLIAM—(W)C-416;
  (ee)F-65; (or)F-174; (W)F-342;
  (ee)G-161; (M)G-327; (ee)H-27

HARVEY, AUGUST—(CB)G-472
HARVEY, JOHN—(CB)G-361
HARVEY, JOSEPH—(CB)G-54
HARVEY, JOSHUA—(CB)G-380
HATAWAY, FRANCIS—(ee)G-144
HATHAWAY, DAVID—(W)C-206;
  (or)D-11; (F)E-201
HATHAWAY, EDMOND—(ee)D-11;
  (ee)D-61
HATHAWAY, FRANCIS—(W)D-11
HATHAWAY, THOMAS—(W)C-540;
  (W)D-11; (ee)E-174
HATHEAWAY, EDMOND—(W)B-232
HATLOCK, JOHN—(F)F-75
HATTAWAY, CHARLES—(CB)G-101
HATTAWAY, DAVID—(or)F-158
HATTAWAY, EDMUND—(A)F-24;
  (M)F-158; (W)F-161; (M)G-232
HATTAWAY, FRANCIS—(ee)F-158;
  (CB)G-174; (or)H-107
HATTAWAY, THOMAS—(ee)B-232;
  (M)F-158; (ee)F-161; (W)F-161;
  (M)G-254; (CB)G-381; (M)G-406;
  (W)H-136
HATTAWAY, THOS.—(ee)G-163;
  (M)G-318; (CB)G-333
HATTAWAY, WILLIAM—(W)H-107
HATTERWAY, DAVID—(M)G-163
HATTERWAY, EDMUND—(ee)G-162
HATTERWAY, THOMAS—(M)G-255
HATTEWAY, FRANCIS—(ee)F-509
HATTEWAY, THOMAS—(CB)G-163
HATTOCK, ADMIRAL—(CB)G-15
HATTOCK, JOHN—(ee)C-406;
  (or)D-34; (ee)D-34; (or)E-279;
  (F)E-279; (ee)H-183
HATTOCK, WILLIAM—(ee)E-279;
  (CB)G-15
HATTOCK, WILLM—(W)H-50
HATTON, JOHN—(W)F-364;
  (ee)G-137; (CB)G-137; (ee)G-138;
  (M)G-139; (CB)G-233; (ee)G-402;
  (CB)G-402
HATTUCK, JOHN—(or)C-404;
  (ee)E-172
HATWAY, DAVID—(A)B-376;
  (ee)C-207
HAUS, JAMES—(W)E-9
HAVEN, JOHN—(M)F-568
HAY, ELEXANDER—(W)H-166
HAYES, WILLIAM—(ee)E-261
HAYS, WILLIAM—(ee)C-310;
  (or)F-116; (or)F-419
HEARN, JAMES—(W)E-241; (A)F-94;
  (F)F-440
HEARN, JOHN—(W)F-94; (or)F-440;
  (ee)F-533; (M)G-276
HEARN, MASON—(or)F-533
HELLEN, WILLIAM—(ee)F-247;
  (CB)G-20; (CB)G-168
HELLEN, WM.—(CB)G-444
HENINTON, JOHN—(ee)E-153

HENLY, JOSEPH—(W)F-286
HENNINGTON, HENRY—(W)H-96
HENNINGTON, JOHN—(ee)F-192
HENNINGTON, JONATHAN—
  (ee)B-157
HERENTON, JOHN—(ee)E-109
HERN, BENJAMIN—(M)G-384
HERRINGTON, EPHRAIM—(ee)F-311;
  (ee)G-44
HERRINGTON, JAMES—(W)F-395
HERRINGTON, JOHN—(or)F-406;
  (F)F-532
HERRINGTON, JONATHAN—
  (CB)G-404
HERRINGTON, PAUL—(ee)C-72;
  (or)E-331; (F)F-311; (CB)G-13;
  (W)H-144
HERRINGTON, SARAH—(or)E-331
HERRINGTON, TIMOTHY—(W)F-358
HERRINTON, EPHRAIM—(CB)G-120
HERRINTON, JOHN—(or)F-349;
  (M)G-223
HEWELL, THOMAS—(ee)B-326
HICKMAN, JESSE—(CB)G-381
HICKMAN, JOSEPH—(ee)B-492;
  (W)C-244; (ee)G-381
HIGHSMITH, JOHN—(or)B-310;
  (ee)B-335; (ee)F-31; (or)F-187
HILL, CHARITY—(or)H-43
HILL, JAMES—(W)F-2; (W)H-20
HILL, JOHN—(W)F-196
HILL, JOSHUA—(M)G-127; (or)H-43
HINES, DAVID—(W)D-165; (W)D-167;
  (W)D-168; (W)D-169; (ee)F-329;
  (ee)F-400; (CB)G-325; (CB)G-327;
  (ee)G-362; (M)G-362; (ee)G-434;
  (ee)G-435; (or)H-163
HINES, HENRY—(W)H-29
HINES, JAMES—(W)D-167; (W)D-168;
  (CB)C-434
HINES, JOHN—(W)F-312; (W)H-36
HINES, PETER—(W)D-165; (W)D-167;
  (W)D-168; (W)E-292; (W)E-296;
  (W)F-372; (W)F-388; (W)H-68
HININTON, JONATHAN—(W)F-192
HINTON, NOAH—(W)E-204
HOBSON, FRANCES—(W)E-12
HOBSON, FRANCIS—(A)B-19;
  (W)B-99; (W)B-372; (W)C-5;
  (W)C-136; (or)C-145; (ee)C-146;
  (ee)C-147; (or)C-172; (W)C-176;
  (W)D-102; (ee)E-10; (or)E-52;
  (M)E-220; (F)F-173; (or)F-423
HODGE, ELIAS—(M)G-146
HODGES, BENJ.—(M)G-214
HODGES, BENJAMIN—(F)D-19;
  (F)E-164; (F)E-166; (ee)G-209
HODGES, ELEAZAR—(or)E-164;
  (or)D-2; (F)D-20
HODGES, ELEAZER—(or)E-166
HODGES, ELIAS—(or)B-494;
  (or)C-216; (M)D-2; (F)D-20;

(F)D-26; (F)E-110; (M)F-132;
  (F)H-109
HODGES, FLOYD—(W)E-164;
  (CB)G-81; (CB)G-187
HODGES, HENRY—(ee)E-110;
  (ee)B-494; (ee)D-54; (W)E-50;
  (ee)E-222; (ee)G-80; (CB)G-105;
  (ee)G-208; (CB)G-274; (W)H-109
HODGES, HILLARY—(ee)F-479
HODGES, HILLERY—(M)G-470
HODGES, HOWEL—(W)B-228
HODGES, HOWELL—(ee)F-537;
  (or)F-554; (ee)G-301; (or)H-109
HODGES, JAMES—(CB)G-274
HODGES, JOHN—(W)B-93; (or)B-266;
  (or)B-228; (F)B-425; (A)B-494;
  (ee)C-68; (or)D-26; (ee)D-138;
  (W)E-164; (F)F-73; (W)F-90:
  (or)F-391; (or)F-537; (F)F-554;
  (CB)G-84; (or)H-26; (F)H-109
HODGES, MATHEW—(W)E-164;
  (ee)E-166; (ee)G-80; (ee)G-81;
  (ee)G-82; (ee)G-83; (ee)G-84;
  (ee)G-85; (ee)G-86; (M)G-213;
  (M)G-241; (M)G-246; (M)G-450
HODGES, MATTHEW—(W)B-494;
  (W)D-26; (W)D-54; (ee)D-58;
  (M)G-208
HODGES, MOSES—(W)F-504;
  (CB)G-422; (W)H-34
HODGES, PORTLOCK—(ee)F-342
HODGES, ROBERT—(W)B-228;
  (A)C-195; (W)D-26; (W)E-50;
  (ee)E-164; (CB)G-187; (M)G-209;
  (ee)G-213; (ee)G-214; (F)H-35
HODGES, SOGER—(ee)D-2; (or)D-20
HODGES, SARAH—(or)F-319
HODGES, THOMAS—(or)F-319;
  (ee)F-504
HODGES, WILLIAM—(CB)G-80;
  (CB)G-81; (ee)G-371
HOLIDAY, JOSEPH—(ee)E-7
HOLLAND, ANN—(M)C-458
HOLLAND, ELIZABETH—(or)E-184
HOLLAND, JOHN—(or)B-52; (ee)B-56;
  (ee)B-119; (F)C-5; (F)C-30;
  (F)C-268; (F)C-430; (or)C-481;
  (F)D-94; (F)E-52; (M)F-113;
  (W)F-543; (M)G-143
HOLLAND, PHILLIP—(W)F-319
  (A)H-166
HOLLAND, RICHARD—(ee)C-296
HOLLAND, SPEAR—(or)E-184
HOLLAND, SPEIR—(W)C-530;
  (or)D-94; (ee)D-103; (ee)F-469
HOLLAND, SPIER—(CB)G-149
HOLLAND, STEPHEN—(W)E-105
HOMES, JOHN—(CB)G-260;
  (CB)G-417; (CB)G-427
HOOKS, JOHN—(W)D-22
HOPKINS, ARNAL—(or)C-1; (W)C-146
HOPKINS, ARNALD—(ee)C-172

HOPKINS, WILLIAM—(W)C-1;
(W)C-323; (ee)G-374; (CB)G-387;
(W)H-98
HORNE, JOHN—(CB)G-294
HOUSE, THOMAS—(ee)B-305;
(ee)G-433
HOUSE, WILLIAM—(CB)G-182
HOVER, JOHN—(F)E-109
HOWEL, CALEB—(F)C-312
HOWELL, CALEB—(F)F-116
HOWELL, GRIFFETH—(W)E-261;
(W)F-47
HOWEL, GRIFFITH—(W)E-34
HOWELL, JOSEPH—(M)F-358
HOWL, JAMES—(or)C-173
HUDSON, JOHN HOLADAY—(ee)F-48
HUDSON, JOHN HOLLADAY—
(or)F-122
HUDSON, LEWIS—(ee)C-435
HULL, BENJAMIN—(ee)C-306;
(ee)C-345; (F)F-290
HULL, JOSHUA—(W)D-17
HULL, PETER—(W)B-428
HULL, WILLIAM—(W)D-93
HUMBER, JAMES—(W)H-164
HURLEY, JOHN—(F)H-63
HUSEY, SAMNEL—(CB)G-249
HUSSEY, SAMDEL—(ee)E-150
HUSSY, SAMUEL—(M)G-325

I

INGLIS, JAMES—(or)E-80
INGLIS, MARY—(or)E-80
INGRAM, JOHN—(W)C-276;
(or)C-286; (ee)C-364; (or)D-90
INGRIM, JOHN—(ee)C-240
IRWIN, HENRY—(ee)E-52; (or)F-173
ISLER, FREDERICK—(W)B-447
IVEY, THOMAS—(A)F-415; (A)H-101

J

JACKSON, GEORGE—(M)D-74
JACKSON, JOHN—(W)F-568
JACKSON, JOSEPH—(or)E-109;
(ee)E-331; (or)F-311
JACKSON, UARY—(ee)F-261;
(or)F-495
JAMES, ABSALOM—(or)E-10; (F)H-34
JAMES, ABSALUM—(or)C-132
JAMES, HENRY—(CB)G-193;
(ee)G-238
JAMES, JOHN—(W)C-280; (W)C-334;
(or)C-335; (CB)G-129; (ee)G-131;
(CB)G-192
JAMES, JOSEPH—(M)G-179
JAMES, JOSHUA—(W)E-232;
(W)U-391; (ee)G-193; (CB)G-238;
(CB)G-460
JAMES, LEMUEL—(A)C-68;
(ee)C-278; (or)C-333; (ee)F-289;

(ee)G-129; (ee)G-130; (M)G-179;
(M)G-192; (M)G-193; (M)G-460
JAMES, MATHEW—(CB)G-129;
(CB)G-192
JAMES, SAMUEL—(or)F-408
JAMES, SOLOMON—(A)B-193;
(or)D-100; (A)E-9; (A)E-329;
(F)F-522
JAMES, THOMAS—(ee)F-102;
(M)G-119; (CB)G-281; (CB)G-282;
(ee)G-312; (ee)G-313; (M)G-361
JAMES, WILLIAM—(CB)G-179;
(CB)G-193; (CB)G-238; (CB)G-460
JAMES, WM.—(CB)G-234
JARREL, HENRY—(or)F-378
JEFFERSON, JOHN—(W)H-74
JEFFREY, OSBORN—(A)E-16;
(A)E-78
JEFFREYS, OSBORN—(or)E-81
JEFFEREYS, SIMON—(W)E-81
JENKINS, HENRY—(ee)B-113
JERRELL, HENRY—(A)F-244
JOHNSON, AMOS—(W)H-66
JOHNSON, ANNA—(W)E-133
JOHNSON, DANIEL—(ee)C-511;
(F)E-49; (ee)H-34; (F)H-80
JOHNSON, ELIZABETH—(or)B-443
JOHNSON, JAMES—(ee)F-543;
(or)F-544; (W)H-66
JOHNSON, JOHN—(F)D-100
JOHNSON, MATTHIAS—(W)F-309;
(W)F-319; (or)H-34
JOHNSON, NATHAN—(ee)B-277;
(or)B-287; (or)B-443; (ee)B-478;
(F)C-210; (F)F-403
JOHNSON, PRISCILLA—(or)E-49;
(W)F-145
JOHNSON, WILLIAM—(W)F-65
JOHNSTON, ELIZABETH—(or)D-13
JOHNSTON, JACOB—(ee)F-388
JOHNSTON, JAMES—(ee)B-121;
(W)B-220; (W)C-512; (ee)G-92;
(M)G-471; (ee)H-40; (or)H-40
JOHNSTON, JOHN—(A)D-74;
(F)F-522
JOHNSTON, MARY—(ee)F-372
JOHNSTON, NATHAN—(A)B-145;
(ee)B-452; (or)D-13; (or)D-27;
(or)F-382
JOHNSTON, PETER—(W)B-250;
(W)C-314
JOHNSTON, PRISCILLA—(or)E-41
JOHNSTON, WILLIAM—(W)E-1;
(W)F-379; (ee)G-286
JOHNSTON, WILMOUTH—(W)B-44
JOHNSTON, WM.—(M)G-252
JOINER, ABRAHAM—(ee)F-159;
(CB)G-92
JOINER, ISRAEL—(M)G-201;
(ee)G-237; (CB)G-286; (ee)G-334;
(ee)G-335
JOINER, JOHN—(W)E-254; (W)F-

(or)F-550; (or)H-63
LANIER, NATHANIEL—(ee)E-29;
(W)E-120; (W)E-198; (ee)F-96;
(or)F-167; (or)F-376; (or)F-405;
(W)F-489; (or)F-550; (ee)G-170;
(ee)G-171; (ee)G-346; (W)H-7;
(ee)H-10; (W)H-69
LANIER, SETH—(CB)G-269;
(ee)G-270; (CB)G-372; (M)G-382;
(CB)G-446; (ee)G-447; (ee)H-12
LANIER, WILLIAM—(ee)C-160;
(W)F-203; (CB)G-270; (CB)G-445;
(ee)G-448
LANIER, WM.—(ee)G-269; (CB)G-441;
(M)G-448
LATHAM, JAMES—(ee)B-222;
(W)B-485; (ee)B-496; (ee)C-127;
(ee)D-39; (ee)D-40; (ee)D-170;
(W)E-6; (W)E-262; (ee)F-290;
(ee)F-419; (ee)G-49; (ee)G-50;
(ee)G-51; (M)G-372; (M)G-445
LATHINGHOUSE, ANDREW—
(CB)G-146
LATHINGHOUSE, THOMAS—
(ee)G-146
LATHINGHOUSE, YOUNG—(CB)G-146
LATTINGHOUSE, THOMAS—(M)G-76
LAUGHAN, ADAM—(ee)C-81
LEE, JOHN—(A)F-94; (M)G-342
LEE, STEPHEN—(W)H-98
LEGATE, JOHN—(ee)D-109; (W)F-551
LEGETT, ABSALOM—(W)D-159
LESLIE, JOHN—(W)E-19; (W)E-115;
(W)E-282
LESLIE, JNO—(W)D-47
LESSLIE, ANN—(M)C-458
LESSLIE, APSLEY—(ee)F-367
LESSLIE, JOHN—(W)C-220;
(or)C-458; (ee)D-119; (M)F-367
LESSLIE, NANCY—(M)F-367
LESTER, JEREMIAH—(ee)G-90;
(ee)G-91; (ee)H-29; (or)H-143
LEWIS, GEORGE—(F)C-241
LEWIS, JOHN—(W)F-415; (W)F-438;
(ee)H-10; (or)H-85
LEWIS, MATTHEW—(CB)G-416
LEWIS, NATHAN—(CB)G-113
LEWIS, PETER—(or)F-45
LEWIS, THOMAS—(CB)G-276
LEWIS, WILLIAM—(ee)B-81;
(or)F-346
LILLINGTON, ALEXANDER—
(F)E-141; (or)E-224
LILLINGTON, JOHN—(F)B-52;
(F)E-141
LILLINGTON, JOHN ALEXANDER—
(F)B-52
LILLINGTON, SARAH—(W)E-224
LILLINGTON, SARAH PORTER—
(F)B-52
LITTEL, GEORGE—(W)C-7; (ee)C-27;
(W)H-104

LITTEL, JAMES—(ee)B-410
LITTEL, JOSIAH—(W)B-410; (ee)C-7
LITTEL, THOMAS—(or)B-410;
(or)C-7; (or)C-27
LITTEL, WILLIAM—(W)H-104
LITTLE, BENJAMIN—(W)C-416
LITTLE, ELISABETH—(or)C-130
LITTLE, ELIZABETH—(or)F-67
LITTLE, FREDERICK—(W)H-80
LITTLE, GEORGE—(ee)G-240
LITTLE, ISAAC—(W)D-49; (ee)G-132;
(CB)G-215
LITTLE, JACOB—(or)C-51; (or)C-62;
(W)D-155; (W)E-29; (W)H-18;
(W)H-24; (W)H-185
LITTLE, JAMES—(W)C-52; (or)D-49;
(ee)E-29; (A)E-137; (W)F-24;
(A)H-10
LITTLE, JOHN—(A)C-51; (ee)C-62;
(A)C-130; (W)E-29; (or)E-55;
(ee)E-107; (W)F-52; (M)G-191;
(CB)G-348; (ee)H-18
LITTLE, JOSEPH—(ee)C-51;
(or)C-130; (ee)C-136; (W)D-102;
(ee)F-24; (or)F-67; (M)G-162;
(A)H-10; (ee)H-85
LITTLE, JOSIAH—(F)B-102;
(W)D-161; (W)E-15; (M)E-55;
(F)E-107; (W)F-163; (CB)G-272;
(CB)G-273; (ee)G-285; (CB)G-317;
(W)H-104
LITTLE, MATTHEW—(W)F-267
LITTLE, PLEASANT—(W)F-577;
(W)H-185
LITTLE, THOMAS—(or)B-102;
(ee)B-126; (ee)B-177; (A)H-11
LITTLE, WILLIAM—(F)E-286;
(CB)G-202; (CF)G-240; (ee)G-241
LOCKHART, DANIEL—(A)E-244;
(M)F-126; (W)F-142; (W)F-159
LOCKHART, HANNAH—(or)E-78;
(or)E-328
LOCKHART, JAMES—(ee)E-16;
(or)E-78; (W)E-81; (ee)E-84;
(ee)E-187; (W)E-237; (or)E-328;
(W)F-18; (or)F-249
LOCKHART, JOEL—(CB)G-61
LOCKHART, LENINGTON—(F)E-232
LOCKHART, LILLINGTON—(F)E-94
LOCKHART, LINNINTON—(F)E-271
LOW, JOHN—(CB)G-103
LOYD, JOSEPH—(or)C-251
LUTER, JEREMIAH—(W)F-543
LUTER, MATHEW—(ee)E-220
LUTER, MATTHEW—(W)F-312;
(W)F-487; (M)G-403

M

MACCLAIN, CHARLES—(W)B-436
MACE, WILLIAM—(or)B-73;
(ee)B-438; (ee)B-475; (or)C-343;

(F)C-343; (F)F-178
MACKLAIN, DAIIEL—(W)F-379
MACLAIN, DANIEL—(ee)G-275
MACNEMAR, LARENCE—(W)B-488
MALLET, MARY—(W)E-44
MANCOR, JAMES—(ee)C-117;
(or)C-121; (W)C-289; (or)D-24
MANING, JOHN—(ee)F-571
MANING, LYDIA—(or)F-110
MANING, MOSES—(W)D-85;
(or)F-110; (or)F-114; (or)F-119
MANING, SAMUEL—(ee)F-110
MANING, SARAH—(W)F-110
MANING, THOMAS—(W)D-64;
(W)F-110
MANNIN, MOSES—(A)F-191
MANNIN, SAMUEL—(or)F-191
MANNING, REUBEN—(ee)E-204;
(or)F-184; (M)G-140; (CB)G-164;
(CB)G-433
MARIONER, SARAH—(ee)G-452
MARTIN, JOSEPH—(CB)G-216
MARTIN, JOSHUA—(ee)H-140
MARTIN, PETER—(ee)F-524;
(M)G-145; (CB)G-266; (A)H-149
MARTIN, WILLIAM—(M)G-83
MASS, MICAL—(or)F-35
MATHEWS, BENJAMIN—(F)D-47;
(F)D-61; (A)F-300
MATHES, JOSEPH—(CB)G-35
MATHIS, BENJAMIN—(F)D-18
MATHIS, WILLIAM—(W)H-61
MATTHEWS, WM.—(W)B-10
MAUBLY, PATRICK—(F)C-127
MAUL, WILLIAM—(F)F-99
MAULE, JOHN—(ee)C-514
MAULE, PATRICK—(F)B-222;
(F)C-160; (F)C-345; (F)F-69;
(F)F-153; (F)H-137
MAULE, SARAH—(F)B-222; (F)F-69
MAUN, HARDEE—(ee)E-49
MAY, BANJAN—(W)D-63
MAY, BATHAIA—(or)C-2
MAY, BENJ.—(M)G-94
MAY, BENJAMIN—(W)B-392;
(W)C-74; (ee)C-394; (ee)C-493;
(ee)C-502; (ee)C-507; (W)D-106;
(W)D-151; (ee)E-87; (W)E-289;
(ee)F-14; (W)F-29; (W)F-40;
(W)F-147; (ee)F-168; (or)F-468;
(W)F-471; (ee)F-578; (ee)G-9;
(CB)G-148; (M)G-196; (M)G-244;
(ee)G-256; (ee)G-257; (ee)G-258;
(ee)G-259; (ee)G-364; (M)G-425;
(CB)G-449; (W)H-14; (W)H-57;
(ee)H-73; (ee)H-74; (ee)H-76;
(ee)H-77; (A)H-81; (W)H-95
MAY, CELIA—(F)H-74
MAY, GEORGE—(or)F-471
MAY, HARDY—(W)E-264
MAY, JAMES—(W)C-542; (W)D-102;
(W)E-87; (or)E-125; (A)F-63;

(W)F-142; (ee)F-157; (W)F-157;
(or)F-312; (ee)F-358; (ee)F-471;
(CB)G-10; (M)G-92; (ee)G-321;
(ee)G-322; (M)G-471; (or)H-130
MAY, JOHN—(F)D-106; (M)E-23;
(F)E-80; (F)E-87; (W)E-264;
(M)F-29; (A)F-476; (M)G-5;
(M)G-197; (CB)G-248; (M)G-250;
(CB)G-257; (M)G-258; (CB)G-259;
(ee)G-338; (CB)G-364; (W)H-73;
(F)H-74; (ee)H-156
MAY, JUREL—(M)G-364
MAY, MARK—(M)G-111
MAY, MARY—(or)C-193
MAY, NATHAN—(or)C-193; (CB)G-2
MAY, PETER—(CB)G-287; (ee)G-331
(A)H-96
MAY, RICHARD—(or)C-2
MAY, SAMUEL—(W)F-157; (M)G-1
(ee)G-287; (CB)G-331
MAY, SELAH—(M)D-106; (F)E-87
MAY, WILLIAM—(CB)G-287;
(CB)G-374; (ee)G-387; (W)H-98
MAY, WM.—(CB)G-331
MAYE, BENJAMIN—(W)C-284
MAYO, AMOS—(ee)F-487
MAYO, BENJAMIN—(W)B-242;
(W)B-445
MAYO, BETHANY—(W)F-342
MAYO, HARDY—(ee)H-136
MAYO, JAMES—(W)B-113; (ee)B-47
(W)C-146; (W)C-172; (or)C-280;
(W)C-323; (ee)C-324; (A)C-416;
(F)C-416; (A)E-11; (F)E-317;
(F)H-84; (or)H-98
MAYO, JOHN—(ee)B-141; (or)B-242
(or)B-252; (W)B-392; (or)B-445;
(ee)C-250; (ee)C-292; (A)C-303;
(ee)C-485; (F)D-87; (or)D-119;
(A)E-241; (or)E-263; (ee)G-190;
(W)H-56; (or)H-136
MAYO, MARK—(W)H-82
MAYO, MARY—(W)B-242
MAYO, NATHAN—(ee)B-63;
(W)C-172; (W)C-224; (W)C-244;
(ee)C-402; (or)D-21; (or)E-220;
(or)E-241; (W)F-232
MAYO, PETER—(ee)E-99; (ee)B-104
(M)E-220; (ee)F-521
MAYO, RICHARD—(F)B-283;
(ee)B-285; (or)B-438; (or)B-475;
(ee)C-139; (or)C-205; (or)D-92
MAYO, THOMAS—(W)D-119
MAYO, WILLIAM—(M)D-21; (F)E-2
(or)F-487
MEAKS, JAMES—(W)D-159
MEBILL, THOMAS—(W)D-56
MEEKS, FRANCES—(A)E-38;
(A)F-24; (A)H-10
MEEKS, FRANCIS—(ee)D-57;
(W)H-147
MEEKS, JAMES—(ee)E-31;

(ee)E-38; (or)F-24; (ee)F-63
MEEKS, JOHN—(or)B-376; (or)C-223;
  (ee)C-223; (or)C-264; (or)D-57;
  (F)D-61; (or)E-38; (F)F-24;
  (M)G-162
MEEKS, MATHEW—(W)F-24
MEEKS, NATHAN—(W)D-57;
  (ee)H-147
MEEKS, ROBERT—(CB)G-162;
  (CB)G-232; (CB)G-254; (CB)G-255;
  (CB)G-354
MEEKS, SIMON—(ee)G-254
MEEKS, WALTER—(ee)C-264;
  (W)(A)E-38; (A)F-24; (A)H-10;
  (or)H-147
MEERCER, JACOB—(W)E-252
MERCER, CHRISTOPHER—(W)-40;
  (W)C-182; (F)F-165
MERCER, JACOB—(ee)B-550;
  (A)F-165; (or)H-103; (ee)H-103
MERCER, JOHN—(or)B-71; (W)H-103
MERCER, JOSEPH—(W)B-71;
  (ee)B-149; (or)B-256; (or)B-378;
  (or)B-384; (or)B-420; (F)C-400
MERCER, JOSHUA—(or)B-270
MERCER, SARAH—(or)F-165
MERCER, SHADRACK—(W)D-105;
  (W)F-165
MERCER, THOMAS—(F)B-296;
  (ee)B-528; (or)B-550; (or)C-40;
  (ee)D-105; (or)D-162; (W)E-43;
  (or)F-164; (or)F-165; (W)F-165;
  (F)F-165; (F)F-578; (A)H-103
MESSER, JEREMIAH—(ee)H-164
MICHALSON, JAMES—(CB)G-429
MILBURN, JOHN—(ee)H-107
MILLER, WILLIAM—(W)E-190
MILLISON, JACOB—(CB)G-38
MILLS, ANTHONY—(or)D-60;
  (ee)F-234; (F)F-464; (CB)G-297;
  (CB)G-299; (F)H-117
MILLS, DAVID—(A)F-99; (or)F-197;
  (ee)F-293; (or)F-498; (M)G-409;
  (ee)H-75; (F)H-146
MILLS, FEDERICK—(ee)F-37;
  (or)H-75
MILLS, FEDRICK—(CB)G-14
MILLS, FREDERICK—(ee)E-317;
  (ee)G-28; (ee)G-296; (CB)G-409
MILLS, HENRY—(ee)G-408
MILLS, ISAAC—(ee)C-143; (ee)C-513;
  (M)G-409
MILLS, JOHN—(F)B-388; (or)C-12;
  (ee)C-12; (or)C-143; (A)D-67;
  (A)E-42
MILLS, NASBE—(ee)C-280
MILLS, NESBY—(ee)B-57; (W)D-34;
  (or)E-75; (ee)E-284; (F)E-317;
  (or)F-323; (CB)G-408; (ee)G-409;
  (ee)H-50; (F)H-67
MILLS, NEZBY—(F)D-37
MITCHEL, WILLIAM—(A)D-49;

(M)G-191
MITCHELL, MARY—(or)B-289
MITCHELL, WILLIAM—(F)B-254;
  (or)B-289; (ee)D-155; (A)E-137
MITCHELL, MARK—(W)F-48
MIZELL, WILLIAM—(or)C-368;
  (W)F-122
MIZZELL, WILLIAM—(F)E-100
MOBBEY, BIGARS—(or)E-56
MOBILE, AZARIAH—(M)G-380
MOBLEY, AZARIAH—(ee)G-356
MOBLEY, BIGARS—(W)C-520
MOBLEY, BIGERS—(W)D-100
MOBLEY, JOHN—(ee)C-5
MOBLEY, MIDDLETON—(W)C-5;
  (or)C-519; (W)D-25
MOBLEY, MIDLTON—(ee)C-18
MOBLEY, WILLIAM—(ee)C-510;
  (or)D-100
MONER, ABEL—(CB)G-432
MONER, WM.—(CB)G-432
MOOR, ABRAHAM—(ee)C-177
MOOR, ARTHUR—(M)B-447
MOOR, CALEB—(CB)G-336
MOOR, ED—(W)C-278
MOOR, EDWARD—(M)G-336
MOOR, JACOB—(F)C-38
MOOR, JAMES—(M)G-244
MOOR, MATTHIAS—(W)B-396;
  (ee)C-187; (ee)F-341
MOOR, MOSES—(or)C-38; (CB)G-336
MOOR, NATHAN—(ee)B-420
MOOR, SAMUEL—(A)C-187;
  (or)C-239; (M)F-341
MOOR, THOMAS—(ee)B-71; (or)B-296;
  (or)C-177; (or)C-183; (or)C-276
MOOR, WILLIAM—(W)B-256;
  (W)B-296; (W)B-406; (or)C-154;
  (or)C-174
MOORE, ABRAHAM—(W)D-128;
  (W)H-74
MOORE, ARTHUR—(W)D-96;
  (ee)G-252; (ee)G-253; (M)G-306;
  (CB)G-320
MOORE, AURTHER—(W)C-258
MOORE, CALEB—(CB)G-173
MOORE, CANNADY—(CB)G-439
MOORE, ED—(W)C-340
MOORE, EDMUND—(CB)G-456
MOORE, EDWARD—(W)B-310;
  (ee)C-25; (ee)G-456; (ee)G-457;
  (ee)G-458
MOORE, ELIJAH—(M)G-306
MOORE, ELISHA—(ee)E-24; (CB)G-66;
  (CB)G-252
MOORE, GEORGE—(or)E-234;
  (or)F-506
MOORE, HENRY—(W)D-160; (ee)G-6;
  (M)G-295; (M)G-414; (or)H-56;
  (or)H-62
MOORE, JACOB—(CB)G-337
MOORE, JAMES—(ee)E-258;

(F)E-317; (F)F-108; (W)F-299;
(or)F-320; (CB)G-40; (CB)G-56;
(CB)G-58; (ee)G-250; (M)G-284;
(F)H-38; (or)H-174
MOYE, JOSHUA—(W)F-374
MOYE, PETER—(CB)G-3
MOYE, PHILLANEY—(W)F-202
MOYE, RICHARD—(W)C-519;
(W)D-18; (W)E-37; (ee)E-40;
(W)F-202; (W)F-259; (W)F-299;
(ee)G-58; (CB)G-474; (W)H-92
MOYE, RUTH JONES—(F)E-153
MOYE, WILL—(CB)G-60
MOYE, WILLIAM—(CB)G-57
MUNDEN, ISAAC—(W)E-33
MUNDEN, JOHN—(ee)B-316;
(W)C-200; (ee)D-137; (or)E-33;
(W)F-134; (or)F-199
MUNDEN, STEPHEN—(A)B-169;
(ee)B-266; (ee)E-33; (ee)F-134;
(ee)F-136
MUNDIN, CORNELIUS—(W)F-515
MUNDIN, ISAAC—(W)F-515;
(or)H-141
MUNDIN, JOHN—(W)E-40; (F)F-54
MUNDIN, STEPHEN—(or)F-50;
(F)F-54; (or)F-538; (or)F-555;
(F)H-79

Mc

McCAFFIE, AZARIAH—(ee)H-22
McCASKEY, JOHN—(W)C-251
McCLELLAN, WILLIAM—(W)E-88;
(ee)F-1
McDANIEL, RANDAL—(ee)G-441;
(CB)G-445; (CB)G-269
McDEARMAN, JOHN—(CB)G-390
McDONALD, BENJ.—(CB)G-357
McDONALD, RANDAL—(ee)F-203
McDONALD, RANDOLPH—(CB)G-446
McGOUNDS, GEORGE—(ee)D-136
McGOWNS, GEORGE—(or)H-129;
(or)F-295, (ee)G-18; (ee)G-30
McGOWNS, JOHN—(CB)G-30
McGOWNS, WILLIAM—(ee)F-295
McGOWNS, WM.—(CB)G-30
McHENERY, WILLIAM—(or)E-90
McKENNEY, ROSLIN—(W)D-143
McKNIGHT, THOMAS—(or)C-440;
(ee)C-442
McLAM, DANIEL—(or)C-301
McLAM, WILLIAM—(ee)C-301
McNAMAR, FRANCIS—(or)E-30
McNEMAR, FRANCIS—(ee)C-32;
(ee)C-77; (ee)C-101; (or)C-195
McNEMAR, LARENCE—(W)C-84;
(or)C-94
McNEMAR, LAWRENCE—(ee)B-418
McSWAIN, EDWARD—(W)C-262

N

NEALSON, GILES—(W)E-39
NEALSON, JOHN—(W)E-39
NELSON, DANIEL—(CB)G-108
NELSON, GILES—(ee)H-127
NELSON, HARDY—(W)E-2
NELSON, JAMES—(ee)E-39;
(W)E-282; (CB)G-59; (CB)G-87;
(CB)G-442; (W)H-127
NELSON, JOHN—(W)C-22; (ee)C-88;
(W)C-314; (or)D-143; (ee)E-282;
(CB)G-89; (ee)G-442; (ee)H-41;
(ee)H-45; (or)H-127
NELSON, MARTHA—(or)E-60
NELSON, MARTIN—(ee)B-434;
(W)B-477; (ee)C-22; (W)C-234;
(ee)D-33; (or)E-21; (F)E-21;
(or)F-92; (W)F-240; (ee)G-59;
(CB)G-87; (CB)G-108; (ee)G-142;
(M)G-414; (or)H-41; (F)H-41;
(or)H-45; (F)H-45
NELSON, MARY—(W)B-477
NELSON, NATHAN—(W)D-33;
(ee)F-154; (ee)G-188; (M)G-307;
(CB)G-351
NELSON, PETER—(W)B-434;
(A)C-22; (ee)C-362; (or)E-39;
(or)H-89
NELSON, SAMUEL—(ee)E-21;
(CB)G-59; (ee)G-87; (ee)G-108;
(M)G-442
NELSAN, SARAH—(M)E-21
NELSON, WILLIAM—(or)E-60
NEUSOM, SIMON—(ee)B-423;
(or)H-20
NEWTON, ANN—(or)C-442
NEWTON, JOHN—(ee)C-483;
(or)F-353; (F)H-64
NEWTON, NATHANIEL—(or)C-442
NEWTON, SARAH—(or)H-64
NEWTON, WALTER—(W)C-484;
(ee)F-353; (M)G-332
NEWTON, WILLIAM—(W)C-212;
(W)C-484
NICHOLS, BARSHABEA—(W)F-20
NICHOLS, MARY—(or)F-181
NICHOLS, WILLIAM—(or)F-181;
(or)F-356; (W)H-30
NICHOLSON, BENJ.—(M)G-112;
(ee)G-329; (M)G-443
NICHOLSON, BENJAMIN—(ee)G-431
NICHOLSON, JAMES—(CB)G-152;
(CB)G-329
NICHOLSON, JOEL—(CB)G-110;
(CB)G-112; (ee)G-330; (CB)G-473
NICHOLSON, JONATHAN—
(CB)G-368; (CB)G-443
NICHOLSON, REUBEN—(CB)G-443
NICHOLSON, WILLIS—(CB)G-473
NICHOLSON, WM.—(CB)G-112;
(CB)G-329; (CB)G-403; (CB)G-406;
(ee)G-429; (ee)G-473

RILEY, TIMOTHY—(W)H-160
RINGGOLD, THOMAS—(ee)F-406;
 (W)H-22; (W)H-25
RINGGOLD, THOS.—(W)H-83
RINGOLD, THOMAS—(ee)F-433
RINGOLD, THOS.—(CB)G-42;
 (CB)G-352
RIVES, ELIZABETH—(W)B-88
RIVES, PETER—(W)B-73; (ee)B-88;
 (A)C-300; (ee)D-106; (or)E-29;
 (ee)C-224; (W)H-83
RIVES, RICHARD—(ee)E-51;
 (ee)E-190; (or)E-276
RIVES, ROBERT—(W)E-29;
 (CB)G-224
ROACH, CHARLES—(or)E-315
ROACH, ELIZABETH—(or)E-315
ROBBERSON, JOHN—(W)F-52
ROBERSON, JOHN—(CB)G-225;
 (ee)G-226; (ee)G-227; (ee)G-228;
 (ee)G-229
ROBERSON, SOVERON—(ee)G-225
ROBERSON, WILLIAM—(M)G-225;
 (CB)G-227; (ee)H-153
ROBINSON, AMAY—(or)F-140
ROBINSON, JOHN—(or)F-140
ROBINSON, SOLOMON—(ee)C-524
ROBINSON, SOVERIN—(CB)G219
ROBSON, ANNE—(ee)G-407
ROBSON, JAMES—(or)F-304;
 (CB)G-107
ROBSON, JOHN—(W)C-248;
 (W)F-529; (M)G-314
ROBSON, NOAH—(or)F-301
ROBSON, SOLOMON—(ee)C-64;
 (or)C-433; (M)F-301; (F)F-304
ROBSON, SOEREIGN—(W)C-433;
 (W)F-301
ROBSON, WILLIAM—(W)C-168;
 (ee)C-433; (ee)E-178; (W)E-315;
 (W)F-205; (W)F-301; (W)F-304;
 (W)F-529; (ee)G-219; (ee)G-220;
 (ee)G-221; (ee)G-222; (ee)G-223;
 (ee)G-403; (W)H-45
ROBSON, WM.—(M)G-191; (W)H-116
RODGERS, WILLIAM—(W)F-121
ROGERS, ABSALOM—(ee)F-190;
 (ee)H-33
ROGERS, ABSOLUM—(or)C-285;
 (W)F-335
ROGER, DANIEL—(ee)B-102;
 (A)C-285; (or)C-517; (ee)E-55;
 (or)E-107; (W)E-204; (or)F-335;
 (CB)G-342
ROGERS, HENRY—(W)H-33
ROGERS, ISAAC—(M)G-145;
 (ee)G-266
ROGERS, JOHN—(ee)C-380; (or)H-33
ROGERS, JOSEPH—(ee) C-380;
 (or)D-4; (W)H-33
ROGERS, MARY—(or)C-410; (W)D-37

ROGERS, MARY PRICE—(ee)C-380
ROGERS, ROBERT—(ee)B-485;
 (A)D-22
ROGERS, STEPHEN—(W)F-578
ROGERS, WILLIAM—(ee)C-285;
 (ee)G-463
ROPER, THOMAS—(F)E-286
ROSS, HUGH—(or)H-71
ROSS, LEAVIN—(CB)G-459
ROSS, WILLIAM—(or)H-71
ROUNDTREE, CHRISTIEN—(W)C-48
ROUNDTREE, FRANCIS—(A)B-496;
 (W)C-48; (ee)D-85; (ee)F-306;
 (or)F-478; (or)F-484
ROUNDTREE, JESSEE—(ee)F-474
ROUNDTREE, JOHN—(W)F-478
ROUNDTREE, MOAB—(W)F-478
ROUNDTREE, OBED—(W)D-40
ROUNDTREE, WILLIAM—(W)F-474
ROUNTREEE, FERIL—(or)F-512
ROUNTREE, FRANCES—(or)F-69;
 (F)F-203; (ee)F-276; (ee)F-278;
 (or)F-310;(or)H-25
ROUNTREE, JACOB—(W)H-22
ROUNTREE, JESSE—(or)F-81;
 (or)F-203
ROUNTREE, MOAB—(ee)F-316;
 (W)H-25; (W)H-26; (W)H-31;
 (W)F-10
ROUNTREE, OBED—(W)F10;
 (or)F-512; (or)H-31
ROUNTREE, REUBEN—(W)F-119;
 (W)F-203; (W)H-31
ROUNTREE, WILLIAM—(CB)G-100;
 (ee)H-54; (ee)H-55; (W)H-83;
 (ee)H-118
ROWLINS, JAMES—(W)F-58
RYLAND, PHILIP—(or)D-116;
 (or)D-117; (F)E-1

S

SALTER, ALEXANDER—(F)E-48
SALTER, ANN—(W)F-391
SALTER, CLARE—(or)C-327
SALTER, CLAREY—(or)F-454
SALTER, EDMUND—(F)F-73
SALTER, EDWARD—(W)B-237;
 (F)B-387; (F)B-325; (ee)B-430;
 (or)C-10; (F)C-10; (W)C-13;
 (or)C-42; (or)C-44; (W)C-122;
 (W)C-144; (or)C-219; (ee)C-219;
 (ee)C-354; (ee)C-381; (W)D-2;
 (ee)D-7; (or)D-19; (F)D-19;
 (F)D-66; (F)D-81; (F)D-132;
 (F)D-134; (W)D-134; (F)E-27;
 (or)E-48; (M)E-113; (W)E-135;
 (F)E-198; (W)E-265; (W)F-73;
 (ee)F-80; (or)F-363; (W)F-391;
 (ee)F-450; (or)F-451; (CB)G-102;
 (M)G-175; (M)G-177; (CB)G-190;
 (CB)G-209; (M)G-213; (CB)G-288;

(M)G-295; (CB)G-324; (M)G-394;
(M)G-414; (or)H-13; (ee)H-56;
(or)H-97; (or)H-126; (F)H-126
SALTER, JAMES—(W)F-155
SALTER, JOHN—(or)D-132; (or)E-64;
(W)F-73; (M)F-126; (ee)F-454;
(W)F-541; (CB)G-34; (ee)G-52;
(ee)G-102; (CB)G-159; (M)G-351;
(ee)H-36; (or)H-39
SALTER, ROBERT—(W)C-11;
(ee)C-42; (ee)C-44; (W)C-118;
(W)C-122; (W)C-156; (or)C-327;
(ee)C-381; (W)D-134; (or)E-94;
(W)E-127; (W)F-173; (ee)F-270;
(or)F-364; (or)F-367; (or)F-450;
(ee)F-451; (ee)F-453; (or)F-454;
(or)F-541; (ee)G-38; (M)G-233;
(F)H-13; (F)H-126
SALTER, THOMAS—(W)C-382;
(or)D-134; (or)F-154; (or)F-209
SANDERS, BENJAMIN—(F)F-48
SANDERS, JOHN—(W)C-502;
(W)D-151
SANDERS, ROBERT—(ee)E-203;
(ee)F-335
SAUGHAN, ADAMS—(or)D-64
SAUNDERS, BENJAMIN—(F)C-173;
(or)C-246
SAUNDERS, ROBERT—(M)G-384
SAUNDERS, SIMON—(W)C-246
SAVAGE, JNO.—(W)B-514
SAYLOR, SIMON—(W)F-4
SCARBOROUGH, WILLIAM—
(W)B-398
SCOTT, MATHEW—(W)D-74;
(ee)D-102
SCOTT, MATTHEW—(ee)D-19
SEABROOK, DANIEL—(W)F-535
SELLARS, THOMAS—(F)D-28
SERMAN, EDWARD—(ee)B-546
SERMON, SAMUEL—(M)G-359
SERMON, THOMAS—(M)G-451
SESSION, SARAH—(or)F-574
SESSION, WALTER—(or)D-95;
(A)F-61; (or)F-351 (M)G-136
SESSIONS, WALTER—(ee)H-15
SESSIONS, WILLIAM—(CB)G-239
SESSIONS, WM.—(CB)G-243
SHANNON, ANN—(or)E-120
SHANNON, JOHN—(ee)B-22
SHEPARD, ANN—(W)F-287
SHEPARD, SOLOMON—(ee)F-287;
(ee)G-246; (ee)G-247
SHEPHERD, ELIZABETH—(or)H-112
SHEPHERD, JORDAN—(W)H-109
SHEPHERD, SOLOMON—(ee)H-111
SHEPPARD, JAMES—(CB)G-461
SHEPPARD, JORDAN—(CB)G-461
SHEPPARD, SOLOMON—(ee)G-461;
(ee)H-35
SHEPPARD, THOMAS—(W)H-109
SHERROD, WILLIAM—(ee)H-92

SHIELD, THOMAS—(or)F-201
SHIELD, WILLIAM—(or)F-201;
(M)F-201
SHIELDS, JAMES—(or)B-388;
(or)E-42
SHIVERS, JAMES—(or)H-40
SHIVERS, JESSEE—(ee)H-40
SHIVERS, JONAS—(W)D-8; (M)G-2
(M)G-227; (ee)G-261
SHUTE, GILES—(ee)H-64; (W)H-97
SHUTE, JACOB—(W)H-64
SIKES, JOHN—(W)E-52; (W)F-423
SIKES, SAMPSON—(W)F-423
SIKES, SAMSON—(W)E-52
SIMMONS, SAMUEL—(ee)G-20;
(CB)G-451; (CB)G-462; (or)H-191
SIMMONS, THOMAS—(W)E-8
SIMONS, SAMUEL—(ee)G-453
SIMPSON, ELIZABETH—(W)B-234;
(W)C-135; (W)F-11; (W)H-50
SIMPSON, ICHABOD—(ee)C-533;
(ee)E-105; (or)E-127; (F)H-53
SIMPSON, JOHN—(W)B-234;
(ee)B-388; (W)B-434; (or)C-72;
(or)C-81; (W)C-135; (ee)C-237;
(W)C-292; (or)C-316; (ee)C-329;
(ee)C-372; (ee)C-404; (ee)C-408;
(ee)C-531; (ee)C-535; (ee)C-540;
(ee)D-37; (or)D-50; (ee)D-67;
(or)D-68; (or)D-71; (ee)D-72;
(or)D-104; (ee)D-116; (ee)D-117;
(ee)D-143; (ee)D-144; (or)E-1;
(or)E-19; (or)E-20; (ee)E-42;
(ee)E-48; (ee)E-72; (ee)E-73;
(ee)E-75; (or)E-115; (or)E-133;
(or)E-269; (or)E-282; (F)E-284;
(or)E-317; (ee)E-322; (F)E-331;
(F)F-75; (or)F-111; (ee)F-238;
(F)F-280; (F)F-292; (F)F-311;
(ee)F-323; (ee)F-324; (F)F-410;
(or)F-450; (M)G-183; (M)G-195;
(ee)G-355; (M)G395; (M)G-419;
(ee)H-12; (ee)H-13; (W)H-22;
(or)H-50; (or)H-53; (or)H-67;
(or)H-125; (W)F-323
SIRMAN, EDWARD—(or)E-3;
(W)E-104; (W)F-59; (ee)G-124;
(CB)G-199; (ee)H-53
SIRMAN, ELI—(W)F-501; (CB)G-12
SIRMAN, JOHN—(ee)E-104; (W)F-1
(W)F-261; (or)F-278; (W)F-306;
(ee)F-310; (W)F-495; (CB)G-26;
- (W)H-24
SIRMAN, LEVY—(W)F-186;
(CB)G-237; (CB)G-334
SIRMANS, THOMAS—(M)G-453
SLADE, JOSEPH—(A)F-186;
(CB)G-99; (CB)G-122; (or)H-181
SLADE, MAJOR—(W)D-24; (ee)H-
SLATER, SAMPSON—(ee)G-4;
(ee)G-5; (ee)G-18; (CB)G-20
SLATER, SAMSON—(CB)G-105

SLATOR, JOHN—(or)E-96; (ee)E-115
SLAUGHTER, CHARITY—(M)D-141
SLAUGHTER, JOHN—(ee)B-366;
  (ee)C-174; (or)D-141; (F)F-263;
  (ee)G-347
SLAUGHTER, SAMPSON—(ee)F-185;
  (ee)F-263
SLAUGHTER, SAMSON—(ee)D-141
SLAUGHTER, SAMUEL—(CB)G-347;
  (CB)G-452
SLAUGHTER, WILLIAM—(W)C-186;
  (or)F-263; (M)G-105
SLAUTER, SAMPSON—(CB)G-41
SLAUTER, WILLIAM—(ee)G-18
SMITH, ANNEY—(W)H-64
SMITH, BENJ.—(CB)G-39; (CB)G-161;
  (CB)G-217
SMITH, BENJAMIN—(ee)C-128;
  (or)C-430; (ee)E-213; (CB)G-172;
  (CB)G-263; (ee)G-316; (ee)G-414;
  (or)H-21
SMITH, CHARLES—(CB)G-408
SMITH, DANIEL—(W)C-340
SMITH, DAVID—(OR)C-5; (ee)C-30;
  (F)C-270; (F)C-479; (M)F-560
SMITH, EDWARD—(W)C-278;
  (W)C-510; (W)D-25
SMITH, ELIZABETH—(W)C-78
SMITH, GEORGE—(A)E-46
SMITH, HARRY—(ee)F-35; (or)F-368
SMITH, HENRY—(W)C-282; (ee)F-368;
  (ee)F-560; (CB)G-208
SMITH, JAMES—(M)C-251; (W)F-22;
  (A)F-45; (F)F-161; (ee)F-346;
  (or)F-519
SMITH, JOB—(CB)G-188; (ee)G-307;
  (CB)G-316
SMITH, JOHN—(W)C-5; (W)C-124;
  (W)C-282; (or)E-227; (or)F-284
SMITH, JOSEPH—(ee)F-501
SMITH, LEWIS—(ee)G-248; (W)H-76
SMITH, MARY—(W)D-37; (M)F-284
SMITH, RICHARD—(F)B-52; (A)B-494;
  (ee)D-100; (or)F-522
SMITH, SAMUEL—(ee)D-60;
  (ee)E-159; (or)F-104; (or)F-492;
  (M)G-299; (F)H-117
SMITH, SARAH—(or)H21
SMITH, SOLOMON—(CB)G-365;
  (CB)G-449
SMITH, THOMAS—(CB)G-88;
  (CB)G-188
SMITH, WILLIAM—(or)B-226;
  (or)C-30; (ee)C-94; (or)C-101;
  (ee)C-277; (or)C-430; (or)C-485;
  (or)D-159; (or)F-316; (or)F-501;
  (or)F-519
SMITH, WM.—(CB)G-289; (M)G-450
SMITHWICK, EDMUND—(W)D-8
SMITHWICK, SAMUEL—(W)D-102
SMYTH, HENRY—(W)H-146

SMYTH, SAMUEL—(W)B-307;
  (ee)B-400; (ee)C-232; (ee)C-537;
  (or)E-69
SNOAD, HENRY—(or)C-8; (F)C-398;
  (F)E-286
SNOAD, JOHN—(F)C-47; (F)D-170;
  (F)E-93; (F)E-286
SNOAD, WILLIAM—(F)E-93; (F)E-286
SPAIN, AGUSTIAN—(ee)F-415
SPAIN, DRURY—(ee)C-243; (W)D-21;
  (or)D-121; (CB)G-229; (ee)H-101
SPAIN, MILDRED—(or)D-122
SPARKMAN, JESSE—(ee)B-65;
  (ee)C-132; (or)C-310; (F)D-74;
  (F)D-78
SPEAR, ELISABETH—(W)D-102
SPEER, WM.—(ee)G-187
SPEIR, APSLEY—(M)C-242
SPEIR, JAMES—(CB)G-23; (M)G-395
SPEIR, JOHN—(W)B-52; (or)B-123;
  (ee)B-210; (W)B-249; (W)C-11;
  (W)C-21; (W)C-44; (F)C-242;
  (F)C-327; (W)D-32; (W)H-24
SPEIR, WILLIAM—(ee)B-52;
  (or)B-119; (ee)B-153; (ee)B-181;
  (or)C-20; (or)C-45; (or)C-483;
  (ee)D-32; (F)D-94; (A)E-27;
  (ee)E-286; (ee)F-84; (or)F-134;
  (F)F-321; (M)G-385; (F)H-64;
  (or)H-112
SPEIR, WM.—(M)G-208; (F)F-353;
  (F)F-558
SPENCER, SAMUEL—(W)B-91
SPIER, JAMES—(W)H-161
SPIER, WILLIAM—(or)F-86;
  (ee)F-108; (or)F-136
SPILLER, JAMES—(ee)F-535
SPIVEY, CALEB—(or)C-345; (W)D-22;
  (or)D-40; (or)D-170
SPIVEY, JAMES—(M)G-100;
  (ee)G-128; (ee)H-24
SPIVY, CALEB—(ee)C-47
STAFFORD, EDWARD—(or)C-150;
  (or)C-152
STAFFORD, JOSHUA—(F)D-35
STAFFORD, RICHARD—(W)D-10
STAFFORD, SAMUEL—(W)D-106;
  (W)E-44; (W)E-87; (ee)E-194;
  (or)E-273; (ee)E-276; (W)F-399
  (M)G-170; (M)G-171; (M)G-435;
  (W)H-7; (ee)H-29; (W)H-155
STAFFORD, WILLIAM—(A)B-22;
  (ee)B-361; (or)B-421; (or)C-106;
  (F)D-118; (or)E-44; (or)E-46;
  (F)E-181; (or)E-194; (F)E-273;
  (F)F-65; (F)F-174; (F)F-257;
  (F)F-338; (F)F-408; (F)F-489;
  (F)H-132
STAFFORD, WM.—(F)B-275; (F)C-278;
  (F)C-411

STAFFORDS, WILLIAM—(F)E-1
STANCEL, GODFREY—(A)B-113;
  (ee)E-315
STANCEL, WILLIAM—(or)F-344
STANCELL, GODFREY—(ee)F-267
STANCELL, JOHN—(ee)F-267;
  (F)F-267
STANCELL, SARAH—(or)F-267
STANCIL, GODFREY—(ee)G-110;
  (ee)G-111; (ee)G-112; (CB)G-330;
  (ee)G-443
STANCIL, PETER—(F)D-47; (F)D-61
STANCIL, WILLIAM—(F)D-47;
  (F)D-61; (or)F-222
STANCILL, GODFREY—(A)D-25
STANSELL, GODFREY—(W)B-372;
  (W)C-176; (ee)C-536; (W)D-100
STANSELL, SAMUEL—(ee)C-108;
  (or)C-340
STANSELL, WILLIAM—(or)B-65;
  (or)B-240; (or)C-370; (ee)C-453;
  (or)C-500; (or)C-505; (ee)B-69;
  (M)E-45
STANSILL, WILLIAM—(F)D-18;
  (F)E-8
STEAVENS, JOHN—(F)B-482;
  (M)D-21
STEAVENS, WILLIAM—(F)B-482
STEPHENS, JOSEPH—(W)C-230;
  (CB)G-142
STEPHENS, WILLIAM—(M)D-121
STEVENS, HARDEE—(ee)G-299
STEVENS, JOHN—(F)C-243
STEVENS, WILLIAM—(M)B-408;
  (F)B-492; (F)C-243
STEWART, ALEX—(W)B-1;
  (W)B-410; (W)B-485; (W)C-46;
  (ee)D-74; (ee)D-75; (W)D-84;
  (W_D-170; (W)E-137; (W)F-153;
  (ee)F-422; (F)H-111; (M)H-112
STEWART, ALEXANDER—(or)B-222;
  (or)B-496; (W)E-27; (W)E-69;
  (ee)E-141; (or)F-290
STEWART, ANNE—(W)F-291
STEWART, JAMES—(W)F-102
STEWART, ROBERT—(M)F-386
STEWART, WILLIAM—(CB)G-86
STEWART, WM.—(CB)G-246
STOCKDALE, JAMES—(W)F-557
STOCKS, ISAAC—(W)B-292;
  (W)B-374;(W)B-412; (ee)B-473;
  (or)C-84; (ee)C-471; (ee)D-50;
  (or)F-410; (ee)F-418; (ee)G-27;
  (CB)G-27; (ee)G-436; (CB)G-436
STOCKS, JOHN—(W)B-292; (ee)B-307;
  (or)B-374; (F)B-428; (or)C-302;
  (ee)C-337; (W)C-472; (ee)D-114;
  (F)D-136; (ee)E-133; (or)E-215;
  (F)F-352; (ee)F-410
STOCKS, MARCUS—(W)C-244
STOKES, DAVID—(W)F-171

STOKES, DRURY—(W)F-318;
  (W)F-554
STOKES, ELIZABETH—(M)E-121
STOKES, HENRY—(ee)F-176;
  (CB)G-157
STOKES, JAMES—(ee)E-121
STOKES, JOHN—(or)B-385;
  (W)C-166; (F)D-35; (ee)E-263
STOKES, MARCUS—(ee)B-482;
  (ee)D-121; (M)G-381
STOKES, MARY—(W)F-145;
  (W)F-479
STOKES, READING—(M)G-231
STOKES, REDEN—(ee)F-177
STOKES, SAMUEL—(ee)B-214;
  (or)B-261; (F)C-123; (F)E-116;
  (or)E-121; (or)F-142; (F)F-145;
  (or)F-176; (or)F-177; (or)F-315;
  (F)F-315; (F)F-343; (ee)F-399;
  (ee)G-23; (CB)G-231; (M)G-326;
  (W)H-32; (F)H-161
STOKES, SARAH—(or)F-316;
  (W)F-491
STOKES, SUSANNA—(W)F-491;
  (W)F-176
STOKES, WILLIAM—(or)E-237
STONE, PRUDENCE—(or)D-35
STONE, RICHARD—(M)B-214;
  (or)D-35
STUART, GEORGE—(W)F-56
STUART, JAMES—(W)E-108
STUCKEY, WILLIAM—(M)G-349
STURDAVANT, MATTHEW—(ee)E-7
STURDIVANT, HENRY—(W)E-328;
  (CB)G-46
STURDIVANT, MATHEW—(W)D-13;
  (or)E-16
STURDIVANT, MATTHEW—
  (ee)B-443; (ee)D-27; (W)E-41;
  (ee)E-81; (W)F-382; (ee)F-491;
  (M)G-61
STURDIVANT, TABITHA—(or)E-16
SUGG, ALLEN—(W)B-307: (W)B-40
  (W)D-23; (W)E-120; (W)F-96;
  (or)F-144; (W)H-36
SUGG, AQUILLA—(or)B-398;
  (ee)C-481
SUGG, GEORGE—(F)B-300; (F)B-398
  (F)D-93; (M)E-229; (F)F-144;
  (F)F-556; (ee)G-410; (W)H-27;
  (ee)H-39
SUGG, JAMES—(W)D-99
SUGG, JOEL—(W)C-384; (W)E-294;
  (W)F-80; (ee)F-404; (A)F-491;
  (or)F-556; (ee)G-55; (ee)G-332;
  (ee)H-8; (or)H-27; (or)H-99
SUGG, JOHN—(W)E-16
SUGGS, GEORGE—(A)B-289
SULAVANT, JOSEPH—(ee)C-40
SULEVANT, JOSEPH—(ee)E-43
SULLAVAN, JOSEPH—(A)B-506

SULLIVAN, JOSEPH—(ee)C-271
SULLIVANT, JOSEPH—(W)B-550;
  (or)C-394; (or)D-105; (or)F-168
SUMERELL, EDWARD—(or)E-11
SUMERELL, THOMAS—(F)D-92
SUMERILL, THOMAS—(A)H-20
SUMERLING, THOMAS—(ee)C-205
SUMMERLIN, FLOWERS—(ee)G-318
SUMMERLIN, JACOB—(M)G-276
SUMMERLIN, THOS.—(CB)G-212
SUMMERLING, THOMAS—(M)G-211;
  (ee)G-242
SUMRELL, HENRY—(or)F-94
SUMRILL, THOMAS (or)C-208
SURMON, THOS.—(ee)G-359
SUTE, JILES—(CB)G-332
SUTHERLAND, DON—(W)H-20
SUTTEN, BENJAMIN—(W)F-35;
  (ee)F-43
SUTTON, BENJAMIN—(ee)F-331;
  (or)F-393
SUTTON, DAVID—(or)E-172
SUTTON, JACOB—(ee)F-374
SUTTON, MARY—(M)F-374
SUTTON, SHADRICH—(W)F-378
SUTTON, SOLOMON—(ee)F-194;
  (M)F-374; (M)G-300
SUTTON, HOMAS—(A)D-91
SWAIN, STEPHEN—(W)D-120;
  (ee)E-329; (or)F-527
SWAN, STEPHEN—(W)F-46
SWANNER, JAMES—(CB)G-319
SWANNER, JESSE—(CB)G-203;
  (ee)G-317
SWEARINGEN, SAMUEL—(W)B-220;
  (F)C-387
SWEARINGGANE, SAMUEL—
  (A)B-398
SWEARINGHAM, SAMUEL—(F)H-80
SWEARINGHAM, THOS.—(F)H-80
SWINDELL, JOHN—(OR)C-262
SWINSON, ELSIE—(or)F-48
SWINSON, JOHN—(or)B-379;
  (W)C-173; (or)C-198; (or)D-135;
  (or)F-48
SWINSON, LEVI—(W)C-174;
  (ee)D-135

T

TAGGART, THOMAS—(W)E-105
TANT, HENRY—(M)G-216
TANTON, HENRY—(ee)G-150
TAUNT, DORCAS—(or)H-159
TAUNT, ELIZABETH—(or)H-159
TAUNT, JOHN—(F)H-159
TAUNTON, HENRY—(M)G-430
TAYLER, JOHN—(F)D-71
TAYLOR, CHARLES—(ee)C-234;
  (M)H-125
TAYLOR, DINAH—(M)C-234

TAYLOR, EMANUEL—(M)H-125
TAYLOR, JACOB—(or)C-464; (F)D-65
  (F)E-324; (F)F-92; (M)G-169;
  (W)H-167
TAYLOR, JEREMIAH—(M)G-369
TAYLOR, JOHN—(ee)B-304; (A)C-134
  (or)C-237; (CB)G-367; (ee)G-369;
  (ee)G-370
TAYLOR, JONATH—(W)F-98
TAYLOR, JONATHAN—(ee)C-54;
  (or)F-1; (or)F-217; (M)G-176
TAYLOR, JOSHUA—(or)F-334;
  (CB)G-182
TAYLOR, LISCOMB—(ee)C-234
TAYLOR, NANCY—(ee)C-234
TAYLOR, SARAH—(ee)C-234;
  (ee)H-125
TAYLOR, SIMON—(or)B-434;
  (ee)B-497; (M)D-50; (ee)G-169;
  (ee)G-194; (ee)G-195; (ee)G-344;
  (M)G-414
TAYLOR, WILLIAM—(or)B-304;
  (F)B-434; (or)C-234; (F)C-404;
  (or)C-406; (or)C-419; (F)C-464;
  (or)D-33; (or)D-50; (ee)D-50;
  (F)D-65; (F)D-144; (F)E-67;
  (F)E-324; (F)F-75; (F)F-92;
  (F)F-111; (CB)G-370; (CB)G-384
TAYLOR, WILLIAM MOORING—
  (ee)H-24
TAYLOR, WM.—(F)H-9
TAYLOW, WILLIAM—(F)C-404
TEAL, BRADBURY—(CB)G-200;
  (ee)H-116
TEAL, WILLIAM—(CB)G-200;
  (M)G-229; (M)G-465; (or)H-116
TEEL, BRADBURY—(CB)G-96;
  (CB)G-229;2(W)H-18
TEEL, EMMANUEL—(A)D-166
TEEL, EMANUEL—(ee)H-45
TEEL, HARDEE—(ee)C-246
TEEL, WILLIAM—(or)C-6; (W)D-8;
  (CB)G-96
TEEL, WM.—(CB)G-261
THAIN, JAMES—(W)B-408
THIGPEN, JOSEPH—(ee)H-58;
  (A)H-73
THIGPEN, JOSHUA—(ee)G-365
THOMAS, ABEL—(ee)F-181;
  (CB)G-354; (ee)G-406
THOMAS, ABELL—(W)H-107
THOMAS, ABLE—(ee)E-162;
  (CB)G-255
THOMPSON, JOHN—(or)E-88;
  (ee)E-100
THOMSON, ROBERT—(W)C-202
TILDESLEY, CHARLES—(CB)G-419
TILDESLEY, THOMAS—(ee)G-419
TILDESLEY, THOS.—(W)H-46
TILLESBY, CHARLES—(CB)G-89
TINDALE, CHARLES—(ee)C-199

(CB)G-186; (M)G-233
TUCKER, REDDICK—(ee)F-551
TUCKER, RITE—(CB)G-467
TUCKER, SARAH—(or)F-551;
(M)G-467
TUCKER, TALLY—(ee)F-551
TUCKER, WRIGHT—(ee)F-551
TURNAGE, GEORGE—(F)F-299
TURNAGE, ISAAC—(ee)F-374
TURNAGE, JAMES—(ee)C-505;
(or)E-8; (or)E-45
TURNAGE, SELAH—(M)F-374
TURNAGE, WILLIAM—(ee)C-466;
(ee)D-61; (ee)F-299; (or)F-300
TURNER, ABRAHAM—(CB)G-454
TURNER, WILLIAM—(CB)G-347
TURNER, WM.—(CB)G-359;
(CB)G-452; (CB)G-453; (ee)G-454;
(ee)G-455
TUTEN, NEHEMIAH—(W)D-160;
(ee)F-208; (CB)G-337; (CB)G-353;
(CB)G-363
TUTEN, PEARSON—(A)F-99;
(ee)F-104; (W)F-293; (or)F-458;
(or)F-464; (M)G-408; (ee)H-19;
(ee)H-52; (ee)H-117; (ee)H-120;
(ee)H-135; (ee)H-138; (ee)H-146;
(ee)H-189
TUTEN, SHADE—(CB)G-442
TUTEN, SHADRACK—(ee)H-89
TUTEN, THOMAS—(or)D-144;
(F)F-111; (W)F-140; (ee)F-420
TUTEN, WILLIAM—(W)H-135;
(W)H-138
TUTTLE, PEARSON—(W)F-99
TUTTLE, PEARSON—(ee)G-443
TYSON, AARON—(or)F-205; (or)H-88
TYSON, ABRAHAM—(ee)B-44;
(ee)B-129; (W)B-475
TYSON, BETHENY—(or)F-400
TYSON, CORNELIUS—(F)F-383;
(F)H-138
TYSON, EDMUND—(F)E-1; (A)E-44;
(M)G-149
TYSON, HEZEKIAH—(W)H-88
TYSON, JACOB—(W)D-108
TYSON, JOHN—(W)D-108; (or)F-400
TYSON, MATTHIAS—(A)B-44
TYSON, MOSES—(ee)B-462; (A)E-44
TYSON, THOMAS—(or)C-185;
(or)C-258
TYSON, WILLIAM—(or)H-88

U

None

V

VALE, EDWARD—(F)B-414
VANCE, DAVID—(W)F-61

VANCE, DAVIS—(W)F-351; (ee)G-114
VERNON, JOHN—(F)D-106
VINE, SAMUEL—(F)C-222
VINES, JOHN—(W)F-182;
(W)H-103; (W)H-164
VINES, SAMUEL—(or)F-578;
(ee)H-132
VINES, WILLIAM—(ee)F-164;
(ee)F-165; (W)F-182; (M)F-578
VINSON, JOHN—(ee)F-512; (W)H-54
VINSON, JOSIAH—(W)F-512

W

WAIN, JOHN—(F)F-129
WAINWRIGHT, DANIEL—(W)H-96
WAINWRIGHT, JAMES—(W)F-321
WAINWRIGHT, JOHN—(CB)G-267
WALDROM, CHARLES—(ee)F-173;
(W)H-136
WALDRON, CHARLES—(CB)G-374
WALDRON, CHAS.—(CB)G-387
WALES, JACOB—(ee)F-355
WALES, JOSEPH—(F)D-41
WALIS, CALEB—(F)E-112
WALKER, DANIEL—(ee)H-61
WALL, HOWELL—(or)C-214
WALL, JAMES—(or)F-118
WALL, JOHN—(CB)G-116
WALL, JOSEPH—(or)C-66; (or)C-83;
(or)F-131; (ee)G-115; (CB)G-115;
(ee)G-116; (CB)G-411; (W)H-159
WALLACE, CALEB—(F)D-13;
(F)F-314; (M)F-358; (F)F-471;
(CB)G-424; (B)G-430; (F)H-130
WALLACE, JOHN—(ee)G-289;
(M)G-361
WALLACE, RICHARD—(CB)G-53;
(CB)G-68; (CB)G-289; (CB)G-390
WALLACE, THOMAS—(F)B-299;
(A)B-533; (A)E-185; (ee)F-441;
(M)G-322; (ee)G-424; (ee)G-425;
(M)G-434; (A)H-7; (ee)H-20
WALLACE, WILLIAM—(ee)H-98;
(W)H-99
WALLAS, THOMAS—(W)F-479;
(or)F-479
WALLER, JACOB—(W)F-395;
(or)F-433
WALLER, SARAH—(or)F-433
WALLICE, JOHN—(W)E-15
WALLIS, AFFIAH—(or)C-384
WALLIS, ANN—(or)B-478; (or)B-480
WALLIS, CALEB—(ee)B-32; (ee)B-36;
(or)B-67; (or)B-79; (or)B-250;
(or)B-299; (or)M-478; (or)B-480;
(or)C-226; (ee)C-383
WALLIS, JOHN—(M)G-193; (ee)G-290
WALLIS, RICHARD—(CB)G-290
WALLIS, THOMAS—(ee)B-79;
(ee)B-392; (ee)C-152; (or)C-383;

(A) C-264
WROTTEN, NEHEMIAH—(ee) F-443
WYNN, WATKINSON—(W) F-572

Y

YOUBANK, JOHN—(CB) G-385
YOUBANKS, GEORGE—(ee) G-385

X

None

Z

None

www.ingramcontent.com/pod-product-compliance
Lightning Source LLC
Chambersburg PA
CBHW031127020426
42333CB00012B/270